A Love That Could Not Wait:
The Remarkable Story of Knights of Bahá'u'lláh Catherine Heward Huxtable and Clifford Huxtable

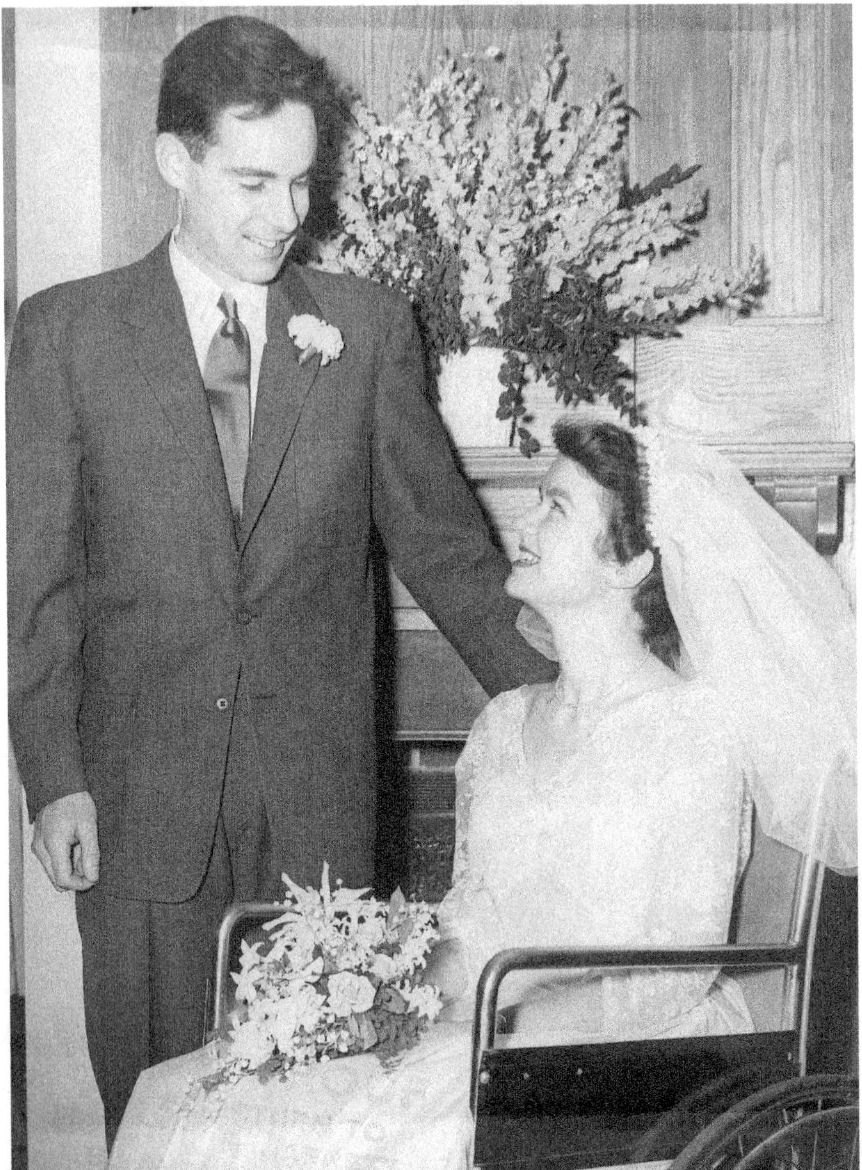

A LOVE THAT COULD NOT WAIT

The Remarkable Story of Knights of Bahá'u'lláh
Catherine Heward Huxtable and Clifford Stanley
Huxtable

J. A. McLean

ONE VOICE PRESS • ESSEX, MARYLAND

A Love That Could Not Wait: The Story of Knights of Bahá'u'lláh Catherine Heward Huxtable and Clifford Huxtable.
J. A. McLean
Text © 2016 by J. A. McLean

All rights reserved. Except as permitted under U.S. Copyright Act of 1976, no part of this publication may be reproduced, distributed, or transmitted in any form or by any means, or stored in a database or retrieval system, without the prior written permission of the publisher.

All photographs reproduced by kind permission of Clifford Huxtable.
Vine Infinity Symbol copyright © John Bigl | Dreamstime.com.

Book design by Kathleen Lehman.
Text set in 11-pt. Adobe Garamond Pro and 16-pt. Litania.

Published by One Voice Press, LLC
Essex, Maryland
www.onevoicepress.com

ISBN-13: 978-1-940135-40-3
ISBN-10: 1-940135-40-0
epub: 978-1-940135-39-7
Kindle: 978-1-940135-41-0

Printed in the United States of America.

First Edition: July 2016
10 9 8 7 6 5 4 3 2 1

This book is dedicated to the memory of
Francis St. George Spendlove (1897-1962)

Mentor and Spiritual Father to Catherine Heward and Clifford Huxtable

"They that have forsaken their country for the purpose of teaching Our Cause—these shall the Faithful Spirit strengthen through its power.... Whoso hath attained their presence will glory in their meeting, and all that dwell in every land will be illumined by their memory."

—Bahá'u'lláh

The Dancer

Catherine Rudyerd Heward Huxtable (1932-1967)
Knight of Bahá'u'lláh (Gulf Islands, British Columbia, Canada)

This frailest, seated girl who'd choose to dance,
Yet cheats ungracious nature's cumbering trial,
Gallops her mount without a backward glance,
Knows well she will be with us but a while
And undeterred by body's withering blight
Achieves the valorous victory of a Knight.

Wariest bird, the shadow ever near,
Outpours her song—we would not have it end—
Lavishes joy, nor deigns to squander tears,
So imminent reunion with the Friend.
Departing then, example left a trust,
To Africa* consigns her fragrant dust.

She dances now, enthroned in love's fair keep.
We see her vacant chair and do not weep.

—Roger White

*St. Helena Island, South Atlantic

"Only by centering myself in the Covenant of God can my life or death have any significance. If I have a private prayer, it's this: Let my life and death count in the Faith!"

— From the letters of Catherine Huxtable

ACKNOWLEDGEMENTS

I would like to extend my warmest thanks to a number of friends without whose cooperation this book could not have been written. I am above all grateful to Catherine's husband, Cliff Huxtable of St. Helena Island, who entrusted me with telling the remarkable story of his life with Catherine. Cliff provided the necessary tools that have enabled me to complete my task: a file of Huxtable correspondence, some 170 photographs, a transcript of a 1978 talk he made on St. Helena at the request of the Universal House of Justice, and a tape-recorded talk he gave on Salt Spring Island that I recorded on July 31, 1998. Not only did Cliff share many recollections of his life with Catherine, but he also answered my ongoing questions for some fifteen months, as I checked factual information and verified my subjective perceptions surrounding the Huxtables' life together. I thank Cliff for reviewing the entire manuscript, for correcting my errors, and for permitting me to quote from letters that he and Catherine wrote to friends during their courtship, early marriage and later from their pioneering posts. Meeting Cliff again on Salt Spring Island, on July 9, 2015, after some 17 years, and visiting with him the sites of the three homes that he and Catherine had occupied during their stay on the island, was a special delight.

I am grateful to Don and Diana Dainty of Ottawa, who first awakened my interest in the Huxtables' story. The Daintys provided me with a packet of some twenty letters written to them by the Huxtables in the late 1950s and early 1960s. These letters, along with our conversations about Catherine and Cliff years ago, sparked my initial interest and enabled me to begin research into the Huxtables' story. The Daintys shared their remembrances of the Huxtables in the Introduction and made themselves available for in-person and telephone interviews. Douglas Martin, former member of the Canadian National Spiritual Assembly and the Universal House of Justice, shared his recollections of the Huxtables and made a few suggestions regarding the orientation of their story.

Michael Rochester of St. John's, Newfoundland provided all the letters of

Catherine's correspondence with him during the summer of 1952, and one letter from 1957. Michael also provided letters written by Cliff to him in 1952, and letters from the Huxtables written from St. Helena Island, as well as the eulogy Michael delivered on behalf of the National Spiritual Assembly at Catherine's national memorial service in Toronto in 1967. He also explained the process by which the Huxtables were named Knights of Bahá'u'lláh for the Gulf Islands, British Columbia, by the Universal House of Justice in 1969, and he also gave this book a thorough pre-publication review. Had it not been for Michael's close attention and interest, this narrative could not have taken its present form. He also provided pertinent historical information about the lives and record of service of Bahá'ís belonging to his generation, information that would have otherwise proven difficult to obtain. Thanks are due also to Michael's wife, Elizabeth Rochester, for sharing her impressions of Catherine, and for providing the description of the firesides in Forest Hill Village attended by the Huxtables, hosted by Elizabeth and her mother, Jessie Harkness Manser. The Daintys and Rochesters also supplied details of the Forest Hill Village Bahá'ís of the early 1950s.

My uncle Ronald Nablo, formerly of Salt Spring Island, British Columbia, now of Belize, Central America, the surviving spouse of my aunt Edna Halsted Nablo, shared his memories of the Huxtables during their stay in Toronto, as did his sister, Nora Moore of Qualicum Beach, British Columbia. My thanks are also due to Marlene Macke, of St. Mary's, Ontario, who was generous enough to have shared her notes of a tape-recorded interview with Cliff Huxtable that took place in Oshawa, Ontario, on August 7, 2000. The reminiscences of the late Bernice Boulding Crooks of Saturna Island, British Columbia, who served as Catherine's companion-helper in Regina, Saskatchewan, from the summer of 1958 until Bernice's marriage on Salt Spring Island (1961), provided a more complete picture of their life on Salt Spring Island.

Accomplished artist, Joyce Frances Devlin, of Burritts Rapids, Ontario, shared her impressions of Catherine and Cliff during an in-person interview. David Spendlove of Ottawa, clarified information pertaining to the life and career of his distinguished father, Francis St. George Spendlove, the Bahá'í teacher who played a vital role in Cliff and Catherine's decision to join the Bahá'í

Acknowledgements iii

Faith in 1952. Husayn Banani, former longstanding member of the Canadian National Spiritual Assembly, shared his recollections of the Huxtables' fireside on Salt Spring Island, British Columbia, during which Fletcher Bennett decided to become a Bahá'í. My telephone interviews with Fletcher's wife, the late Elinor Bennett of Sidney, British Columbia, and the information she sent me, were very useful in filling in the gaps of the Huxtables' early days on Salt Spring Island, and the circumstances surrounding the formation of the first Local Spiritual Assembly of the Gulf Islands at Riḍván (April 21), 1964.

Ann Kerr Linden of Toronto and Eileen Collins of Sherwood Park, Alberta, the sister of poet Roger White, took part in telephone interviews and email correspondence that provided biographical information on Catherine's late teenage years and the Huxtables' stay in Regina, Saskatchewan from 1957–1959. I thank Ann for sending black and white photos of the Huxtables and their friends. I am grateful to the Reverend Pamela Webster of Ely, Minnesota, for sharing recollections of her friendship with Catherine from 1949–1950, her visit with Catherine on Salt Spring Island in the summer of 1965, and details of their correspondence. Sara Griffiths, archivist of First Unitarian Toronto, was helpful in determining that Catherine Heward's name was found on the church rolls before she became a Bahá'í in 1952. Robert "Bob" Guillet, Cliff's fellow-student at the University of Toronto, who was present at the freshman dance when Cliff met Catherine in 1950, was kind enough to provide some details about their first year at the University of Toronto in a telephone interview.

I extend my thanks to the Archives Department at the Bahá'í National Center of Canada for providing me with a copy of a letter written to Catherine on behalf of Shoghi Effendi, copies of Catherine's correspondence with Rúḥíyyih Khánum, and other letters written to the Huxtables. I extend my thanks to Roger M. Dahl, Archivist of the National Bahá'í Archives of the United States, for forwarding information on the life of John Leonard, Knight of Bahá'u'lláh for the Falkland Islands, one of Catherine's Bahá'í teachers. Pauline Igao of the Falkland Islands was kind enough to provide me with a succinct pen portrait of John Leonard. I am grateful to the Local Spiritual Assembly of the Bahá'ís of Salt Spring Island, British Columbia, for sending me a copy of one of Catherine's inspiring letters, written from the island of St. Helena to the Baháʼís of Salt Spring Island, just seven months before her death. Cindy Wrate Newkirk was kind enough to send me some cards and letters written by the Huxtables between 1966 and 1969 that she discovered in the correspondence of her mother, the late Enid Wrate of Salt Spring Island. Last but not least, I would like to thank my congenial copy editor, Norma E. Hoyle of Abbotsford, British Columbia, who simplified my sometimes convoluted prose and improved the mechanics of earlier drafts.

TABLE OF CONTENTS

The Scope of This Book ∞ 12
Catherine's Early and Formative Years ∞ 20
The Freshman Dance, Unitarianism, The Bahá'í Faith ∞ 35
The Summer Letters to Michael Rochester ∞ 51
Courtship and Marriage ∞ 72
Regina, Saskatchewan ∞ 82
West to the Gulf Islands ∞ 99
Adieu Salt Spring ∞ 134
St. Helena Island ∞ 146
Death and Resurrection ∞ 161
A Life Remembered ∞ 179
Afterword ∞ 189
Tributes to Catherine and Cliff ∞ 191
Memorable Quotations ∞ 193
Appendix 1: A Child Meets Catherine Heward Huxtable ∞ 196
Appendix 2: How the Huxtables Were Named Knights ∞ 198
Appendix 3: Timeline of the Lives of the Huxtables ∞ 200
Appendix 4: Written on Her Gravestone ∞ 204

PREFACE

At age thirty-five, Catherine Heward Huxtable died from the deadly effects of muscular dystrophy. Attended by her husband, Clifford "Cliff" Huxtable (1932–), Catherine passed away in 1967 at home on the remote island of St. Helena in the South Atlantic, the third and last pioneering post the Huxtables shared as a couple. Their story deserves special mention in the annals of the Ten Year Plan/World Crusade (1953–1963), not only because the Huxtables pioneered to distant lands, but more importantly because Catherine served the Bahá'í Faith while living with the challenges imposed by a physical disability that confined her to a wheelchair. With each passing year, she grew weaker, but the gradual ebbing of Catherine's powers could not dampen her determination to pioneer. No more apt description of the Huxtables' spiritual mettle can be found than in the noble title "Knight of Bahá'u'lláh" chosen by Shoghi Effendi (1897–1957), the former head and Guardian of the Bahá'í Faith, to designate the cohort of believers who were the first to settle in countries, territories and islands without Bahá'í residents.

The circumstances of Catherine's life and early death (1932–1967), and the services she accomplished with her husband, are known now only to a dwindling number of their close friends. I have written this book in light of the urgent need to record the memories of those who can still contribute to telling the story of these courageous pioneers. I have done my best in the pages that follow to respect Cliff Huxtable's request to give Catherine's life preeminence, but except for her childhood and youth, theirs is unavoidably a story shared. For what they achieved, they achieved together. Without the outstanding supportive role played by Cliff, Catherine could never have accomplished her most cherished desire.

While this narrative details the Huxtables' contribution to winning the goals of the Ten Year World Crusade and subsequent Nine Year Plan (1964–1973), it intends a larger human interest: to convey the impact of Catherine's magnetically luminous personality and the lasting impression her courage made on those who knew her well—and even on those who met her only in passing. Beyond her

Bahá'í-specific service, Catherine's exemplary spirituality should be of interest to readers of any religious background.

Despite the idealism reflected in the title "Knight of Bahá'u'lláh", this narrative also recalls the severe tests and difficulties these pioneers had to face, particularly on Salt Spring Island and St. Helena Island. And yet, despite the formidable obstacles they encountered, the Huxtables experienced real joy and satisfaction in accomplishing their goals. Their life together reflects that commingling of joy and sorrow that is the inevitable destiny of all who share the human condition.

This story could not have been written had the Huxtables not arisen to serve the world religion to which they were entirely committed. In that sense, this narrative begins with action. However, when viewed in the longer perspective of the distant future, their story will be read as the experience of one couple among many who contributed to laying the early foundations of a united global society. For the peaceful world that will undoubtedly come into being, after the crises and catastrophes of this age have passed, will have been built, much as a larger-than-life mosaic is assembled by many hands, by the individual and collective efforts of countless numbers of dedicated Bahá'ís found in every land. This mission we gladly share with any and all like-minded collaborators who work for the spiritualization and the unification of our "strangely disordered world"—to use Shoghi Effendi's apt phrase.

A few among the Huxtables' contemporaries had already recognized years ago that their life together reflected such love, courage and sacrifice as would make their life-story worth the telling. Now, almost fifty years after Catherine's death, I am happy to say that their story has been told. Setting out their record of service has turned out to be a journey of search and discovery, of surprise and delight, for which I feel a mingled sense of both satisfaction and gratitude. The time spent over these past fifteen months has been very much the proverbial labor of love; but any labor I have expended has been more than amply refreshed and rewarded, by piecing their story together, by the inspiration provided by their words and deeds, and by the friendships made and renewed as I researched the story of their lives.

Preface

Finally, may *A Love That Could Not Wait* serve to inspire and strengthen anyone who has been unusually burdened by life's adverse circumstances. Accepting affliction with courage and grace, seizing the opportunities that life presents, and living life to the fullest, regardless of the length of our years, are surely the outstanding lessons of Catherine's life. The story of the wheelchair pioneer who, with the assistance of her helpmate, defied her disability confirms that her oft-repeated prayer to make her life count in the Faith she loved so well was not said in vain.

                                    Almonte, Ontario, Canada
                                    May 4, 2016

INTRODUCTION

It gives us great pleasure to accept Jack McLean's invitation to remember our friends, Catherine and Cliff Huxtable, in this book about their life together, *A Love That Could Not Wait*. So little is generally known about the Knights of Bahá'u'lláh, and their great contribution to the establishment of the Bahá'í Faith around the globe during the years 1953–1963, that a book like this one comes as a welcome addition to understanding the strength of character and the sacrifices that were required in those years, to open virgin territories to the Bahá'í Faith, and to establish Local Spiritual Assemblies there.

As for Catherine, words are simply inadequate to express the graciousness and warmth of her character, especially her warm outgoing sociability, and her very attractive personality. She was sincerely interested in people and engaged them easily in conversation. No wonder that we, along with numerous other friends, were very glad to share this friendship during the early days (1950s) of the then Toronto and nearby Forest Hill Village Bahá'í communities. We continue to be grateful for having made Catherine and Cliff's acquaintance in those early days, while we were learning and deepening together in our knowledge of the Bahá'í Faith, and participating happily in the affairs of the Bahá'í community.

One surprising coincidence of our relationship with the Huxtables occurred in 1955, when Don Dainty oversaw, as a representative of the Toronto Bahá'í Spiritual Assembly, the Bahá'í marriage ceremony of Cliff and Catherine in the Hewards' family home. As a member of the Toronto Assembly, Cliff likewise later officiated at the marriage ceremony for us in Diana's family home the following year. What a mutual pleasure for both families!

Among those early Bahá'í friends were included individuals who have been mentioned in the following pages: the Huxtables of course; Douglas Martin, who became a respected member of the National Spiritual Assembly of the Bahá'ís of Canada and the Universal House of Justice; highly regarded Hand of the Cause John Robarts and his gifted wife Audrey FitzGerald Robarts and their children, Nina, Patrick, Gerald and Aldie. The Robarts family became overseas and homefront pioneers and early prominent administrators and respected and valued members of the Bahá'í Faith; Alice Hall, and Elizabeth Manser Rochester and her mother Jessie Harkness Manser all held hospitable fireside meetings for the community in Forest Hill Village, and, as Jack has pointed out in the pages that follow, it was at Elizabeth's and her mother's firesides that the spiritual turning-point came when Catherine and Cliff met our wise and knowledgeable university advisor and teacher, George Spendlove.

In the Fall of 1955, Don and I departed for St. Catharines, Ontario, to take up new jobs and help support the growth of a new Spiritual Assembly in that location. From that time onward, we carried on an extended correspondence with the Huxtables, as they set out on their courageous series of settlements: first to Regina, Saskatchewan, then west to Salt Spring Island, British Columbia, off the coast of Vancouver Island. Facing many tests and challenges, they bravely persevered and shared their stories through our friendly exchange of letters. Meeting Cliff and other close friends at National Conventions was also a memorable reunion for Don.

The arrival of the Huxtables' son, Gavin, on Salt Spring Island, came a year or two after the birth of our second child, Catherine. To honor Catherine Huxtable, we had named our daughter after her, as it was unusual for someone with muscular dystrophy to live long enough to have a child. Later, we marveled at Catherine's ability to happily raise a child from a wheelchair for the first five years of Gavin's life.

After a series of remarkable situations and much prayer and consultation with their advisors, details that Jack has set out below, Cliff and Catherine decided that St. Helena Island in the South Atlantic Ocean, off the coast of south-west Africa, might provide a better climate and environment for them both, as well as a place to find affordable help for Catherine. Their many friends were amazed once more by their courage to set out across the ocean to a tiny island with high hopes that they might be able to be well-settled and to be of service to their beloved Faith. We had the pleasure of a visit from them in Ottawa in 1966, as they traveled across Canada en route to their chosen destination. May God hold them in His special care, always!

Don and Diana Dainty, Ottawa

∞ 1 ∞
The Scope of This Book

Knights of Bahá'u'lláh

"Knight of Bahá'u'lláh" is a title of spiritual nobility bestowed by Shoghi Effendi (1897–1957), the head and Guardian of the Bahá'í Faith, on a 254-member contingent of "pioneers" who opened 121 countries, territories and islands previously uninhabited by Bahá'ís during the Ten Year World Plan/Crusade (1953–1963).[1] (The title was limited to the period of the Ten Year Plan.) The Huxtables became Knights of Bahá'u'lláh for opening the southern Gulf Islands of British Columbia to the Bahá'í Faith in October, 1959.

The Indispensable Presence of Cliff Huxtable (1932–)

Catherine Huxtable credited two people for making her life circumstances bearable: her mother, Helen Bury Heward, whom she described as her "generous, long-suffering helper"[2] and her husband Cliff, who added a new spiritual dimension to her life by introducing her to the Bahá'í Faith after their meeting in the fall of 1950. (I should not neglect to mention the care provided by her older sister Julia in the years of childhood and youth.) Catherine's service to the Bahá'í Faith could not have been rendered without the devotion, love and support of Cliff Huxtable. Cliff's life of service as a Bahá'í pioneer on St. Helena Island has continued to this day—at this writing (2015), some forty-eight years after Catherine's death.

Catherine and Cliff were tested and purified in a common crucible. Throughout their twelve-year marriage, Cliff also had to contend with long stretches of illness and exhaustion; he fully shared Catherine's suffering, and to no lesser degree, her heroism. He reached the breaking point, more than once, under the weight of the considerable stresses that each relocation in the pioneering field involved with a disabled person: moving long distances, finding work and accommodation, setting up house, employing live-in caregivers, being a husband and provider to his wife, and later father to their son, Gavin, while having to endure the distress of knowing all the while that their life together would be cut short.

The Period Covered: Whole Life (1932–1967)

The chronology of this book spans the thirty-five years from Catherine's birth in England to her death on the island of St. Helena in the South Atlantic, best known to history as Napoleon Bonaparte's place of exile in 1815, until his death six years later. Although this book provides some pre-Bahá'í background on Catherine's life in chapter 2, the narrative highlights especially the fifteen-year period beginning when Catherine joined the Bahá'í Faith in 1952, as a twenty-year-old young woman in Toronto, until her death. It does not delve into the history of the Bahá'í community on St. Helena following her passing. However, a brief Afterword is provided that updates the reader on some of the actors included in this story and provides a sense of closure.

Sources

The main sources for this story have been handwritten letters, three transcripts of tape-recorded talks, in-person and telephone interviews, email correspondence and Internet research. Notes were taken during all telephone interviews. Catherine Huxtable was a prolific and devoted correspondent, and without her letters, it would have been impossible to write this book in its present form. Cliff's letters were no less valuable; they have helped to round out the picture of their life together. These letters have been the primary source in safeguarding the memories of the Huxtables' everyday lives as new Bahá'ís, as a couple engaged to be married, husband and wife, young pioneers, and parents. The letters also record the ongoing trials they faced and the joys they experienced.

This correspondence throws open a window on Catherine's engaging and lively personality, both in its human and spiritual aspects. It expresses the heroism of her spirit, the frankness of her occasional frustrations and periodic discouragements, and her active engagement with teaching the Bahá'í Faith. The letters entrusted to me by the Daintys and Michael Rochester amount to some 250 pages. Together with the Huxtable papers and transcripts, and the material found in the Canadian Bahá'í National Archives, excluding interviews, emails and Internet research, the written sources for this book amount to approximately 500 pages, written over a fifteen-year period from 1952–1967.

Besides the information provided by Cliff Huxtable, the basic facts of Catherine's life and personality have been gleaned from three foundational articles. "A Conqueror for St. Helena" (1974), written by Catherine's brother-in-law, Weston "Wes" Huxtable (1931–2001), gives an excellent overview of Catherine's life. I hasten to mention that Wes's use of the triumphant word "conqueror" has nothing to do with proselytizing St. Helenians. His intention was clearly to convey that Catherine had learned to conquer herself, particularly her initial horror of the wheelchair and the feelings of self-pity that she once felt in her early teenaged years. Roger White's "In Memoriam" article from *The Bahá'í World* (1963–1968) gives an eloquent, sensitive and succinct presentation of Catherine's spirituality and the effect of her magnetic presence on those who knew and loved her. Paisley Glen's finely written "In Memoriam" appreciation of Catherine's life and faith, "Catherine Heward Huxtable (1932–1967)", published in the Canadian Bahá'í News (1967), was another welcome source.

The transcript of Cliff Huxtable's 1978 talk on St. Helena Island has been a valuable aid in giving an overview of their life together. The transcript of my tape-recording of a 1998 talk given by Cliff at my parents' former home, at 131 Mt. Baker Crescent on Salt Spring Island, contains important personal details of their stay there, not found elsewhere, covering the years when they opened the Gulf Islands to the Bahá'í Faith in October of 1959, until their departure in October of 1965. I could not have imagined when I recorded Cliff's 1998 talk, that some sixteen years later when I began this book, the information it contained would help to frame the narrative of their six-year stay on the island. Marlene Macke's transcript of her interview with Cliff in the year 2000 revealed some previously unknown anecdotal information about the life of the Huxtables' spiritual father, the eminent teacher, Francis St. George Spendlove.

The information that forms the life story of the Huxtables until the time of Catherine's death in 1967 has been reconstructed largely from living eye-witnesses who participated, directly or indirectly, in the narrative that is related below.

Their story is well documented by copious first-person correspondence, email exchanges and in-person and telephone interviews. Although the documents that came into my hands have enabled me to reconstruct the lives of the Huxtables, some unavoidable gaps and errors of my own making may exist in the pages that follow. We have to remember also that human memory is fallible when it comes to recalling events that took place as far back as sixty-five years ago. And, even if the participant accurately recalls the event, this does not mean that every detail of the recollection is accurate. Fortunately, the recollections of the participants whom I consulted, despite the passage of time, remained fresh, with but few exceptions. I can affirm, consequently, that this narrative is largely true-to-life. When I was not sure of the facts, I have alerted the reader, or I followed the surgeon's maxim, "When in doubt, cut it out."

The Special Nature of Spiritual Biographies

Stories about Bahá'ís belong to a niche category of literature. Unlike other biographies, they are not written for the mass market. What interest they do create is generated by the fact that the reader shares a common bond of faith with the subject(s) of the book and its author. Although the story of the Huxtables consists of what would normally be viewed as mundane events, the extraordinary things performed by otherwise ordinary people become especially important because the protagonists performed them for the fulfillment of the Divine Plan, as a service to humanity, and ultimately, for the sake of God. Because of this high motivation, and because pioneers inevitably face difficulties in accomplishing their goal, these events come to assume a special significance. Their history becomes sacred history, but one that possesses a very human face. Spiritual biographies also reveal their own lessons regarding the workings of the special dynamic that operates in the lives of those who are willing to leave their homes to shoulder the sometimes lonely and demanding task of spreading the Bahá'í Revelation in faraway places. As time passes, these biographies will no doubt attract greater attention, as future writers and historians reconstruct earlier periods of Bahá'í micro or macro history, even as they seek to discover the spiritual mettle that defined the lives of those whose Faith they share. To the extent that the community becomes curious about the lives of their co-religionists of former times, will these stories help them to assess the contribution made by their spiritual forebears and to inspire present and future readers in their own efforts to serve the Bahá'í Faith.

The Story as "History" and Moral Purpose

I maintain that the purported clash between "history" and moral purpose is one of those false dichotomies that has caught the attention of alert readers in the Bahá'í community. In the pages that follow, I have consciously avoided mythologizing the lives of the Huxtables—especially Catherine—just as I have rejected the negative stereotype of the saint as a grave, humorless, penitent whose life was a constant trial. The Huxtables' life together was indeed full of troubles, but despite Catherine's occasional discouragement and periodic depressions—what she called a "spiritual slump"—her radiance and serenity shone through the clouds that had temporarily blocked her sun. This statement is just as much a reflection of history as it is of spirituality. In attempting to balance Catherine's highly evolved spirituality with her humanity, I have respected the accuracy demanded of the historical researcher, by maintaining fidelity to the original source documents. At the same time, I have been motivated by the empathetic human interest of the creative writer, and the engaged stance of a committed believer.

The following narrative is not complicated. Its story line is easily plotted: Catherine's birth in England; Cliff and Catherine's youth in Toronto; their meeting, courtship and marriage; pioneering to Regina, then to Salt Spring Island where their son Gavin was born; pioneering again to St. Helena Island where Catherine died. The writer's challenge in narrating such a story is to engage and sustain the reader's interest throughout the mundane business of moving house, finding companion-helpers for Catherine, while Cliff looked for and found gainful employment in each new location. Nevertheless, I have attempted to capture the sense of adventure they clearly felt, the courage and sacrifice involved, the divine confirmations they always received, as well as the joy that our pioneers felt as they achieved success in their community-building activities and in their life circumstances.

Writers and readers of this genre of literature are conscious of the familiar, usually academic critique of the lives of "saints" as hagiography—a biography that praises too much. Be that as it may, it is nonetheless true that many Bahá'ís of their generation thought that Catherine fitted the description of a "saint." I have written saint in inverted commas because to write about Catherine's saintly nature invokes at the same time her warm humanity: her love of the arts; her radiant smile; her welcoming hospitality; her mischievous, self-deprecating sense of humor; her childlike enthusiasm; her disdain for disrespect; her fine sensitivity; her penetrating insights into human nature; and, despite her gentility, the iron will that did not impose or dictate.

In the end, writing about a couple like the Huxtables is a tricky business: if I praise too much, I may repel the reader by creating a certain spiritual fatigue or credibility gap; if I praise too little, the reader will ask why their story is worth recording in the first place. Although my admiration for the lead characters in this story is, on the evidence, fully justified, it is neither naïve nor blind to human frailties, as a few sections of this story will reveal. Because I want especially to set out their accomplishments, I have felt no need to satisfy some questionable demand for "balance and objectivity" by referencing certain particularities of their humanity, either in their family life or with each other. Some of their experiences are simply too personal and private to record, and it would be unseemly and unwise to do so.

I have, of course, relied heavily on the documentation that came into my hands to reconstruct the Huxtables' story. Yet the following story required a more creative approach than simply reproducing exact quotations or making paraphrases of the source documents. Although this story is based on the actual events that formed the life experiences of Cliff and Catherine Huxtable, creating and sustaining reader-interest has required a considerable sifting and synthesizing of the raw material and an imaginative reconstruction of the events that does not violate historical accuracy.

Necessary Digressions

I should alert the reader to a few digressions that became necessary in the following narrative. For example, when I discuss the role played by George

Spendlove, the teacher who had the greatest impact in deepening the faith of Catherine and Cliff, I have provided some additional biographical information. I have also provided some context for the roles played by John Leonard, Pamela Webster, Ann Kerr Linden, Wes Huxtable, Michael Rochester, Angus and Roberta "Bobbie" Cowan and Winnifred Harvey. While Catherine and Cliff remain the main characters throughout, this information has been necessary to assist the reader in understanding the positive effect these individuals had on the then young couple. (I should note that John Leonard influenced especially Catherine.)

Insider Language and Use of Special Terms

Regarding the Bahá'í terminology found in this book, I have used insider language with such words and phrases as "Knight of Bahá'u'lláh," "fireside," "pioneer," "believer," "fellow-believer" or "the friends," the last phrase being the familiar way Bahá'ís, like Quakers, refer to one another. I sometimes abbreviate the Bahá'í Faith simply to "the Faith." Although the meaning of most of these words and phrases will be obvious from the context, I have provided an explanation when necessary. The title "Hand of the Cause of God," or simply "Hand of the Cause," refers to one of a total of fifty distinguished teachers who were appointed or mentioned for propagating and protecting the Bahá'í Faith, either posthumously or during the lifetimes of the Prophet-Founder Bahá'u'lláh (1817–1892), His son 'Abdu'l-Bahá during His ministry (1892–1921), and during the ministry of the Guardian of the Bahá'í Faith, Shoghi Effendi (1921–1957).[3] For dates, I have used the Common Era, i.e. the Christian calendar. For the local and national institutions of the Bahá'í Faith, the Local Spiritual Assembly and the National Spiritual Assembly, I will sometimes use the abbreviations LSA and NSA rather than writing them in full. When referring to Salt Spring Island and St. Helena Island, I have sometimes opted for the more colloquial expressions "Salt Spring" and "St. Helena." Regarding chapter 6, opinions vary as to what constitutes the currently shifting politically correct terms for the Aboriginal peoples of Canada. During the Huxtables' two-year stay in Regina (1957–1959), the term "Indian" was widely used; we find this word reflected in Catherine's letters, and I have quoted it as such. But I also use interchangeably and without prejudice today's words, "Aboriginal," "First Nations" and "Indigenous."

The Title of this Book

In 1998 author Janet Ruhe-Schoen published at Palabra Press condensed biographies of eight women (Lua Getsinger, May Maxwell, Martha Root, Keith Ransom-Kehler, Dr. Susan Moody, Dorothy Baker, Ella Bailey, Marion Jack) and one man, Hyde Dunn. The title of that book is *A Love Which Does Not Wait*. When the similarity of the two titles was brought to my attention, I decided, upon reflection, to maintain the present title because it expresses best the spirit that moved a young disabled woman to action, a woman who was only too keenly aware that her life would be cut short.

∞ 2 ∞
Catherine's Early and Formative Years: England and Toronto (1932-1950)

Her British-Canadian Ancestry and Privileged Family Background[4]

Before narrating Catherine Heward Huxtable's life with Cliff, I shall set out her family background. This information is worthy of mention for two reasons: first, it will be of historical interest to some readers. This material provides a larger picture that situates Catherine's life within a social context; second, the fact that a woman in a wheelchair willingly abandoned the protected and affluent lifestyle that she knew in Toronto, with its conveniently located medical services, for the formidable challenges of the pioneering field, is evidence, not only of her strong spirit of courage and independence, but also of complete dedication to her chosen Faith.

Although it was Catherine Huxtable's fate to have been diagnosed in childhood with a type of muscular dystrophy that was expected to limit her lifespan to about twenty years, she was fortunate to have been born into affluence. Catherine's care was uppermost in her parents' mind. Their upper-class status allowed the Hewards to provide her with the best care and medical attention that was available at the time. Her Canadian father, Lieutenant-Colonel Stephen A. Heward, and Mrs. Helen Bury Heward, her English mother, were able to afford the services of a Scottish cook, long retained by the Hewards, who also looked after Catherine's care requirements. When Catherine was a child and young teenager, this task was also shouldered by her elder sister, Julia Wynne. When Julia married the Orillia radiologist, Dr. James Norman Harvie (1920–1979), whose father had been the town doctor, the care she had provided was supplied in turn by a Norwegian lady of reputable character.

Catherine's father, Stephen Augustus Heward (1868–1958), was educated in Switzerland, England and Toronto. His first profession was that of architect, but in 1897, after opening an office in Toronto, he abandoned this occupation sometime after 1900. He chose instead a military career.[5] The Hewards were once prominent in Orillia, a town eighty-three miles (133 km.) north of Toronto, where they owned Heward's Point, on the southwest shore of Lake Couchiching. It was there that they enjoyed their summer home, "Edinswold," where they were neighbors of the famous Canadian humorist, writer and political scientist, Stephen Leacock, to whom the Hewards had sold an adjacent piece of land on the eastern side of their property. Sometime in the pre–1840 history of Upper Canada, today's Province of Ontario, the Hewards owned a huge tract of land, including what is now part of western Toronto. It extended ninety miles (145 km.) north to Lake Couchiching.

Colonel Heward's ancestors had been members of the influential and wealthy Family Compact, a group of male elites of British descent who, despite the name, were unrelated. They formed an oligarchy, a Tory clique that controlled the political, religious, judicial and economic life of Upper Canada from circa 1810–1840. Their power dissolved after the rebellions of 1837 in Upper and Lower Canada (Ontario and Quebec). A prosperous Loyalist family from New England, the Hewards had fled the rebellious American colonies and moved to Toronto and Montreal, taking their family fortune with them. Catherine's mother Helen was reported to have descended from a de Rudyerd, a prominent knight who fought at the Battle of Hastings in 1066. The Burys acquired their wealth through land holdings. Their assets were maintained in the nineteenth and early twentieth centuries through banking in northern England and real estate development around Branksome near Bournemouth, the resort town on the southwest coast of England.

Birth in Charlwood, Surrey, Childhood and Youth in Toronto (1932–1949)[6]

Catherine Heward was born on January 6, 1932, at Charlwood House, a Tudor style home in the small village of Charlwood, Surrey, one of the greenest and most affluent home counties in England. Located on the southwest border of greater London, even today Surrey still ranks high for its choice quality of English life. After serving as an artillery captain in World War I, Captain Heward returned to Canada and was appointed commander and Lieutenant-Colonel of the Halifax artillery. Circa 1930, Colonel Heward retired to the gentleman's life

2 ∞ Catherine's Early and Formative Years

in Charlwood where Catherine was born in 1932, when he was sixty-four years old. Anticipating World War II in Europe, and with estates to settle in Canada, the Colonel and Helen Heward returned to Toronto in 1939, when Catherine was seven years old.

It would have helped to complete this narrative to have known something of Catherine's personality in childhood, but no one from her original family is still living. Only one story has survived; it was transmitted to me by Cliff Huxtable: "She told me she had been very willful as a baby. One day in England, the family had left her in the pram while they walked off a little way. She was mad as hops, screamed and cried and shook the very substantial pram until she had knocked it over and fell out. I am very pleased she had later developed spiritually. Catherine could be very determined in the nicest way."[7]

Catherine received her primary education at Havergal College (Anglican), a private school for girls and young women located in the Lawrence Park area of midtown Toronto. Havergal College, despite the name for a post-secondary institution, accepted junior students. Catherine entered Havergal at the age of seven, and followed through until her graduation from the eighth grade in 1945. Secondary education followed at Bishop Strachan School for girls (Anglican), one of Canada's top private schools, in what was then still known as Toronto's Forest Hill Village. The curriculum at both schools included not only the usual tuition in academics, but also a program in music and amateur dramatics. Her love of the arts was to remain strong throughout her life. While she could walk, Catherine had a normal social life, but faced with steadily worsening health, she was forced to abandon formal schooling during her teenaged years.

Her Rejection of Class Distinction and Other Forms of Prejudice

Although Catherine Heward accepted her privileged family background, she rejected any notion of class distinction that blighted the attitude of some of her parents' generation. In her eyes, her socio-economic background was of little consequence to her personal identity and character formation. Because she was an egalitarian in her view of social class, and unlike her class-conscious parents, she rejected any barrier that stood in the way of anyone who sought her company. In today's parlance, Catherine was fully a "people person." Indeed, she made no secret of the fact that she loved people. Her open view of society was to facilitate later her acceptance of the Bahá'í teachings, with their progressive stance on social and gender equality, and the condemnation of any form of racial, religious or class prejudice. But it was especially the answers she found to life's great questions, both the imponderables and the known, that attracted her to the Bahá'í teachings.

Diagnosis of Muscular Dystrophy: The Heward Family Home, 7 Clarendon Crescent, Toronto

Catherine Heward grew up in a large, three-story house at 7 Clarendon Crescent, a short secluded street on the escarpment just south of Forest Hill Village, overlooking the Nordheimer Ravine and lower Toronto. For easy access, Catherine's room was located immediately to the left on the main floor when one entered the house. A beautiful magnolia tree once stood in the back yard, but the Heward property has since gone the way of "progress," replaced today by an apartment block. In 1941, when she was nine years old, Catherine almost succumbed to a near fatal attack of scarlet fever.[8] After recovering from the serious illness, the young girl was observed to be falling frequently. She tired easily, had a poor sense of balance, and unlike other children, she was unable to run. Consultations with doctors followed. When she was ten years old, during a visit to their summer home in Orillia, the doctors diagnosed a type of muscular dystrophy that usually strikes male children. Mrs. Heward hid her grief following the medical consultation that day; she did not attempt to explain anything to her child about her illness in the months that followed. Only later did Catherine learn the name of the disease that was slowly claiming her body. Between the ages of ten and fifteen, her back, arm and leg muscles gradually weakened, a degenerative condition that continued for the rest of her natural life. As her disease progressed, her social world necessarily became more restricted. She became dependent upon her parents, sister and friends for outings and receptions, and they did their best to keep Catherine connected to the outside world.

2 ∞ Catherine's Early and Formative Years

Her Childhood Friend Madeleine Ashlin Davis, Beloved "Stouge"

During her childhood years, and throughout the rest of her life, Catherine maintained the closest sisterly friendship with a beloved classmate who also went to Havergal, Madeleine Ashlin, later Davis. The schoolgirls met when Catherine was eight years old: they became the greatest of friends and confidants. Like Catherine, Madeleine came from a privileged background. She was the granddaughter of Chief Justice Francis Alexander Anglin, the first Chief Justice appointed after Canadian confederation in 1867.[9] Catherine and Madeleine's playful sense of humor was evident early on in their friendship. The two girls jokingly called one another "stouge." (Madeleine's spelling). Between them, Mrs. Heward became "Mrs. Stouge" and Colonel Heward was "Colonel Stouge." The nickname for Catherine's parents was probably her way of finding some relief from the strict protocols and formalities that regulated the British–Canadian household in which she grew up. Madeleine's father sported a monocle, which contributed to his air of pomposity, but despite his consciously cultivated British–Canadian identity, he was approachable and friendly.[10]

Her Battle with the Wheelchair, Withdrawal from School, Madeleine Ashlin's Departure for Brazil

By age fifteen Catherine was forced into a wheelchair, and although she fought back for two more years to avoid its regular use, it was a losing battle. She was horrified at the prospect of such a restricted life: "At first I used a wheelchair only when I was alone. Then I conquered my horror of being a cripple," she recounted in a magazine interview when she was twenty-one years old. (The word "cripple," pejorative today, was in common usage in the 1950s.) Catherine had not only horror to overcome, but feelings of self-pity. In the same interview, she declared: "I don't feel sorry for myself now. All people have their problems."[11] Until the end of her life, although she was weak in her upper body, Catherine was able to feed herself, but she needed both hands to drink a cup of tea. She was right-handed, and when she wanted to shake hands, she used the left hand to support the right arm.[12] The gradual invasion of muscular dystrophy, although it is generally not painful, and does not affect the mind, leaves the patient progressively debilitated; everyday living becomes a struggle.

Catherine's forced withdrawal from Bishop Strachan School at age seventeen (1949), and Madeleine Ashlin's move to Brazil (1950) after she graduated from Havergal College, where Madeleine had been boarding, had a temporary depressing effect on Catherine. Years before Madeleine's father had secured a position with the Brazilian Traction Light and Power Company in Rio de Janeiro and later São Paulo. It was time for Madeleine to join her father.[13] Catherine's withdrawal from school did not, however, signal an abrupt end to social intercourse. When her health permitted, through the care of Mrs. Heward and her older sister Julia, and with a small circle of close friends, Catherine's cultural and artistic interests were nourished. She enjoyed occasional lectures, the art gallery, the theatre, concerts, movies, and ballets. She lived not far from the Royal Ontario Museum, to which the Hewards were generous patrons. It was there that George Spendlove, one of the outstanding Bahá'í teachers of his generation, served as curator. As associate professor, he also taught archaeology at the University of Toronto. (More will be written in chapter 3 of George Spendlove's key contribution to Catherine Heward's and Cliff Huxtable's spiritual awakening and his outstanding contribution to the Toronto Bahá'í community of his generation.)

Epiphany in England: The Awakening to Life, the Arts, and the Beauty of Trees (1949)

After withdrawing from school, Catherine made a consolation sea-voyage to England with her mother and sister Julia. She was seventeen years old, an age when an adolescent's self-identity is still in the process of flux and formation. It turned out to be a trip that was to have a significant impact on Catherine's developing self-esteem and personal identity formation. The trip to England gave fresh wings to her sagging spirits. Catherine's outlook on life was invigorated and strengthened during the trip to her mother's native land, where she met her English relatives and visited London.

In England, Catherine came to realize that her life was far from over. Just as significantly, she was able to perceive that the people who passed through her life did not look down on her as being a pitiable "cripple". Instead, with a growing

2 ∞ Catherine's Early and Formative Years

sense of self-confidence, she observed that people were actually attracted to her—and with good reason. One of her close friends commented on her beautiful, luminous face, sparkling brown eyes, "gorgeous" auburn hair, and the radiant smile that would fill a room.[14] (References to her radiant smile were frequent among interviewees.) This realization was significant because she used to feel that being confined to a wheelchair constituted a barrier to making new acquaintances. It was a false perception that she gradually dispelled over the ensuing years. After her marriage to Clifford Huxtable in 1955, and by the time that they had pioneered to the Gulf Islands, British Columbia, in October, 1959, she came to realize that being in a wheelchair actually predisposed strangers to be drawn to her.[15]

Catherine greatly loved both classical and popular music, but being the artist and craftsperson that she was, she was naturally strongly visual. During the 1949 trip to England, her sense of perception grew suddenly sharper. This phenomenon was probably due to the relief that her new outlook on life afforded, with its enhanced sense of self-esteem. More significantly, we can also view this development as a reflection of an expanding spiritual consciousness that manifested itself in a more acute awareness of the ambient world. In this case, Catherine became suddenly more conscious of one of the most ubiquitous objects in nature—trees. Nor was it her visual sense alone that sharpened. Her appreciation of Beethoven's music and Brahms's First Symphony began at this same time, although she also enjoyed popular music and jazz. She liked Benny Goodman, "the King of Swing," and his sextet. The 1948 Capitol Records catchy tune, "He's got a fine brown frame," sung and played by jazz pianist and songstress, Nellie Lutcher, was one of her favorites.

In one of her letters to Cliff's close friend and fellow-student Michael Rochester, letters that will be explored more fully in chapter 4, Catherine explained the phenomenon of increased awareness that she suddenly experienced in England. On September 8, 1952, she wrote:

> It was about three years ago, at about this time of year, that my eyes were first opened to the astonishing beauty of trees. Before that, although I had always been a great nature lover,

trees in general were something I could never appreciate. Then I went to England for a trip, and I began to live. At the same time, while there, Beethoven really began to mean something to me, and I suddenly found myself looking at the English trees—and almost gasping at their variety and shape and colour, etc. etc. And, wonder of wonders, when I returned across the ocean, I discovered that Canadian trees were beautiful *too*!! But each year when autumn rolls around again, I ache to see once more the New Forest and London's Hyde Park, in yellow-leafed misty splendour. [underlining in original]

Catherine Heward's Friendship With Ann Kerr Linden

Included in the circle of Catherine's teenaged friends was Ann Kerr Linden, née Cartwright.[16] Like the other testimonials presented in this book, Ann bore witness to Catherine's authentic, admirable spirituality. Now well into her senior years, Ann is at this writing (2015) still working as a psychiatric social worker in Toronto. Her recollections are particularly pertinent because, like Pamela Ball Webster, who met Catherine in late 1949 when Catherine was seventeen years old, Ann is one of the few friends still living who knew Catherine the year before she met Cliff Huxtable in the fall of 1950. (We will return to Catherine's friendship with Pamela in chapter 3.)

Prompted by a kindness to widen Catherine's circle of friends, Pamela introduced Ann to Catherine. Catherine and Ann began to correspond. The two young women met at the Heward's large three-story home under the watchful eye of Mrs. Heward. Ann felt that Mrs. Heward did not entirely approve of her friendship with Catherine, an impression that Catherine later confirmed, but no attempt was made by the Hewards to interfere. Cliff Huxtable later recalled that the Hewards "had the good qualities of their class, but Catherine was free of its limitations."[17]

As their friendship developed, Catherine and Ann grew close enough that they spoke intimately on life-issues. Ann recalled that Catherine impressed her as a "very sensitive, introverted young woman, and you felt the presence of a strong interior life." Despite the restrictions on her mobility that curtailed to some extent her social life, Ann confirmed that Catherine was far from being a recluse. The young Miss Heward, despite her contemplative nature, was vitally interested in people. Ann remarked on Catherine's strong interest in the arts, including film and music. Catherine's cousin, the actor Wey Robinson, and film-maker Don Owen, who later produced the National Film Board of Canada's first successful full-length feature, *Nobody Waved Goodbye* (1964), figured among her friends and acquaintances. Don Owen was a member of the youth group at First Unitarian Toronto that Catherine later joined through Pamela Webster.

Ann felt sufficiently at ease during one conversation to ask Catherine how she was able to cope with the severe limitations imposed by muscular dystrophy. Catherine responded that listening to a Beethoven string quartet, and watching Hollywood musicals at the cinema, gave her an exhilarating feeling of liberation, and allowed her to participate vicariously in the activities of the able-bodied. What Catherine most wanted to do was to dance, a desire that was realized during a singular, extraordinary visitation with Cliff on the third evening following her death on St. Helena Island. (See chapter 10). Like most other women of her generation, Ann reported that Catherine was interested in future prospects: "She was very beautiful and men found her attractive. She dated occasionally, but this was not unusual. Most of us dated in those days because we were naturally interested in marriage."

Her Artistic Petit Point

Catherine had hoped to earn her livelihood through her artistic ability. Weston Huxtable, Catherine's brother-in-law, wrote that after leaving school, Catherine "enrolled in a commercial art course but wasn't able to finish it because her arms were too weak to draw anywhere but at a desk, depriving her of the freedom of movement she felt essential for an artist."[18] Although the Hewards were sufficiently wealthy to have relieved Catherine of the need to earn a living, she insisted on being financially independent. Not long after she was forced to abandon her commercial art course, Catherine found employment through one of the handicrafts: petit point or needlework. As the first of their "physically handicapped" employees, she was able to earn a limited income by working for Marina Creations, "specialists in exquisite luxuries such as hand-made jeweled gloves, scarves and petit point." Catherine also produced finely delicate pictures, evening bags and earrings in the miniature craft.[19] Pamela Webster once observed Catherine painting in miniature. She was astonished by her ability to paint using only one eyelash that was affixed to a small implement![20] Despite muscular dystrophy, her fine motor skills were highly developed. With the money she earned and saved, Catherine was eventually able to purchase a Ford Prefect car, imported from the United Kingdom.[21]

The Testimony of Ann Kerr Linden: "Her Faith was Palpable."

About a decade after their meeting, when Ann and her Danish husband Sven Kerr had settled in West Vancouver, the Huxtables motored west from Regina to stay with the Kerrs during the Huxtables' summer vacation in 1958. When they were on their way to settle in the Gulf Islands the following year, the Huxtables were received again by the Kerrs. Ann was finely attuned to the quality of Catherine's faith. In a telephone interview on April 8, 2014, she gave the author a succinct appreciation of what she felt in Catherine's presence: "Her faith was palpable. She didn't have to say anything, but you felt it, although people who were meeting her for the first time may not have been initially aware of what it was they were feeling. The quality and strength of her faith increased as time went on. It was real. There was a radiance. Her faith developed through her deep suffering and her reliance on prayer. You could feel that she was a person who had suffered intensely. She was at times in despair about what she was facing, and she experienced fear, frustration and worry, but she was not sunk by it. She was connected to God."

"My Calamity is My Providence": Catherine's and Cliff's Respective Searches for Meaning

"O SON OF MAN! My calamity is My providence, outwardly it is fire and vengeance, but inwardly it is light and mercy. Hasten thereunto that thou mayest become an eternal light and an immortal spirit. This is My command unto thee, do thou observe it." Bahá'u'lláh

The Diagnosis of Muscular Dystrophy

Both Catherine and Cliff had been visited by traumatic life events that would eventually lead them to the Bahá'í Faith, and to unite them in marriage. Their common spiritual search was driven by a "desperate need to find reality."[22] Catherine's traumatic life event was, of course, the diagnosis of muscular dystrophy. As we have seen above, Catherine initially found it unbearable to realize that her physical disability would shorten her life drastically.[23] She eventually learned that the doctors had estimated her lifespan at twenty years, a prognosis that turned out to be fifteen years short of the mark. Being a sensitive soul who was inclined to a strong interior life, Catherine began to seek spiritual comfort, courage and empowerment to help her face disability and premature death. That search included especially finding some deeper significance to her life-situation. I emphasize the truth-and-empowerment motivation of Catherine's search. If it were comfort alone that she were seeking, she could have found it in any number of religions. Catherine found the Bahá'í spiritual philosophy on facing tests and difficulties, life's challenges and learning experiences, to be particularly helpful to someone in her situation.[24]

Although she became a Unitarian in 1950, when she was eighteen years old, within the next two years Catherine became dissatisfied with the lack of spiritual substance that she found in the teachings of the Unitarian Church, despite its progressive belief in social justice. In a church that admits in the same congregation, agnostics, atheists and theists, she found the teachings of the church too intellectually dry for her personal brand of spirituality. Not all Unitarians believed in the soul or the afterlife, whereas Miss Heward was a strong theist who believed in an immortal human essence. Her life situation impelled her to find answers to such profound questions as the purpose of life, the existence of the soul and the afterlife, and the meaning of suffering. Despite its promotion of the independent search for truth, a belief that is shared with Bahá'ís, she was not able to find in

Universalist Unitarianism any personally significant spiritual philosophy for one who was facing early death. One Unitarian even suggested to her that death had the practical effect of "making room for others." Although this remark was not intended to be malicious, it discouraged Catherine's sensitive spirit.[25]

Cliff and the Near-Fatal Accident in East Toronto

While Catherine was coming to grips with the challenging circumstances confronting her, Cliff was dealing with the aftermath of a weighty test of his own—a serious accident that he had unintentionally caused. On August 17, 1949, when Cliff was sixteen years old, he found summer employment in a small crew of Ontario Hydro workers whose job it was to maintain the base of cedar poles that carried the main power lines. One summer afternoon, the crew's work schedule had taken them to east Toronto, to the north side of the main highway that ran eastward to Oshawa and Kingston. They came upon a highway bridge spanning a wide, deep ravine with a narrow stream running through it. The power line left the highway, ran down into the ravine and up again to join the road. Cliff and his co-worker Russ followed the line down into the ravine. After completing their task, they climbed back up the steep slope to continue their maintenance-work along the highway. Since the two young men were working well ahead of their follow-up crew, they stopped to enjoy the view. They were about one hundred feet directly above the stream.

In a relaxed moment, Cliff picked up a smooth, round rock and said to Russ: "I bet I can get this rock into that stream." Before throwing the rock, Cliff looked carefully along and down the slope. He had a clear view to the edge of the stream; it was mostly bare ground, covered with some scattered, stunted shrubs. Satisfied that no one was below, he stepped back, then moved forward to launch the rock and followed through to watch it land. The rock fell short of the stream. Cliff could not have known that, invisible from above, an eight-year-old boy had been hiding near the edge of the stream as he played "cowboys and Indians." As seemingly impossible as were the chances, the stone struck the boy on the back of the head. As the boy's hysterical mother and others rushed to the scene, Cliff plunged down the bank feet first. Cliff took the wheel of the mother's 1936 Plymouth and sped up the dirt road leading to the top of the steep slope. Reaching the highway, he drove as fast as he could to a nearby doctor's office. The doctor followed Cliff back to the ravine in his own car, where the grim-faced physician bandaged the boy's head. They sped away to the Emergency department at the Toronto East General Hospital, where the doctors performed emergency surgery. Fortunately, the lad survived the operation, but several other operations became necessary to restore his health. Much later the doctors decided to insert a metal plate to fortify the skull.

On that terrible evening, Cliff desperately wanted to speak to only one person: Hiles Carter, his "spiritually aware" high school science teacher. It looked at first as if fate had conspired against their meeting that night. Cliff had recently received a postcard from Hiles, who was on holiday in the Canadian Maritimes. He seemed to be inaccessible. Unbeknownst to Cliff, his teacher had just returned to Toronto, when he heard of the accident on the radio as he was unpacking the family car. Hiles phoned immediately to offer his help. That night Cliff and his science teacher walked the streets of Toronto, far into the night. During some long, anxious hours, Hiles patiently listened while the young man talked himself out. During that conversation, Hiles helped Cliff to better understand his unarticulated aspiration to pray. Cliff takes up the narrative in his own words:

> I wanted to pray but really did not know how. He asked what I wished for deep in my heart as an outcome of this tragedy, then said, 'That is your prayer.' He suggested there were no accidents, that God was real, and that if we sought it there was good in everything. He further suggested that if I earnestly sought the good, I would one day look back on this dreadful event with deep gratitude to God. This was the effective beginning of my spiritual education.[26]

Cliff and his family paid a heavy price for the accident. Following an investigation, the police determined that criminal negligence was not a factor, but because the medical expenses could not be covered by his financially limited parents, the boy's family initiated a civil suit. This legal action consumed an insurance policy held by Cliff's father, as well as his life savings to that point. Emotional recovery for Cliff was slow. His social life remained a blank for the next two years. Cliff tended to be a loner. He reflected some twenty-nine years later, however, that the accident turned out to be a minor "miracle,"[27] because it eventually caused a profound change in his life. The Huxtables' friend, my aunt Edna Halsted Nablo, was convinced that the accident was the proverbial blessing-in-disguise. She believed that the Huxtables' marriage was one of the compensations of Providence for the tragic accident that had taken place in Cliff's youth.[28] Edna's conviction was not without foundation. The accident later helped to forge a compassionate bond between Catherine and Cliff, no less than Catherine's paralysis, a bond that, coupled with the Bahá'í Faith and their mutual love, brought them together in marriage. As for Cliff, the series of events that eventually brought him together with Catherine began in that unhappy moment of his life.

The Role of Cliff's Brother Weston Huxtable (1931–2001)

Although the conversation with Hiles Carter was a significant turning-point in Cliff's life, a moment that first made him conscious of the reality of prayer, he continued to grapple with the after-effects of the accident. His older brother, Wes, who first introduced him to the Bahá'í Faith, was helpful during this distressful period by encouraging him to examine the Bahá'í teachings, and to find the remedy to his psychological distress, rather than to remain fixated on the past. To help Cliff move forward, after Wes had listened to his younger brother pour out his troubles one more time into the early hours of the morning, he attempted to make a break-through by asking pointedly: "Cliff, are you in love with your troubles or do you want to solve them?" Wes's question "hit home." It became another turning-point conversation.

Wes had graduated from Forest Hill Collegiate (Toronto), where he became a committed Bahá'í through his classmate Gerald Robarts, one of the three sons of the future Hand of the Cause of God John Robarts and his wife Audrey FitzGerald Robarts.[29] After he had enrolled at the University of Toronto, when faced with criticism from the rest of the Huxtable family because of his recent conversion, Wes switched universities and enrolled at Queen's University in Kingston, Ontario. At Queen's he joined a small group of new Bahá'ís and Bahá'ís in-the-making. Despite the family's initial rejection of Wes's newfound Faith, Cliff began to examine surreptitiously the Bahá'í books his brother had brought home from university. When the therapeutic conversation mentioned above with his brother took place, Cliff had been attending firesides occasionally for some two years. By the time he was eighteen years old, Cliff was determined that he would make it his purpose in life to help others, although it was not clear to him precisely how his humanitarian motive could be accomplished. Cliff's conversations with his high school mentor, Hiles Carter, and his brother Wes were to have unsuspected, far-reaching consequences for Cliff and Catherine's acceptance of the Bahá'í Faith, their conjugal life, their spiritual development, and for the many other lives that in turn would eventually be touched by them.

∞ 3 ∞
The Freshman Dance, Unitarianism, The Bahá'í Faith (1950–1952)

The Freshman Dance: Victoria College, University of Toronto (1950)

    The stage was now set for a romance that would determine the course of Catherine's and Cliff's lives together until the time of Catherine's passing in 1967. The scene was the 1950 Fall Freshman Dance at Victoria College where Cliff had registered. Catherine went on a dare. Since she was in a wheelchair, she had never before attended a public dance. Because he could borrow his father's car, Cliff, who was still investigating the Bahá'í Faith, went along at the urging of Bob Guillet, a fellow student who was studying geology, but Cliff had not really been keen to go. They arrived quite late, and for most of the evening, they simply stood around, eyeing the young women on the other side of the dance hall.

    These freshmen had only recently graduated from high school, and the evening had all the makings of a high school dance. Two rows had formed up, one of "wallflowers" and the other of "stags."[30] The bravest of the brave, for all to see, would venture across the floor to take their chances with a member of the opposite sex. Cliff and his friend fell in with the freshmen and began to watch the dancing. Toward the end of the evening, Cliff noticed a radiant young woman sitting down. It was a moment of instant attraction.

    The young Honors Science student walked across the dance floor in her direction, when he suddenly noticed that the woman who had attracted his attention was in a wheelchair. He retreated to the men's line, but Cliff was persistent. Earlier he had noticed a tall, elegant young woman who had been standing behind Catherine, who was now dancing with a fellow-student enrolled in one of Cliff's science courses. To find out what he could about the beautiful stranger in the wheelchair, Cliff cut in and danced off with her. The woman was Joyce Sachs (later Asquith), one of Catherine's Unitarian friends, who told Catherine that she had been very "chuffed" (Br.=pleased) to be chosen by Cliff, but his only enquiries were for the young woman in the wheelchair. Joyce responded graciously to his questions by saying: "Oh, come over and meet her. She is just like everyone else."

Cliff joined Catherine's group and spent the rest of the evening chatting with her. When the dance was over, the first year students headed over to 7 Clarendon Crescent where they met Mrs. Heward. They spent about an hour there, enjoying one another's company, before breaking up to go their separate ways. As he walked back to his car, Cliff had the strong intuition that Catherine would one day become his wife. Looking back on their first meeting, Catherine wrote in a letter of July 14, 1952, to Cliff's close friend Michael Rochester: "Did I ever tell you that Joyce is as responsible for the meeting of Cliff and I [sic] as is Bob Guillet?"

Pamela Ball Webster and Catherine's Investigation of Unitarianism

Although Pamela Webster and Catherine were in actual personal contact for only about a year, their friendship became determinative for the spiritual path chosen by both women. Catherine's bosom friend, Madeleine Ashlin, had introduced Pamela to Catherine in late 1949. Madeleine and Pamela had roomed together at Toronto's Havergal College for girls in 1948–1949. Catherine had already graduated to secondary studies at Bishop Strachan School the same year that Pamela enrolled at Havergal.[31] Catherine had no close friends in the immediate neighborhood of Clarendon Crescent, and it was Madeleine's intention that Catherine and Pamela would become friends since Pamela lived in the vicinity.[32]

After her withdrawal from school, Catherine's sea-voyage to England in 1949 had been a great spirit-lifter, but Madeleine's departure for Brazil in 1950 had left her feeling lonely and isolated within a family environment that she found at times restrictive. Pamela took Catherine's growing sense of isolation and loss to heart by setting out to improve her social life. More importantly, she also assisted Catherine's early spiritual search by introducing her to the Unitarian church.

Pamela often visited Catherine at home where she partook of the impressive afternoon *thé à l'anglaise* offered by the Hewards. Served on a tea trolley, the Hewards' tea-time offered a fine selection of treats preserved in colorfully decorated biscuit tins. Among the treats, the Hewards served brandy snaps, cylindrical biscuits filled with butter cream or whipped cream spiked with brandy. Pamela observed that "the Hewards had that English respect for eccentricity."[33]

When Catherine and Cliff met at the Fall Freshman dance, Catherine had been attending the Unitarian church at Pamela's invitation. Catherine, who had turned eighteen the previous January, formally joined the Unitarian congregation on October 29, 1950, about two months after the dance. She listed her occupation as "student."[34] Despite her youth and the predominance of Christianity in "Toronto the Good,"[35] Pamela had developed a curiosity about Christianity and non-Christian religions. Hers was an unusual interest for most young people living in the still largely Protestant, Anglo-Saxon city. Catherine and Pamela began to discuss "deeper things that mattered, including spiritual matters."[36] But Pamela had another, more practical motive in introducing Catherine to the Unitarian Fellowship. She knew that some members of the congregation owned cars. They would be able to transport Catherine to church and back, allowing the young woman to experience a more active social life.

Both Pamela and Catherine were gregarious, but the saying that opposites attract may have been a key factor in the friendship of the two young women. Although Catherine and Pamela shared a common interest in spiritual matters, and although they discussed serious life issues, their personalities were distinct. Pamela had been attending St. Paul's Anglican church, but she was such an openly inquisitive and non-conforming spirit that had been expelled from confirmation class by Canon Henry John Cody (1868–1951), Rector of St. Paul's and former President and Chancellor of the University of Toronto, because she asked too many questions. By contrast, although Catherine would learn to be frank, in the first few months after she became a Bahá'í in 1952, she wrote to Michael Rochester: "One of my troubles is that I am inclined to be too timid to express radical ideas unless in answer to a direct question. I have a lot of self-teaching to do this summer, and a great determination to do it."[37] Some two years later, when Catherine introduced Pamela to the Bahá'í Faith, the sensitive Miss Heward would on occasion begin to cry if her more outspoken spiritual companion too openly challenged the Bahá'í teachings. Catherine clearly did not enjoy any dialogue that passed over into contention.[38]

Catherine welcomed Pamela's invitation to attend the First Unitarian Fellowship. They found a breath of fresh air in the church's open spirit of inquiry.

3 ∞ The Freshman Dance, Unitarianism, The Bahá'í Faith

It was a "liberating experience"[39] for both women. Despite the Hewards' social standing and their attendance at one of downtown Toronto's prominent Anglican churches, where the Hewards had their own labeled family pew for generations, Catherine was not attracted to the outward formalism of Anglicanism.[40] Although the church appeared to be entirely satisfying to her parents and her older sister Julia, who "modeled a very patterned devotion"[41] to the Anglican church, Catherine's interiority and sensitivity impelled her to seek a more intimate and direct form of religious experience.

Pamela and Catherine began to attend the First Unitarian Church of Toronto, located at 175 St. Clair Avenue West, at a time when Unitarianism was expanding rapidly in Canada. This expansion took place largely through the influence of the Reverend William Phillip Jenkins (1911–1985), an American who was minister at First Unitarian when Catherine and Pamela were attending. Jenkins was a theistic humanist[42] and outspoken controversialist, well-known in the Toronto media for his forceful views on religion and social issues.[43] He was later to officiate at Catherine and Cliff's 1955 wedding, a service that he performed at other Bahá'í marriage ceremonies before 1958, when Bahá'í marriage was granted legal recognition in the province of Ontario.[44] Both Pamela and Catherine were popular enough with the young Unitarians to have been elected president and vice-president respectively of their youth group. Pamela observed that during her time in the young people's group, Catherine had also demonstrated an ability to plan and to organize.[45]

Much later in life, Pamela was to recollect that their experience at the church was "wonderful in that we could express ourselves freely; the world grew larger."[46] The leader of the senior youth group was a dynamic young man who "encouraged us to think for ourselves."[47]   Pamela appreciated the fact that the youth leader sat at the table with his students, rather than standing up to direct the discussion. She observed that those discussions were their first exercise in critical thinking.[48] Although Catherine did not find complete spiritual fulfillment in the Unitarian church, her exploration of Unitarian beliefs turned out to be an important stepping-stone that would soon lead her, through her dialogue with Cliff Huxtable and other Bahá'í teachers, to the Revelation of Bahá'u'lláh.

Pamela left Toronto on September 16, 1950, to attend university at Wellesley College on the outskirts of Boston where she studied English, history and biblical history for the next four years, followed by a year at the Graduate School of Education at Harvard in Cambridge, Massachusetts. Although Pamela did not live in Toronto again after her departure for Boston, whenever she returned to her native city, she would visit Catherine until the Huxtables left Toronto for Regina in 1957. The two women remained faithful to their friendship; they engaged in frequent correspondence until about a year before Catherine died in 1967.

Meeting Cliff Huxtable was destined to become the major factor that initiated a quantum leap in Catherine's spiritual development. However, Catherine's introduction to Unitarianism became a shorter transition phase in Catherine's life, just as Pamela's introduction to the Bahá'í Faith by Catherine became a longer transition phase in Pamela's life. Ten years later, after eight years of investigation, Pamela would become a Bahá'í for another eight years, but her spiritual path eventually led her to the Episcopalian priesthood. (See chapter 4.)

The Bahá'í Faith: Spiritual Fulfillment and Finding Community

I mentioned above three turning-points in Cliff's life: his conversation with his spiritually aware science teacher, Hiles Carter, after the accident in east Toronto; his talks with his brother Wes, who encouraged him to solve his problems rather than to dwell on the past; and his meeting with Catherine. Catherine's discovery of Unitarianism, and Cliff's interest in the Bahá'í Faith, determined their joint spiritual search and formed the matrix of their early friendship and courtship. (In passing, it bears mention that Cliff was never seriously interested in Unitarianism.) After they met at the Freshman Dance at Victoria College, Cliff joined Catherine in attending the First Unitarian Congregation. They would discuss Unitarian teachings and Reverend Jenkins's stimulating Sunday sermons. During their conversations, Cliff would give the Bahá'í point of view, based on remarks of his brother Wes, and as Cliff understood them from his own readings of Bahá'í books. Cliff introduced Catherine to the Bahá'í Faith, but it was Catherine who encouraged Cliff to investigate the Bahá'í Faith more thoroughly with

3 ∞ The Freshman Dance, Unitarianism, The Bahá'í Faith

her. They attended a weekly Sunday evening fireside in Forest Hill Village at the apartment of Elizabeth Manser (later Rochester), and her mother, Jessie Manser. They also frequented the firesides of John and Audrey Robarts, at the Robarts' home in the same vicinity, and a few firesides at Laura and Victor Davis' home, at 44 Chestnut Park Road in the centrally located, affluent district of Rosedale.

Central to the young couple's attraction to the Bahá'í Faith were the cardinal teachings on the unity of humanity, and "the life and death teachings,"[49] as Cliff referred to them, those teachings that gave insights into the meaning of life and the afterlife, vitally important realities for someone in Catherine and Cliff's situation. They found these Bahá'í teachings intellectually and spiritually satisfying. Cliff recollected: "She gained a deep understanding of the purposes of suffering, also of magnanimity. Even before turning to the Faith, I never heard or sensed 'why me?'"[50] Death was not about "making room for others," as Catherine had been told by one insensitive Unitarian; it was a "messenger of joy", an open door to a glorious journey of the soul that did not end with our last breath. Death was a rebirth from the womb-world into an as yet inconceivable state of joy and liberation in our eternal movement toward the presence of God.[51]

Catherine's spiritual search was no passing intellectual curiosity. It was based on divine love and the intuitive ways of the heart; she was grounded in the immediate experience of spiritual reality. Catherine appreciated the ensemble of the Bahá'í teachings. She perceived in them a coherent whole, like the interlocking parts of a puzzle or an artistic design. Pamela Webster related: "She grasped the system she was interested in holistically."[52] Cliff wrote that she also found appealing "the balance and moderation of the overall picture painted by the teachings and progressive revelation."[53]

I should note that during this period of spiritual search and discovery, the Hewards made no attempt to curb Catherine's interest in Unitarianism or later the Bahá'í Faith. While they clearly loved Catherine and eventually came to appreciate her highly evolved spirituality— especially her sister Julia who cared for Catherine in her difficult childhood years—where they were concerned, they alternately ignored or resisted her spiritual quest. Although the Colonel and Mrs. Heward never asked questions about the Bahá'í Faith, they did not raise objections to or disparage Unitarian or Bahá'í beliefs. For her part, Catherine never attempted to press the Bahá'í Faith on her family. After making some early attempts, she concluded that silence was the wisest course because initiating conversations on any Bahá'í topic would upset the family, particularly her father. Despite the fact that Julia once read two Bahá'í booklets, the family's almost total lack of interest in her newfound faith, notwithstanding the love they felt for one another, remained a frustration and deep disappointment.[54]

The Distinguished Curator and Scholar, Fireside Teacher and Mentor, Francis St. George Spendlove (1897–1962)

Before the inauguration of the current systematic global community-building program based on the "institute process," a program that includes but is not limited to the four "core-activities,"[55] one-on-one teaching and firesides were the main vehicles for teaching the Bahá'í Faith. Although the fireside is no longer the preferred teaching medium that it once was, now that the more comprehensive institute process has become the central engine that drives the expansion of the Bahá'í Faith, it remains effective and widely used. Hosting a fireside every nineteen days was the congenial teaching medium that was highly recommended by the Guardian of the Bahá'í Faith, Shoghi Effendi.[56]

The fireside is sometimes used today as a bridge to invite seekers to participate in the more systematic group learning that takes place in the phased learning of the study circles, or as a link to the devotional meeting. Although local variations exist, the generic fireside consists of a small gathering of invited friends, held in someone's home, during which prayers are said, followed by an informal talk, usually on some aspect of the Bahá'í Faith. The talk is followed by questions and answers and discussion. The evening is topped off with refreshments and socializing.

Between 1950 and 1952, when Catherine Heward and Cliff Huxtable were investigating the Bahá'í Faith, George Spendlove was one of the highly respected and influential fireside teachers for both "contacts", as they were then called, and Bahá'ís. Spendlove was one of a handful of Toronto's earliest active Bahá'ís. In 1936 he joined the staff at the Royal Ontario Museum as curator of

3 ∞ The Freshman Dance, Unitarianism, The Bahá'í Faith

the Japanese and East Indian[57] collections. He gave regular weekly Tuesday night firesides for twenty-two years (1938–1960). Some of the firesides were held at the Bahá'í Centre at 112A Bloor Street, and at the Spendlove home at 463 Lytton Boulevard in North York, firesides that greatly stimulated the teaching work in Toronto, along with the public meetings where he spoke. Douglas Martin, former National Spiritual Assembly member of the Bahá'ís of Canada (1960–1985) and later Universal House of Justice member (1993–2005), attended some of those firesides and was impressed with George Spendlove's profound understanding of the Bahá'í Faith.[58] George's American wife, Dorothy G. Spurr Spendlove, a devoted Christian Scientist, acted as gracious hostess.[59] Shoghi Effendi (1897–1957) was most appreciative of the teaching work that Spendlove was accomplishing. On December 11, 1936, he added his personal post-scriptum to a letter written on his behalf by his brother H. Rabbaní:

> I wish to assure you in person of my deep appreciation of the work you are so devotedly accomplishing in Toronto. My hope, indeed my prayer, is that you may be graciously assisted to establish a group of fervent believers who will form a nucleus and foundation for a flourishing spiritual assembly. Persevere in your pioneering efforts and rest assured. Your true and grateful brother, Shoghi.[60]

As he did for others, George Spendlove played a pivotal role in confirming Catherine and Cliff in the Bahá'í Faith. He was a colorful, eccentric, one-of-a-kind individual whose public speaking style was emphatic, personal and surprisingly blunt. Although he was by nature a gentle, reflective and sensitive person, George had been traumatized by the battles in which he had fought during World War I. At age nineteen, he enlisted as an artillery gunner, an action that exposed him to concussion from exploding shells and later toxic mustard gas, first introduced by the Germans in 1917. After convalescence in a military hospital in England, he returned to Montreal in 1919, where he recovered slowly at his home for another two years. According to Rúhíyyih Khánum, the Bahá'í teachings had helped to heal George's heart from the invisible wounds his spirit had suffered because of his traumatic years of combat.[61] His combat injuries caused drooping eyelids and impaired hearing, among other maladies, for the rest of his life.[62]

George Spendlove spoke in strong, sometimes puzzling, oracular pronouncements that defied contradiction. He was known for his witticisms. One of his most well-known sayings has passed to the wider world: "Be very careful what you pray for; you may get it." His serious demeanor was lightened by a subtle sense of humor. He sometimes smilingly referred to humanity as "homo sap."[63] His convictions were buttressed by fervent daily prayer, but despite his voice of authority, George Spendlove also conveyed the power of the love of God. He was especially sensitive to beauty and refinement. These esthetic qualities were central to his professional life as art curator. To Cliff and Catherine, George became an instructive and loving spiritual father. "George and Catherine just glowed in each other's presence,"[64] recalled Cliff. George Spendlove possessed that rare combination of impressive academic and spiritual credentials, quite sufficient to impress any sincere seeker. He was born the same year as the Guardian (1897), whom he met during his pilgrimages to the holy shrines in Haifa and Acco/Akká in 1933 and 1956. Together with the sincere appreciation and praise from Shoghi Effendi quoted above, he received this note of gratitude from the eminent head of the Bahá'í Faith:

> Dearly beloved co-worker: I wish to assure you in person of the deep debt of gratitude that I feel I owe you in view of your historic services to the Faith. You have upheld the principles of our Faith, spiritual as well as administrative, and with exemplary loyalty, courage and wisdom. I will, from the depths of my heart, supplicate for you the Master's richest blessings. Persevere in your high endeavours. Your true brother, Shoghi.[65]

George's spiritual roots grew strong under the influence of that distinguished founding family of the Bahá'í Faith in Canada, the Maxwells of Montreal.[66] Another distinguished and effective teacher of his day, Rowland Estall, who was born in England in 1906, introduced George to the Bahá'ís, after George discovered a reference to the Faith in a book on comparative religion. Like the true seeker that he was, according to his own testimony, George closeted himself

3 ∞ The Freshman Dance, Unitarianism, The Bahá'í Faith   45

in a hotel room in Montreal with *The Hidden Words*. He abstained from food and drink and engaged in ardent prayer, determined not to leave the room until he knew whether the Bahá'í Faith was the Truth. By morning, he had emerged, a believing Bahá'í.[67] George became a close friend of May Maxwell, "'Abdu'l-Bahá's beloved handmaid, distinguished disciple,"[68] and the younger Mary Sutherland Maxwell, later Hand of the Cause of God, Rúhíyyih K͟hánum, who became the wife, confidant and secretary of Shoghi Effendi, and the leading ambassadress of the Bahá'í Faith after his death on November 4, 1957. Mary Maxwell much admired George Spendlove, her elder by eleven years, with whom she held pleasant, informative conversations that contributed much to her early intellectual development.[69]

Although he became a special instructor or associate professor in the department of Art and Archaeology at the University of Toronto—until 1968 the museum was part of the University of Toronto—he was especially known and respected for his work as collector and art curator at the Royal Ontario Museum. Along with the Modern European Collections, he was responsible for developing the Far Eastern Collection, which featured Chinese bronze, porcelain and other art.[70] In 1952, he was appointed first curator of the magnificent Sigmund Samuel Canadiana Gallery of early Canadian fine art, located on the west side of Queen's Park Crescent. Early Canadian furniture, prints, books and paintings were a "first love." Although George was not primarily a writer but a lecturer, scholar and curator, he was also known in literary circles in Toronto as an author of articles and books on Chinese art and early Canadiana.[71] His numerous honors and distinctions as a fellow and member of royal societies, various academies, groups and associations attest to the excellence that he achieved in his field.

God Becomes Real: Cliff Huxtable Encounters George Spendlove

The fireside at which Cliff met the remarkable phenomenon that was George Spendlove took place at Elizabeth Manser's, one of the well-attended firesides in Toronto. The fireside was assisted and fully supported by Elizabeth's mother, Jessie Harkness Manser. The small apartment in which Jessie and Elizabeth lived was located in Forest Hill Village, on the boundary of Toronto, in a building at 404 Spadina Road. Elizabeth Manser Rochester has observed that some of the university students who attended her firesides during the post-World War II period were seeking answers to troubling questions that had arisen in the aftermath of the then recent global conflict.[72] Miss Manser had become a believer in 1946, a few years before others of her generation, and officially enrolled in 1948. In 1946 Elizabeth attended a fireside given by Bahiyyih Randall Ford (later Winckler), at the nearby home of John and Audrey Robarts. The topic was announced as world government, a favorite subject of Elizabeth, but the fireside "had nothing, so far as I can remember, about world government." Nonetheless, Elizabeth immediately became a believer, as Bahiyyih Ford, unasked, answered all her questions.[73]

Elizabeth's firesides had been poorly attended initially, but because of regular weekly personal telephone invitations, excellent speakers, original topics, and the opportunity provided for warm social interaction among young adults, the firesides soon grew to overflowing. She recalled:

> There were many times when the floor as well as the chairs and couch were blocked with people. It was frequently impossible to walk on the floor because of the crowd, and I remember passing plates of sandwiches out into hands which passed them on. From the way the plates came back empty, my mother sometimes wondered if the kids ate from fireside to fireside.[74]

Although Cliff had been investigating the Bahá'í Faith with Catherine for two years by this time, he had not yet taken the religion seriously. Some of the younger generation living in the early 1950s, perceived the Bahá'í community of that time as being filled with genteel, white-haired seniors, particularly the stereotypical "little old ladies," some of whom were club women.[75] Cliff liked to poke fun at "the delightful little old ladies in the 'sweet Baha'i and Baha'i.'"[76] His jocular attitude turned serious after he met George Spendlove.

It needs to be said that these senior women had contributed significantly

3 ∞ The Freshman Dance, Unitarianism, The Bahá'í Faith

to the establishment of early Bahá'í communities in Canadian cities. Some had met 'Abdu'l-Bahá; others, like Laura Davis, who merits the title of spiritual mother of the Toronto Bahá'í community, had made the pilgrimage during the administration of the Guardian (1922–1957). Her pilgrimage of 1955 has been well reported in Marlene Macke's instructive biography, *Take My Love to the Friends: The Story of Laura R. Davis*.[77]

Professor Spendlove's reputation had preceded him. The little apartment was packed as usual. Nineteen-year-old Cliff Huxtable was sitting cross-legged on the floor just across from the speaker. George began his presentation with a weighty question: "Is there anybody here who really wants to know what they should be doing with their [sic] life?' No response. George repeated the question. This time Cliff put up his hand and replied, "Yes, I do." George looked down at Cliff, gave him the once over and said: "That's the problem with you Clifford. You want to start at the top of the ladder instead of the bottom rung." Cliff recalled that Elizabeth Manser appeared to be discomfited by his challenging, personal approach. Elizabeth indicated, however, during our exchange of emails some sixty odd years later that she had no recollection of being upset by anything George Spendlove said.[78]

George's provocative approach turned out to have served a divine purpose that night. Cliff was not offended, and George went on to speak powerfully on Divine Reality. For others who were attending that fireside, God may have been only an abstract idea, but when George spoke about the Creator, He became real. Cliff remembered the impact of that fireside. As he was walking home, it struck him that the Bahá'í Faith was no social club for little old ladies, and that "all this was vastly real."[79] Cliff added: "George got through to me on the power and reality of God and the whole universal system; he was deep and powerful himself. His special love for Catherine must have been very important to her."[80]

Catherine and Clifford Become Bahá'ís (1952)

Although that Manser fireside became another of those significant turning-points in their lives, it was not there that Cliff and Catherine decided to enroll. That step was taken at the fireside of Audrey and John Robarts at 4 Millbank

Avenue in Forest Hill Village adjacent to the Toronto city limits. Both Catherine and Cliff affirmed their belief in Bahá'u'lláh on the same evening in April, 1952, at the Robarts'.[81] Although the Huxtables left Toronto for Regina some five years later, Cliff continued to cherish throughout his life the memory of George Spendlove, the man who had ignited the spiritual flame within the hearts of Catherine and himself. In a talk on St. Helena Island in March of 1978, eleven years after Catherine's passing, Cliff recalled the contribution that his great teacher had made: "Canada owes him much for the background that he offered its young Bahá'ís."[82] Despite the gratitude that Cliff felt toward George Spendlove, he recognized that Catherine had also led the way to his becoming a believer. In his letter of November 10, 1953, to Gale and Jameson "Jamie" Bond, he remarked: "She has certainly led the way for me and has set a selfless example. I wouldn't be a Bahá'í today if it hadn't been for her. . . . But thank God she and several other people persevered. My hope and prayer is that I may now discharge the trust thus laid upon me."

Despite the fact that Catherine at first felt that her disability might curtail effective Bahá'í service, she did not waste any time in finding opportunities for teaching the Bahá'í Faith. She began giving talks immediately following her enrollment, including a talk given to a group of young people at my parents' newly built home on then rural Martin Grove Road in the township of north Etobicoke, Toronto. Catherine wrote her childhood friend, Madeleine Ashlin, about one radio talk that she gave in Toronto in November or December, 1952.[83] One of those whom Catherine confirmed in the Faith within the next two years was Elizabeth Martin, the wife of Douglas Martin. Douglas has indicated that Elizabeth became a Bahá'í in 1954 because of the hours she spent in the company of Catherine Huxtable. For the Martins, Catherine "incarnated everything about the Faith that was in the process of capturing our hearts."[84]

The Testimonies of Elizabeth Rochester and Pamela Webster

Subjective perceptions color all human interactions. However, commonly shared perceptions clearly exist, as long as these perceptions do not widely diverge, as they do, say, with certain political or historical figures. The most frequent

3 ∞ The Freshman Dance, Unitarianism, The Bahá'í Faith

comments made by those of Catherine's generation refer to her palpable spirituality, smiling face, and radiant personality, qualities that were put to good use in the teaching and pioneering fields. Elizabeth Rochester remembered especially Catherine's sweetness. Her following comment is noteworthy because it indicates that Catherine's sincerity was able to break through Elizabeth's youthful, alert skepticism. Not everyone, I should add, is inclined to be impressed by sweetness. Too much sweetness can easily become cloying, and if it is, as Elizabeth has observed, it may well be masking something else. In her telling comment, Elizabeth made it clear that Catherine's sweetness was neither saccharine nor insincere: "Through her," she wrote, "I learned to appreciate sweetness. She was so very sweet, and, at that stage in my life, I was a little suspicious of sweetness. Always before it had seemed to me to mask something else. But, in Catherine, there was no mask, no hiding of some other feeling; just pure sweetness. I loved her."[85]

Pamela recalled Catherine's comeliness in the days just before she met Cliff, when Miss Heward was seventeen years old. Physically, Catherine resembled her father more than her mother. Her sister Julia was tall and thin, like her mother, while Catherine was shorter—about five feet, six inches tall (167 cm.) according to Cliff[86]—round-faced, and, until the onset of muscular dystrophy, thicker-set by comparison, like her father. Pamela recalled "the beautiful, gorgeous hair, twinkling brown eyes and lovely smile."[87] She observed no active interaction between Catherine and Colonel Heward, who remained silent during social visits and kept largely to himself. Mrs. Heward, however, was fully present, observing, interacting, and either approving or disapproving of Catherine's choice of friends. Mrs. Heward scrutinized Catherine's guests, and although usually not forbidding of her daughter's friendships[88], because she appeared to be severe, Mrs. Heward had the effect of keeping visitors away unless her approval be given.

The young Pamela must have met with Mrs. Heward's approval because she was invited to the Hewards' summer home, Edinswold. Pamela's British ancestry and family background likely went in her favor. Her ancestors were original settlers at Niagara in 1783. Her aunt Katharine L. Ball (d. 1991) was a respected professor at the University of Toronto, the first woman president of its Faculty Club, and a key person in the development of Canadian library science regarding cataloguing and classification.[89]

Pamela remembered Catherine's magnetic, welcoming greeting: "It was illuminating. She would focus directly on her guest. She was very special. She looked at you with understanding and appreciation. She radiated love. It was a great joy to be in her presence."[90] Pamela's words confirmed the understanding of Ann Kerr Linden regarding Catherine's sensitive, artistic personality: "Catherine Heward was very sensitive and emotionally intuitive," she related.[91] Being the "people person" that she was, Catherine possessed a certain ability, like her future husband Cliff, to accurately assess an individual's personality, both its strengths and weaknesses. She was an excellent judge of character.[92]

Although Catherine's letters reveal that she was articulate and intelligent, she was not inclined to delve too deeply into the world of abstract ideas and to make fine intellectual distinctions, a tendency that can easily lead to debate. Perhaps her timidity to express radical ideas, unless she was questioned directly (as she wrote in her letter of June 22, 1952, to Michael Rochester), derived from her experience of growing up in a household governed by parents who did not favor the free expression of unconventional ideas. But it is also quite clear that in becoming a Bahá'í, Catherine possessed her own mind. Although she shied away from confrontation and debate about the Bahá'í Faith, Catherine could become indignant at any display of disrespect. She was ruled neither by convention, conformism nor the subservience that bowed to money or the status quo. "She wasn't cowed by her parents," Pamela said.[93] Her friend affirmed that despite her illness—or perhaps because of it—"she had this passion for independence. This fit perfectly with her pioneering."[94]

It struck Pamela that in Catherine's personality, her capacity to love and her faith state functioned as one: "There were no inconsistencies. Her faith was so enormous that it would fill the room. She had the energy and conviction of a true convert. . . . She stands out so forcefully as someone who distilled from the experience of her faith a great capacity to love. She had a supreme ability to relate to others with love."[95] She affirmed her spiritual search began with Catherine, just as Catherine's had begun with Pamela's: "Catherine sent me on a path of inquiry that would not have developed otherwise. . . . She was one of the most hugely beautiful people I have known."[96]

∞ 4 ∞
The Summer Letters To Michael Rochester: Catherine's Life and Faith (1952)

The Summer Letters Written from Edinswold

On a sunny, cold winter afternoon, I was delighted to find in my post box a packet of 132 pages of Catherine's letters, all handwritten, to a young student in Honors Mathematics, Physics and Chemistry at the University of Toronto. I placed the letters in a large manila envelope and noted the date: January 21, 2014. The sender and the former student were one and the same person. Michael Rochester later became a well-respected geophysicist at Memorial University in St. John's, Newfoundland. For twenty-nine years (1963–1992), he served as a member of Canada's National Spiritual Assembly. Michael had been introduced to the Bahá'í Faith at the University of Toronto by Catherine's future husband, Cliff Huxtable. Michael and Cliff became the closest of friends when they studied together during Cliff's two years of Honors Science. Michael became very fond of Cliff's parents, and the two men have remained close friends despite some sixty years of physical separation.[97]

The summer letters were written from the Heward's large, two-story summer home Edinswold, a cognomen derived from Edin, the name of Colonel Heward's eldest brother, and the old English word for "wooded upland." Edinswold was bordered by a long hedge that surrounded the lawn and demarcated the property from the nearby shoreline of Lake Couchiching, near the town of Orillia, in "cottage country" eighty-four miles (135 km.) north of Toronto. Idle tennis courts from the nineteenth century, a small boathouse and a workman's family cottage completed the grounds.

The Outstanding Traits of her Personality Revealed

The letters of 1952 are such a valuable asset for this narrative because they clearly depict their author's quality of faith and personality. Her 127 pages of ten handwritten letters to "Mike,"[98] dating from June 22 to September 8, together with one five-page letter of March 29, 1957, written from Toronto two years after her marriage to Cliff, indicate that Catherine was a communicator—a prolific correspondent who reveled in expressing her feelings and ideas. These are affectionate, candid, engaging, sometimes emphatic letters, highlighting both spiritual matters and the everyday affairs that were occurring in the lives of Michael, Catherine and Cliff, and Catherine's immediate family.

The letters express Catherine's views about the Bahá'í Faith to the student who became a Bahá'í himself in August of that same summer, while their correspondence was in full swing. Occasional lines of self-deprecating humor lighten the seriousness of her explanations of the Bahá'í teachings. Catherine's expressions of warm affection, unfailing encouragement, spiritual counsel, and the exhilaration born of her recent total commitment to life as a Bahá'í, are conveyed throughout. Although this correspondence openly shares the joy she had by then found in her relationship with Cliff, it also reveals her short-lived but painful struggle over the feasibility of marriage, as she continued to cope with declining health. These letters also record passing appreciations of the new believers whom she had recently met. They also contain certain confidences to Michael regarding painful family-of-origin issues, that for discretion's sake, can only be alluded to here. Besides her love of the arts, it is clear that engaged dialogue, either in writing or *viva voce*, was one of the preferred means by which Catherine came to grips with her illness and personal problems. Letter writing was a natural kind of therapy.

Her Fresh Enthusiasm for the Bahá'í Teachings

The following passages express Catherine's encouragement of Michael, as he pursued his ongoing study of the Bahá'í Faith, and the absolute centrality it took in Catherine's spiritual life. In her letter of June 22, she wrote:

> It makes me so happy to know how graciously you are striving to be able to become a Bahá'í; and the zeal with which you are reading the books really inspires me. I hope you can always keep your fire burning so brightly. I'm glad you are

4 ∞ The Summer Letters to Michael Rochester

having the opportunity this summer provides of thinking long and carefully about all the points you feel unsure about. Don't forget to ask God to help you. I am enclosing a copy of the very wonderful prayer by Bahá'u'lláh which was sent to me at the time that I became a Bahá'í. I think you will like it. It says an awful lot.

Judging by the thanks expressed to Michael for his insights on the questions they discussed, these letters also reveal that the teaching and learning experience of the summer correspondents was a "two way street" on which Catherine and Michael were teaching and learning together. After returning to 7 Clarendon Crescent in Toronto, Catherine wrote on September 8:

> All this, plus the fact that physically my life is almost unbearable at times, makes me more grateful than ever to have something so big and good and all absorbing as the Bahá'í Faith to concentrate on. It, and it alone, makes all else seem unimportant. I fervently hope that I will be able to give to <u>it</u> as much as it has given to <u>me</u>. I sometimes wonder how on earth all the many <u>non</u> Bahá'ís manage to get through their difficult lives <u>without</u> it." [All underlining in this and the following passages is found in the original].

This excerpt from June 30 expresses her ongoing enthusiasm that Michael is making rapid progress in his study: "I am even <u>more</u> thrilled to hear how wonderfully you are progressing along that sometimes bumpy road to becoming a Bahá'í. You already seem so much like one that I'm inclined to think of you as one." In the same context, she writes at length about the utility of Bahá'í pamphlets, which were a common and effective teaching medium in the days before the Internet. Here is just one passage:

> On the subject of pamphlets—golly—when I glanced

through my stack of them, as I just did, I feel like sending you the whole bundle—most of them are so wonderful! However, that would be a bit awkward and you probably wouldn't have time to read them anyway. . . . One other reason I like Bahá'í pamphlets is that I find that often an <u>isolated</u> sentence or two quoted from the scriptures, stands out and creates a much better impact than when one sees it in the midst of a long paragraph or page. They are handy things to carry around with one for occasional reference at odd times of the day.

In the same letter, she expresses some of the challenges she is finding in her strivings to deepen her faith:

> I have been reading a combination of "Bahá'u'lláh and the New Era" and "The Renewal of Civilization". I think the latter is simply wonderful—[David] Hofman expresses himself <u>so</u> well. I find I can only read small amounts at a time—even of these lighter books. There seems so much to try and absorb in teaching oneself, and I reach saturation point very rapidly. I can see now that the summer isn't going to be nearly long enough. I had thought reading up here would be much easier, but although I do have a little more time, nature can be very distracting! But even though my surroundings do not encourage endless reading, they do stimulate meditation and tranquility, and already I feel 80% calmer than I did a couple of weeks ago.

On July 13, one of those much sought-after teaching opportunities arose with her aunt Gwen, her favorite English aunt on her mother's side. Catherine finds consolation in the following reflections that she might not be a fully effective teacher yet. In her letter of July 14 she wrote:

> Yesterday I was very thrilled when an opportunity arose

(after considerable prayer) for me to tell my aunt (the one who is staying with us) quite a bit about the Bahá'í Faith. I did a very blundering job, but she showed considerable interest and I think will be willing to read a little—which I hope will make up for my mistakes. It no longer bothers me unduly when I feel the inadequacies of my teaching. I now feel that if I have been praying for guidance beforehand, God will see to it that I say at least <u>some</u> of the right things, and if the <u>time</u> is right for the person to recognize the Truth, then that person surely will, no matter how poorly I express it. And even if the person doesn't become a believer in the near future, or <u>ever</u>, at least he will know something about the Faith and when the time comes that the Bahá'í name becomes more publicized, and many people will spread wild rumours about it, born of prejudice—well, that person will be <u>less</u> prejudiced because he will <u>know</u> something about it and won't be afraid of it. Dear me! I didn't expect to get quite as involved as that—let's blame it on the heat.

Catherine then quotes for Michael seven handwritten pages from *Your Experience as a Bahá'í*, a booklet that used to be sent to new believers by the Canadian NSA. Within a month or two, Michael would be receiving his own copy. In her letter of June 30, Catherine shares her observations of the novel she had been reading, *A Lamp is Heavy*,[99] by Canadian author Sheila MacKay Russell. Russell obtained a degree in Public Health Nursing, and her novel is a disguised autobiography. The main character is madcap student nurse, Susan Bates, who enters a large American hospital just prior to World War II. Susan ends up both loving and loathing her chosen profession. Catherine comments that through this process "she reaches maturity through all the lessons she learned through contact with different patients, nurses and doctors. Her old conventional, narrow ideas are gradually broken down (quite painfully) until she emerges with many ideas that are very closely akin to Bahá'í ones."

Her reading of Susan's troubles, tragedies and triumphs elicited the following observation that Catherine applied to the Bahá'í Faith: "It made me realize once again the truth in the saying that Bahá'ís don't need to 'convert'—all they have to do is to go out and <u>find</u> people who are already unconsciously Bahá'ís." She deplores the fact, however, that the author makes no mention of religion: "Many novels annoy me because the author completely leaves out any mention of religion in the lives of the people he describes—leaving them hollow."

Michael Rochester Joins the Bahá'í Faith: August 13, 1952

In her letter of July 27, Catherine expresses her delight at the good news she had just received: Michael Rochester had made the decision to become a Bahá'í. (He was not officially enrolled until August 13). Catherine's response expressed her usual unbounded delight; she was "on clouds":

> It is useless for me to try to <u>express</u> how thrilled I was at the news that you have really <u>made</u> the big decision! Let me just say that I have been on clouds for days with the happiness your news brought. It was wonderful too to read all your thoughts and feelings on the subject, because you expressed very beautifully all that I have felt or still do feel but could never put into words.

Catherine's letters to Michael were not a deciding factor in his decision to become a Bahá'í, but they doubtless came as confirmation of the conclusion he had already reached that the Bahá'í teachings were true. In the month of February 1952, Michael had already almost decided that he wanted to formalize his Bahá'í affiliation. I say "almost" because he had one final obstacle to overcome that he explained in the following email:

> I was already a convinced believer by the beginning of February 1952, but I still had some things to work out—in particular I had some concerns about the principle of the Guardianship, which I realized were finally settled one day in

that summer of 1952. . . . I never had any trouble with Shoghi Effendi himself, and greatly relished his World Order letters which I read that spring. Later my appreciation of him was further deepened by talking with Harlan Ober and Ben Weeden at Green Acre, 1954–56.[100]

The turning point in Michael's decision to join the Bahá'í Faith is worth a small digression. It came in a serene, pastoral moment. That summer, to raise money for his tuition fees, the third-year University of Toronto student had been working in a cucumber field on twenty-five acres of farmland near Tilbury, Ontario, owned by his stepfather, Zygmunt Konrad. One sunny day in late July, Michael needed a rest from hoeing and lay down in the field. In this peaceful state of mind, his thoughts turned again to his relationship to the religion he had been studying for the past eight months. In that supine, quiet moment of clarity, there in the unlikely location of a cucumber field, Michael realized that the final obstacle to his becoming a Bahá'í had been removed. Michael's Bahá'í membership was not formalized until a short time later when he received his letter of welcome from the Ontario Teaching Committee. On "Saturday evening," the only date on the letter, he wrote to Catherine: "You will rejoice with me when I tell you the finest news of all—on August 13 I became a Bahá'í in name! Can you imagine the deep inner happiness within me as I contemplate the vast prospect of life as a Bahá'í, fully realizing the changes that have yet to be made and the attendant responsibilities and challenges?"[101]

Both Michael and Catherine continued to explore Bahá'í literature. Her letter of August 1 contains her reflections on Nabíl's narrative, *The Dawnbreakers*:

> I'm glad you have had a look at "The Dawnbreakers" (isn't that a <u>wonderful</u> name?)— I'm longing to read it myself, after having heard Audrey Robarts[102] read a few excerpts from it, and after reading the first part of "God Passes By" which deals all too briefly with the Letters of the Living and the other earliest Bahá'ís. It is almost more than I can bear, and I practically weep,

when I read of the unbelievably diabolical tortures and methods of slaughter that they had to submit to. How they stood it I do not know, except I can only suppose that their courage and faith must have been superhumanly strong from being so close to the light [e.g., the Báb, Bahá'u'lláh]. I want to read more, much more, about the lives and personalities of these unique people, so that they will really come alive to me—at present, I'm afraid, they have an unreal quality about them. It is hard to grasp that one belongs to the very same race as such courageous people when one's own life and the lives of those around you have been so soft and sheltered. I don't know, Mike, whether it is <u>as</u> noble to "live a full life under the teachings, etc.," except that I believe we, today, have a <u>different role</u> to play than the Bahá'ís of the earliest periods, and I guess if <u>we</u> can face up to <u>our</u> challenges and difficulties as well as <u>they</u> did theirs, while then, yes, I guess our lives <u>will</u> be as noble, but in a different way.

Travelling Teacher John Leonard Answers Questions and Removes Doubts

The act of becoming a Bahá'í is usually a process that takes place over time—unless conversion be sudden—and it usually involves the collaboration of more than one person. This process can be compared to the making of a mosaic: it may be that one individual articulates the design and places the tiles, but others will also assist in the work, adding their own unique accents that help to form the overall pattern that leads to that decisive moment of recognition. Although George Spendlove played a principal role in awakening and deepening the spiritual understanding of Catherine and Cliff, other teachers already mentioned, such as John and Audrey Robarts, made their valuable contribution to the formation of Catherine and Cliff's newly emerging Bahá'í identity. For Catherine, John Leonard (1922–2006), who later became a Knight of Bahá'u'lláh for the Falkland Islands, was also one of these souls.

Catherine was impressed with John Leonard's dynamic spirituality.

4 ∞ The Summer Letters to Michael Rochester

In her letter of August 28, 1952, she testifies to the impact that he had on her spiritual formation. She shares with Michael Rochester her warm appreciation of his enthusiastic teaching efforts, and their effect on her finely tuned spiritual receptivity. These three passages show Catherine's usual candor, enthusiasm, humor, and sincerity:

> Last week I was very thrilled to receive a letter from one of my "Spiritual Daddies", John Leonard. He lives in Geneva, N.Y., and was the same person who sent me that beautiful prayer that I sent you earlier this summer. He it was who came up to Toronto to speak at our Naw Ruz Feast and who, two days later, came to see me. He shook me out of my lethargy and made me determined to become a Bahá'í almost immediately, whether Cliff was ready or not. He is a most radiant Bahá'í, with a tremendous faith. For instance: he didn't know Toronto at all and I expected him to have considerable trouble finding my house—especially since he refused to take any instructions over the phone.
>
> When he arrived, I asked him if he'd had much trouble. He looked at me in surprise and said "Of course not! I came <u>straight</u> to your house."—As if to say he was meant to come and see me and he was divinely guided. It was a remarkable afternoon we spent together. I told him all my remaining doubts and questions, and he unhesitatingly gave me <u>exactly</u> the answers I needed. That afternoon has remained <u>vivid</u> in the memories of both John and I [sic]. We have written to each other a few times but this latest letter came as a surprise as I had not heard from him since May. And yet I feel closer than ever to him! That is the most remarkable thing about Bahá'í friendships—the closer than closeness one can feel towards people one hardly knows at all. It is most strange.

I laughed at what John said: "What do you know, and what do you know now that you don't know?" He is wonderful. . . . I wish he could come again to Toronto so that you could meet him. He is now working for a Persian Bahá'í interior decorator. . . . 'A very wonderful and generous man who is teaching me a great deal, and plans to teach me much more. He certainly is a deeply dedicated Bahá'í—has just about totally ruined his health serving the Cause, but goes on with terrific determination. It is really an inspiration to be working for him under the circumstances, and while it isn't all beer and skittles by any means and has some very tough moments, I count myself most fortunate.'. . . John is a man who has very deep personal feelings for Shoghi [Effendi]—he has actually written to him three times during the three years he has been a Bahá'í, and says he received most wonderful replies." [Underlining in the original].

John Leonard was born John Alfred Levy. He grew up in Manhattan, New York. His father, a photographer, changed the family name to Leonard. He became a Bahá'í early in December, 1948, in the Los Angeles area, largely through the teaching efforts of a Bahá'í teacher and pioneer to South America, Mrs. Marcia Stewart (later Atwater). In 1954, he pioneered to the Falkland Islands, a service for which he was named a Knight of Bahá'u'lláh by Shoghi Effendi. Not long after his arrival, he married visiting Paraguayan pioneer, Margaret Mills. Together they formed an effective teaching team. John stayed in the Falklands for no less than fifty-two years. He corresponded with the Huxtables until Catherine died, and following her death he kept in touch with Cliff until his own passing in May, 2006. When he died, the Universal House of Justice paid tribute to his services.[103]

John's long presence in the Falkland Islands, and his notable services to that community, were published as a "potted biography"[104] in *The Dictionary of Falklands Biography* (2008). The article was written by Margo Smallwood, the corresponding secretary (2014) of the Local Spiritual Assembly of Stanley.

Falklander, Pauline Igao, was kind enough to provide me with a very complete pen portrait of John Leonard and the services of his wife Margaret. Along with her anecdotes, Pauline used the following adjectives to describe him, adjectives that I have selected and compressed from her message: "larger-than-life, jovial, doggedly determined, outgoing, chatty, intelligent, cultured, conscientious, scrupulously honest, kind."[105]

Teaching the Bahá'í Faith to her Friend Pamela Ball Webster

I have written in chapters 2 and 3 about Catherine's close friendship with Pamela Ball (later Webster) and how Pamela enlarged the scope of Catherine's world, and engaged her in their mutual investigation of the teachings of the First Unitarian Congregation of Toronto. Pamela knew that Catherine had become a Bahá'í, but she knew very little about the new religion that Miss Heward had joined. For the first time, Catherine was afforded the opportunity of teaching the Bahá'í Faith to the dear friend who visited her the previous weekend at Edinswold. Catherine is still ecstatic as she relates Pamela's visit to Michael in her letter of August 19:

> I am so bubbling over with inner happiness that I must tell you about it before commenting on your letter, even though words seem horribly inadequate to express it all. It was the weekend which sent me soaring, although actually I was calm and happy most of last week. My vision suddenly cleared completely (it was beginning to do so when I wrote to you last) and I could see definite and distinct answers to my prayers . . . I still feel a little breathless with surprise and delight! A very dear friend of mine, Pam Ball, who I see all too seldom because she goes to Wellesley College near Boston, managed to come and stay with me for the weekend. My friendship with Pam (a very rich one) began in late 1949 at a very low point in my life, and it was thanks to her that I started going to the Unitarian church in early 1950 (and incidentally, if I hadn't started going to the Unitarian church I would never have met Joyce Sachs [Asquith]

and consequently Cliff too!)

Catherine goes on to explain how open Pamela was to her exposé of the Bahá'í teachings:

> I had thought Pam to be a Unitarian at heart, but once we started talking about religion, I soon discovered to my relief and happiness, that a lot of her ideas had quite a bit in common with those of my own (Bahá'í, that is), and also that she was still groping around quite a lot for many answers. . . . But she seemed remarkably receptive to many of the ideas and, much to my intense relief, didn't become argumentative or draw away from me, as people are wont to do. And just to prove to you how interested she was, she <u>read two</u> whole books (The Chosen Highway and Renewal of Civilization) while she was here, and read part of two or three others!!!! And entirely on her own accord, without any prompting from me! You could have knocked me over with a feather!

Catherine's total commitment to the Bahá'í Faith becomes evident in the following lines:

> All the time I felt so jubilant inside, because I felt as if I was really doing God's work, and I felt a tremendous awareness that THIS was really the only thing that <u>matters</u>—in <u>my</u> life and in the life of the whole world. This was by far the biggest teaching opportunity I have had so far, and while telling Pam about the Faith I was filled with awe and joy at what a great big beautiful thing this Cause of God <u>is</u>! And oh, how grateful I was to God for giving me this opportunity and for putting the right words into my mouth, and for restoring my confidence in myself, in the Faith, and most of all, in <u>Him</u>.

She goes on to outline Pamela's main "stumbling block" that emerged during their conversation:

> Mind you, I'm not saying that Pam was completely won over— she found the main stumbling block the understanding of the station of Bahá'u'lláh, and she may never become one of our co-workers, but this I am pretty certain of, she <u>will</u> be a friend of the Faith. And quite possibly, if she feels a greater need of a personal religion, she will turn again to renewed study of the Faith, for she is a highly intelligent, thoughtful person. But isn't it <u>wonderful</u>, Mike? Can you understand why I feel so radiant?

Catherine soon received confirmation from Pamela herself that her teaching efforts did not go unrewarded. On just the following day (Wednesday), she received at Edinswold a letter from Pamela that contained these positive and gently humorous lines. Her use of the word "discussings" was intentionally light-hearted:

> Multitudinous thank you very muches for a weekend I will always remember. Already it is a golden patch of sunshine on the path of this summer—and know it will always be so.... Perhaps the most memorable events of the weekend were the readings and small discussings on the Bahá'í Faith which you shared with me. It is a truly amazing revelation to me in countless respects—as I think you were aware. Certainly in the rapid skimming I enjoyed, much of its significance, complexity <u>and</u> simplicity were missed—but a great deal wasn't—and I look forward to studying more. It may be the answer to my search—but I am not ready yet; even so it is good to have an eventual destination in the secret heart's eye.

Pamela's Spiritual Destiny[106]

In hindsight, Catherine's comments on Pamela's spiritual destiny proved to be accurate. Catherine's articulate, questioning and studious friend did in fact study the Bahá'í Faith for eight more years. On May 22, 1960, she became a Bahá'í at the home of Sam and Mimi McClellan in Cambridge, Massachusetts.[107] Her early years as a Bahá'í were full of the enthusiasm of someone who had made a priceless spiritual discovery. Her abundant correspondence with Catherine indicates the heartfelt gratitude Pamela held for her friend and teacher for having guided her to God's latest divine Revelation.[108] For about eight years, she served on the LSA of Bethesda, Maryland. The highlights of that period were meeting such friends as Louise Saymard, who had met 'Abdu'l-Bahá,[109] her joy at having joined a united and active community, and the evening spent in Washington with the distinguished Laura Dreyfus-Barney, née Clifford Barney, the compiler of 'Abdu'l-Bahá's foundational philosophical-theological text, *Some Answered Questions*. In Washington she also met Ali Kuli Khan, the former Iranian diplomat and one-time secretary and translator of 'Abdu'l-Bahá's Arabic and Persian correspondence, who also made early translations of the Bahá'í sacred writings before Shoghi Effendi's authoritative translations became the standard.

Sometime after the late 1960s, Pamela began to take another spiritual path. Much later in life, she was ordained to the priesthood at St. Mary's Episcopal church in Ely, Minnesota in 2010. It did not seem to me, however, based on our several engaging conversations, that Pamela had "renounced" her former religion; instead, she openly acknowledged her debt of gratitude to Catherine, her boundless admiration for her spirituality and her deep appreciation for having been a member of the Bahá'í Faith. Pamela remarked especially on the process of consultation that she had learned as an LSA secretary, a process that serves her well in the exercise of her present functions in the councils of the church. Through her loving-kindness, Pamela opened the door for Catherine to enter a larger world of social and religious intercourse, in which the young Miss Heward began her spiritual search in earnest. Catherine in turn accompanied Pamela on the latter's early investigation of the Bahá'í Faith, an investigation that led her to membership in the Bahá'í community for the greater part of a decade.

Family and Friends: The Hewards, Nora Nablo Moore, Ross Woodman, Cliff Huxtable, Jameson Bond

Although Catherine loved her parents, and her older sister Julia, her letters contain the occasional expressions of her frustrating relations with her "complex and discontented" family. Their virtual total lack of interest in her newly-discovered Bahá'í Faith, about which she was so enthusiastic, and their desultory pattern of affections for one another, not only frustrated Catherine; they temporarily increased her sense of isolation. This does not mean that every day that summer at Edinswold was tension-filled. The following passage indicates that family affections could be cordial for weeks at a time. In her letter of August 12, she writes: "Anyway, during the last few weeks we have been quite a happy family, and there has been the most lovely harmony and companionship between Mum and Julia, in spite of the fact that Mum is in a very run-down condition. And so I am keeping my fingers crossed and praying it will last a while longer." Her letter of August 19 mentions that Colonel Heward had been spared the severity of his usual two summer attacks of "dreadful bouts of asthma" . . . "thanks to the wonderful new drug, Cortisone" . . . "He's really been enjoying life—going fishing in our row boat, clipping hedges, and doing carpentry. It's good not to hear him complaining about anything." Her father's improved health no doubt was soothing balm to family relations.

In her letter of July 14, Catherine mentions Nora Nablo (later Moore)[110], a woman who conveys in person a kindness couched in a quiet, thoughtful dignity. Her comments are typical of the loving appreciations Catherine wrote of her new Bahá'í friends:

> I hope you had an enjoyable trip to Toronto. Nora wrote to me a few days ago, and I gather she benefited from your company most of the time—the Robarts were away, weren't they? I hope this wasn't too much of a disappointment to you, and that your talk with Nora proved stimulating. My affection and admiration for Nora increases steadily all the time now. For some time I didn't notice Nora very much, perhaps because I couldn't

take my eyes off Liz [Manser Rochester] at each Fireside, but in the last few months I have been getting to know Nora and am beginning to appreciate her true worth, which is great.

In her letter of June 22, she mentions Professor Ross Woodman, an academic at the University of Western Ontario in London, who died at the advanced age of ninety-two years, while this book was being written.[111] Ross Woodman went on to produce a lifetime of outstanding literary scholarship, notably on Romanticism and in Bahá'í studies:

> There was also another public meeting at the Museum at which Ross Woodman gave the last in a series of talks. He was very good; he has a marvellous gift of being able to answer questions with amazing force and clarity. London is very lucky to have him, although he must be in a very trying position—that of a Prof. at Western U. where he would probably get kicked out to talk to students about the Faith, yet he has to face all that wonderful material in class every day!

Cliff naturally takes a prominent place in Catherine's summer letters. In her letters of July 14 and August 12, she mentions Cliff's rapid spiritual progress, and a letter of congratulation sent by Jameson Bond:

> Cliff is well and continues to make great progress. He keeps on coming up against tests of various sorts; he is quick to recognize them as such, knows what to do about them and <u>does</u> it! The contrast between this summer and <u>last</u> is really astounding. . . . Cliff and I have had the honour of receiving a wonderful joint letter of congratulations [on becoming Bahá'ís] from none other than Jamie Bond! Although I only had the pleasure of meeting Jamie twice, I am profoundly grateful to him for he played an important part in making Cliff a Bahá'í before

he left Toronto to pioneer.[112] I do hope you meet Jamie someday Mike.[113] He is a most wonderful person—and his face really <u>looks</u> like a Bahá'í. I have heard <u>you</u> compared to Jamie.

Catherine on Herself: Challenges to Health, Love of Autumn, Modern Poetry

As mentioned above, the summer letters give a very good idea of the outstanding personality traits that were coming to the fore as a result of Catherine's recent enrolment or "declaration" of faith, as it was then called. These characteristics were always potentially present in Catherine, but becoming a Bahá'í canalized and brought them into a fuller, actual efflorescence. The following passages allude to struggles with her declining health, her fine sensitivity and love of autumn.

In the letter of August 12, she wrote: "I must admit just keeping cheerful all the time is a full-time job, and not an easy one, even though I am cheerful by nature. As my arms and legs grow weaker and weaker, and the very simplest daily routine becomes more of a supreme physical and emotional strain, I'm inclined to be cranky at times in spite of myself." She wrote on September 8 from Toronto that the arrival of autumn occasioned a deep nostalgia; the trees became "hurtingly beautiful":

> Your depiction of walks in the north woods was vivid and beautiful, to me. I <u>love</u> autumn and ache to see it again—even in the city. The trees in the district in which I live, become hurtingly beautiful. The loveliest sight I can hope to see this autumn is the view overlooking the ravine from the top of the reservoir (where you took me in June)—it is <u>marvellous</u>. To me autumn brings a great feeling of nostalgia and a little sadness—because I have been unhappy in other autumns—but this does not make me love it any the less.

Although Catherine possessed a quick, practical intelligence, she was not inclined to linger long over intellectual analysis. Her letter of September 8, 1952, indicates the frustration she was feeling in understanding the symbolic abstractions of modern poetry:

> A young poet friend of mine has spent many hours trying to explain modern poetry to me which has helped, but I find it very exasperating. I nearly hit the roof upon reading [T.S. Eliot's] "The Cocktail Party". I resent it when these poets make me feel like an ignoramus!! I have never written any verse myself, but the only prize I ever won during my last four years' schooling at B.S.S. [Bishop Strachan School] was for a Scripture essay on the Pyramids which I managed to compose. I used to like writing prose. That liking now expresses itself in these <u>lengthy</u>, highly ungrammatical epistles which I force upon my poor friends. But <u>you</u> encourage me greatly because now I see that I am not the <u>only</u> person who can write a sixteen page letter at the drop of a hat!

Her Inner Struggle Over Courtship and Marriage

From the time of their meeting at the Freshman dance at the University of Toronto, Catherine and Cliff's friendship gradually developed into courtship. While no ambivalence detracted from Cliff's commitment, Catherine was torn by inner struggles. For obvious reasons, if their courtship led to marriage, their union inevitably would have to face a fate that most couples would never willingly embrace. When Catherine and Cliff met, Catherine had almost reached the end of her doctor-predicted lifespan of twenty years. During the summer of 1952, distance temporarily impeded frequent visits, but for lovers distance is no object. Cliff had obtained summer work for Atomic Energy of Canada at their nuclear facilities in Deep River,[114] 110 miles (180 km.) northwest of Ottawa, testing Ottawa River organisms to discover where radioactivity from the cooling water was accumulating, and if it were building up in the food chain. He would hitchhike the 530 miles (853 km.) round trip between Deep River and Toronto each weekend to visit Catherine and to take in a Saturday night movie.

4 ∞ The Summer Letters to Michael Rochester

During the summer, Catherine kept her inner turmoil to herself, undoubtedly to spare Cliff the anguish with which she was wrestling. Although Cliff was not aware of her dilemma, she poured out her heart to Michael Rochester. Keeping what she felt were Cliff's best interests at heart, she was not convinced that the necessary ingredients for a happy marriage, including children and family life, could be fulfilled as long as the menacing presence of muscular dystrophy continued to cast its creeping, dark shadow. Although Catherine wrote openly about her love for Cliff, for a few months her feelings about the relationship and marriage were agonizingly uncertain. In her letter of July 27, Catherine is very positive about the possibility of marriage. After one "marvellous weekend with Cliff," during which the weather was "very kind to us," weather that favored "some lovely drives," she felt that "we are now so sure that we want to marry."

But about six weeks later, she had come to the conclusion that it would not be possible to marry Cliff, as long as she suffered from muscular dystrophy. She broaches the subject with Michael in her letter of August 12, 1952:

> I'd rather like to tell you about one of the things that was bothering me. The more I love Cliff, the more <u>unselfish</u> that love becomes, in its nature, so that more and more I am interested in what is best for <u>him</u>, and in his happiness, regardless of <u>me</u>, and my happiness. The question that keeps coming up to torture my mind with its seeming un-answerability is this: Should I give up Cliff—break off our friendship—for <u>his</u> sake? Now Mike, I am not asking you, or anyone else, to answer this question—<u>no one</u> can answer it <u>for</u> me—even if my friends thought the answer to be "yes", they would be too kind to tell me so. I realize it is something entirely between me and God. This I find very hard. At the <u>best</u> of times I am extremely bad at making decisions, and am used to talking problems over with Cliff and other people to clarify my thoughts. But, as I say, this problem is different. Mind you, even though my love <u>has</u> become fairly selfless, it still completely paralyses me to think of giving him up. [Underlining in original]

Catherine goes on to explain that her dilemma was at bottom what may be described as a heart–head conflict. She engages in an extensive analysis, enumerating the obstacles that would burden Cliff "with worries far too heavy for his youthful shoulders." When she thought about the problem in a detached, rational (intellectual) fashion, she came to the conclusion that she would have to forego marriage, but when she followed her heart (emotional), "the arguments are quite the opposite." Although Catherine works her way through the intricate labyrinth of the battle raging between her mind and heart, she still finds the way to lighten the dialogue. At one point, she pauses to write: "Oh dear—now that I have shaken off my depression, this all sounds rather silly and melodramatic—especially the way I have said it. . . . But it has been a relief to get it off my chest, because it really is a very serious matter, and until I find the right answer, I know it will keep cropping up to bother me."

Judging by her explicit responses to Michael, it was clear that her friend and correspondent provided wise and hopeful advice. He encouraged Catherine to consider their relationship as a providence from God, in which the young couple could attain a greater unity, as these lines reveal: "Surely God has brought you together for some special reason connected with your mutual spiritual growth—to think of one of you without the other's influence is to leave something lacking in the other's character."[115]

Humans Propose but God Will Dispose: Resolution for Catherine's Dilemma

Catherine came to a seemingly firm conclusion only one week later on August 19, 1952: "I will never be able to get married while I have muscular dystrophy." This declaration suggests that Catherine had hoped to find a cure for her disease, and to make her marriage to Cliff conditional upon her becoming well. Cliff naturally shared Catherine's hope that she could be healed. He was motivated in part to study science in the expectation that he might find a cure for muscular dystrophy, but within two years he came to realize that the demands of being a serious bio-medical researcher was not really his calling. Catherine had at one time pinned her hopes on the "Koch treatment." Five years after her marriage to Cliff, and after eight years of medical consultations, Catherine finally decided to take glyoxylide, the experimental homeopathic remedy patented and dispensed by William Koch, PhD, MD (1885–1967). Dr. Koch claimed that he had used injections of glyoxylide successfully to treat cancer.[116] Her physician was not opposed to her trying the remedy, but in the end Catherine discovered that the treatment had no effect: "It made absolutely no impression on my health."[117]

On the eve of the Birth of the Báb (October 20), as they sat in Cliff's car, in front of 7 Clarendon Crescent, preparing to say goodnight, Catherine informed Cliff of her decision. In evident emotional distress, and appearing grave, Catherine looked Cliff in the eyes and suddenly announced that, after much reflection and prayer, she had concluded that the best course for them both was to sever relations. Cliff had no inkling that Catherine had been wrestling with the fate of their relationship: he was stunned. That night, when her sister Julia was putting Catherine to bed, Catherine burst into tears and told her that she had "jilted" Cliff. Fortunately, relief and resolution came quickly. For the entire afternoon of the next day, Cliff received the kind counsel of John Robarts who had invited him to lunch at the Men's Club of the University of Toronto. Cliff recalled the kindness of Mr. Robarts with gratitude: "He counselled me as a wise and loving father leading a much-loved son towards maturity. When we parted, I phoned Catherine to tell her we were going to be alright." When she heard Cliff's consoling reassurances, she burst into another flood of tears.[118]

Catherine's temporary decision to break off her engagement to Cliff, although understandable for someone facing her precarious life-situation, did not persist. Despite the formidable obstacles they faced within the next two years, their love deepened, and their commitment became mutually firm. By 1954 the young couple in their early twenties had banished any and all remaining doubts. They determined to marry and to serve the Bahá'í Faith together, regardless of the number of years that remained to Catherine.

-5-
COURTSHIP AND MARRIAGE:
Life in Toronto (1950–1957)

Courtship and Obtaining Parental Consent to Marry

Catherine and Cliff's courtship began practically from the first moment they met at the Freshman dance at the University of Toronto in the fall of 1950. Cliff's attendance at the Unitarian church was generated mainly by his romantic interest in Catherine. Once Catherine had resolved her dilemma about marrying Cliff (1952), marriage would have to wait until Cliff graduated in 1954 and found a job. The Huxtables' courtship ran concurrently with their spiritual search. As Catherine investigated the teachings of Unitarianism and the Bahá'í Faith, they became gradually familiar with one another's character. The courtship included attending the First Unitarian Church on Sunday mornings, discussing the sermons, followed by lunch with the Hewards and a social visit. They attended Bahá'í firesides in Forest Hill at Elizabeth Manser's and the Robarts, and occasionally in Toronto at Laura and Victor Davis' home in Rosedale. They usually went to a movie on the weekends. Cliff often called in at afternoon tea—a strictly observed English custom at the Hewards'—following his day of classes at the University of Toronto. Cliff recalled that they once went as spectators to an evening dance at Casa Loma, the Gothic Revival castle and gardens in midtown Toronto.[119] This allowed Catherine to enjoy vicariously her great love of dancing. Catherine's appreciation of the arts and music inclined her to introduce Cliff to the "pops" of classical music. There were warm embraces during the courtship, but Cliff remarked that their affections did not include "all the things kids do these days."[120]

According to Bahá'í law, any couple who wishes to marry requires the consent of all living, biological parents.[121] Now pedigree was important to the Hewards. Cliff would have to be acceptable to Catherine's socially conscious, British-Canadian parents. Although he was not upper class, with his solid, professional, middle-class background, his devotion to Catherine, and his reliable and loyal character, he passed muster. His paternal grandfather and great-grandfather had

5 ∞ Courtship and Marriage

both been Methodist ministers. His grandfather, the Reverend Charles Huxtable, ministered for a time in Wakefield, Quebec, north of Ottawa, and his English great-grandfather, the Reverend George Gellard Huxtable, served in the Bahamas and later in Montreal. His father, George Reuben Huxtable, was a chartered accountant, who had articled in Montreal and eventually became a senior executive in Ontario Hydro. His mother, Dorothy, a bright student from Quebec, won a scholarship for university, but the pursuit of post-secondary education met with resistance from her farming father. After her graduation from high school, Mrs. Huxtable became the personal secretary to the chief executive of the Miner Rubber Company in Granby, Quebec.

Regardless of socio-economic status, the Colonel and Mrs. Heward soon came to realize that Cliff and Catherine's relationship was vitally important to their mutual happiness. Although consent from the Hewards was not long in coming, Cliff's parents at first refused. Cliff's mother Dorothy, like any concerned mother, naturally had what she thought were her son's best interests at heart: "She saw what Catherine's disability would do to my life," Cliff observed.[122] It would be the proverbial millstone around her son's neck. Cliff's father Reuben feared that the load would be too heavy for his son to bear. If Cliff were not able to cope with all the demands that marriage to a person with physical disablities would involve, the marriage would fail, and more sorrow would eventually be heaped on both Catherine and Cliff. Mr. and Mrs. Huxtable did not want to wager on marital success.

Looking back on the days following their request for parental consent, Cliff remarked that his parents "did not have a vision of the Faith and its empowerment."[123] But Cliff made it clear to his parents that in the matter of consent, the fate of their proposed marriage was entirely in their hands. In that regard, he emphasized that they were "agents of God." Cliff and Catherine assured the Huxtables that they would abide by their decision. Much fervent prayer followed. Cliff's parents came to realize that the young couple was not to be dissuaded, and within a few months they agreed to the marriage. Cliff remembered: "They reluctantly gave consent and attended our wedding as if it was a funeral."[124]

Cliff later remarked on the wisdom of their having followed Bahá'í law, and maintaining their marital union in the face of severe tests and difficulties: "By our observance of the Marriage Law, when inevitable strains arose, they supported our union. At the end of the day, after my father had passed on, my mother sent me a beautiful letter expressing her admiration and thankfulness to God that I had stayed with it to the end."[125] Although it remains unclear whether the following passage comes from the very letter Cliff mentions, the Archives Department at the Canadian Bahá'í National Center located one of Dorothy Huxtable's letters expressing her thanks. Cliff's mother came across his letter requesting permission to marry Catherine when she was going through drawers and cupboards, making space for Harold Window whom she married in the summer of 1967, six years following the death of Reuben Huxtable in an automobile accident. Dorothy was writing to Cliff a few weeks after Catherine's death. Following so close on the heels of Catherine's passing, her remarks contain no hint of the reluctance Cliff's parents had shown twelve years earlier. On the contrary, the passage of time had completely altered his mother's perspective:

> I re-read the letter you wrote to Dad and me asking our permission to marry Catherine. I gave it to Harold to read, and once more he declared how very much he would like to know you. What a lot of living we have all done since you wrote that letter! And how proud we were, many, many times, of you and Catherine, and thankful that we gave our permission.[126]

The Wedding Photo: May 7, 1955

A framed 5x7 inch black-and-white photograph in my study shows a wedding that took place on May 7, 1955, at 7 Clarendon Crescent, Toronto, at the home of the Hewards. This prized wedding photo pictures a joyous event. At the center of the photo sits a twenty-three-year-old young woman in a wheelchair—a round-faced, brown-eyed bride, with auburn hair and radiant smile, coiffed with a bridal veil, gowned in white, holding a floral bouquet on her lap. Standing to her immediate right is her bridegroom, an elegantly slim young man, wearing a white carnation boutonnière. On his right stands George Spendlove, an older, bald-headed man in a light-colored suit, a spiritual mentor who toasted the health and happiness of the bride and groom. Of the five people in the photo, only George is not smiling; instead he looks searchingly at the camera.

To Catherine's left stands the beaming officiating minister, the Reverend William Phillip Jenkins, the enterprising cleric who helped to establish the Unitarian church in Canada in the years following the Second World War. Reverend Jenkins, despite his unpredictable and controversial comments that were reported in the media, was broad-minded enough to have officiated at a number of Bahá'í marriage ceremonies. To his left stands Ernest Don Dainty, the young chairman of the Toronto Local Spiritual Assembly, who conducted the not yet legally recognized Bahá'í marriage ceremony. A few years later when Don Dainty married Diana Merrick, a role-reversal occurred: it was Cliff who, as chairman, represented the Local Spiritual Assembly at the Dainty's wedding.

This photograph is remarkable for a number of reasons, some banal, others significant. George Spendlove toasted the bride and groom at this wedding with a soft drink, while the non-Bahá'í guests would have raised glasses containing alcoholic beverages. George was already well-known for his witticisms, and he did not disappoint the wedding guests. He proposed the following toast: "We all wish Catherine success in the greatest plastic art known to woman, making a man into a husband."[127] It would have been unusual for a wedding to have had two marriage ceremonies at the same time, one conducted by a Unitarian minister, the other by an officer of the local Bahá'í community.

Cliff's brother, Weston, was best man. Douglas Martin, one of two representatives of the LSA, and A. E. H. Walker served as ushers. Family members and the Heward social circle formed a sizeable number of the Toronto wedding guests. But perhaps the most unusual feature of this wedding was the fact that it took place at all. That it did so became a cause for genuine celebration, and a joy that can be readily perceived in the broad smiles that wreathed the faces of the wedding party that day. Here was a young woman who had been challenged with a physical disability, being married to an able-bodied man. In itself, this circumstance was perhaps unusual for the Toronto of the 1950s. But Providence had foreseen that this bride and groom were being united following their meeting at a university dance that Catherine attended in a wheelchair, and the extraordinary experiences of their individual lives before they met. It was, however, decidedly remarkable that the bride's physicians had estimated that she would not live to see her wedding day, never mind to bear a healthy male child some seven years later.

Julia Heward Harvie wrote to her sister and brother-in-law two days after the wedding while they were away on honeymoon. Her letter contains her impressions of Catherine's appearance. She mentions the "radiance" that is clearly visible in the happy wedding photo:

> Catherine, you looked too good to be true in that dream of an ethereal dress, with your tiny white satin feet peeping out below. I just wish that I could have beheld your face during the Service, but when I saw it after you certainly had that special bridey radiance all over you. I thought the Bahá'í Service was beautiful beyond words, loving both Don Dainty's part and Mr. Spendlove's.[128]

Married Life at the Hewards': Cliff's Professional Life, LSA Service and Firesides (1955–1957)

The Huxtables honeymooned in the vicinity of the "Mother Temple of the West," the Bahá'í house of worship located on the western shore of Lake Michigan in Wilmette, Illinois, a suburban town located just north of Chicago. Because Catherine's mobility had continued to deteriorate, it was not a question of whether or not the newly-weds would strike off on their own, at least not for another two years. The most practical and sensible arrangement would be to have Cliff move into 7 Clarendon Crescent. The Huxtables' domestic life began in the bed-sitting room of a modern, ground floor addition to the family home that had been built for Catherine years earlier. Cliff recalled: "It was a pleasant room with ensuite facilities just off the entrance hall of the house."[129]

Before her muscles became too weak, with Cliff's help Catherine could "walk" for exercise. She did so only in her room at home. Cliff would pull her up from her wheelchair facing himself, and as Catherine balanced herself very

5 ∞ Courtship and Marriage 77

carefully on her feet, while holding Cliff's hands, he would pull her gently forward. As she moved, Catherine would let a foot swing around to take a step. In this manner she could walk short distances, occasionally doing many rounds in their room. This exercise became less frequent over time, and by the time they left Toronto it had practically ceased.[130] Another "walk" they accomplished took place when Catherine carefully balanced herself standing on Cliff's feet, and while she held him in an embrace, they would walk for short distances.

With his background in Honors Science, Cliff found his first job with the Internal Sales desk of Canadian Laboratory Supplies. It was uninspiring work, but it paid the bills. Teaching followed at Western Technical and Commercial High School, just north of Toronto's High Park, a challenging and stimulating vocation Cliff enjoyed. He later took one summer course in teacher training, but it was not until the Huxtables moved to Salt Spring Island that Cliff would complete his education degree at the University of Victoria. Catherine's craftwork continued, but it gradually abated during the early years of their marriage. Late in 1959, the year that they moved to Salt Spring Island in the southern Gulf Islands of British Columbia from Regina, Saskatchewan, Catherine wrote that she had "retired from her *petit point* work."[131]

Despite their restricted space, Catherine and Cliff began their own small firesides that usually consisted of one or two seekers. They were both elected to the Toronto LSA circa 1954 and served on that Assembly until their departure from Toronto for Regina in 1957. Cliff served as chair between 1956 and 1957 and "possibly longer," while Catherine served as secretary. Cliff's duties included officiating at the weddings of Don Dainty and Diana Merrick, and of Marjorie Stee to Stuart Waddell, a Scot who came to their wedding in full highland regalia. It would be a mistake, however, to imagine that because of Catherine's disability, the Huxtables were sitting quietly at home, except for the occasional fireside and regular Local Spiritual Assembly meetings. Married life at the Heward residence proved to be one of the busiest, happiest, and most satisfying periods of their life together. Catherine wrote in her letter of March 29, 1957, to Michael Rochester:

> This has been the busiest, most wonderful year of our

lives. There's much to be said for leading the kind of life you <u>want</u> to lead. We've both had the feeling of doing just that lately. Cliff adores his job [teaching at Western Tech], and has a great deal of fun doing it. We have so many wonderful friends now that we can't keep up with them all. Teaching opportunities abound on all sides. Our fireside is deeply satisfying and stimulating. We rarely have an evening alone at home together any more, but we don't seem to need that so much now, which is good, considering all the wonderful opportunities I mentioned . . . . We seldom get our lights out before midnight—but we seem to be surviving.

In the following lines, Catherine alludes to her weakening health, but despite it all, both she and Cliff were pursuing busy lives:

I had a month-long cold this winter, from exhaustion, but Cliff hasn't been sick since September. . . . My day's getting shorter due to increasing need for rest. I have practically given up my *petit point* work now. I miss the money, but there are so many more interesting things for me to spend my time on now—writing endless letters, doing telephone work for the Assembly, arranging parties (we've given three since the fall and there's another next week for Janet and John),[132] preparing our firesides, planning a project with the Blind.[133] And so the days whiz by.

Catherine also writes of Cliff's increased sociability due to their more frequent contacts with people: "And so you see, he is far from the hermit of former years—it's people, people, people day in and day out, and he loves it!" She concludes her letter of March 29, 1957, with her gratitude for a happy marriage: "It is an incredibly great bounty. I feel thoroughly 'spoiled'—and love it!" Catherine's allusion to Cliff's increased sociability was in large part due to her influence.

The Huxtables' marriage served to heal Cliff from the remaining vestiges of the psychological trauma that resulted from his having almost caused the accidental death of a young boy who was playing under a bridge in east Toronto. The "hermit" syndrome was largely the result of that accident. In the ninth decade of his life, while looking back on that troubled phase of his youth, Cliff was able to declare: "Catherine brought me out of that trauma."[134]

The Call of the Guardian: The Impact of Winnifred Harvey's Pilgrimage (1956)

In her letter of March 29, 1957, to Michael, Catherine tells him of her dreams of Shoghi Effendi, whom she used to call simply "Shoghi" in her earlier letters: "Twice recently I have had vivid and inspiring dreams in which I have met Shoghi Effendi. Unfortunately they do not qualify as visions, and so may never come true—but I can hope!" (As we shall see in chapter 8, Catherine had already received a letter from Shoghi Effendi, responding to her query of how she could best serve the Faith in her weakened condition.)

Within a year of their marriage, a pilgrim returned from Haifa bearing a weighty verbal message from the Guardian to the Bahá'ís of Toronto. His message was consistent with those in his general written communications to the Bahá'í community. The message would set the course of Cliff and Catherine's lives until the time of Catherine's death in 1967. The pilgrim was Winnifred Harvey, a capable, intelligent, deeply thoughtful, well-read Bahá'í. During the ministry of Shoghi Effendi (1922–1957), any returning pilgrim who had the privilege of attaining the presence of the "Sign of God on earth" would be of special interest to the friends on the "home-front." Even though the Guardian always insisted that the purpose of pilgrimage was not to meet him, but to pray in the Bahá'í holy shrines, returning pilgrims had benefitted greatly from any guidance Shoghi Effendi had to offer—guidance that he encouraged the pilgrim to impart on his or her return. Of course, Bahá'ís at home were also most curious to receive the impressions that the appointee and successor of 'Abdu'l-Bahá had made on the pilgrim's heart and mind.

Winnifred Harvey had become a Bahá'í in 1940 while she was living in

Ottawa, shortly after her departure from Winnipeg, where she had been taught the Faith by Rowland Estall (1906–1993), "one of the most effective Canadian Bahá'í teachers" of his day. The same year she moved to Ottawa (1940), Winnifred found employment in the Dominion Bureau of Statistics where she rose to a senior position. She was the first resident Bahá'í in the nation's capital.[135] On a trip to Montreal, while she was taking tea with Lorol Schopflocher, wife of the philanthropist, Canadian-Jewish-German, later Hand of the Cause of God, Siegfried "Freddie" Schopflocher (1877–1953),[136] and other women members of the Bahá'í community, including one unnamed senior woman who had met 'Abdu'l-Bahá, Winnifred had "a sudden experience of conviction and joined the Faith."[137] She served on the Canadian National Spiritual Assembly from 1950–1961. Winnifred organized successful firesides in Ottawa, and later served on the first Local Spiritual Assembly of that city from the time of its formation in 1948 until the early 1960s when she moved to nearby Vanier (Eastview), a town that is now included within the municipal boundaries of Ottawa. During the mid 1960s, she pioneered across the Ottawa river to French-speaking Hull, Quebec. In 1970 she left Canada to serve at the Bahá'í World Center as a statistician and later as bookstore manager. At the time of her death in 1990, Winnifred had served in Haifa for twenty years.[138]

Winnifred communicated the Guardian's clear directive to Catherine and Cliff, as well as to the Local Spiritual Assembly of the Bahá'ís of Toronto. In late 1956, following her pilgrimage, Winnifred spoke at a well-attended meeting of the Toronto Bahá'í community where she again emphatically delivered the Guardian's message—"disperse!" According to "Recollections," the transcript of Cliff's 1978 tape-recorded talk, Cliff related the conversation that took place between the Guardian and Winnifred at the pilgrims' table in the second Western Pilgrim House[139] located at 10 Haparsim Street, formerly Persian Street: "What is the largest community in Canada?" the Guardian inquired. "Toronto," she answered. "And how many Bahá'ís are in Toronto?" "Fifty or more," replied Winnifred. "Tell them to disperse!" the Guardian ordered. "Tell them this is a message from me."[140] In issuing this directive, Shoghi Effendi was characteristically emphatic. His voice boomed like thunder.

5 ∞ Courtship and Marriage

Answering the Call

As members of the LSA, Cliff and Catherine felt a special responsibility to encourage the friends in Toronto to respond to Shoghi Effendi's message, but for a whole year, the Guardian's message met with little direct action. Despite the Guardian's urgent call, the Huxtables felt that they could not pioneer because of Catherine's condition. But as time passed, faced with the lack of response from the Toronto Bahá'ís, they began to contemplate a pioneer move. The terrible event that moved them to action was the sudden death of Shoghi Effendi in the early hours of November 4, 1957. With the Guardian's passing, the situation became "doubly critical." Cliff Huxtable remembered that the Bahá'ís who lived during the prosecution of the Ten Year World Crusade/Plan (1953–1963), were keenly aware that the election of the Universal House of Justice was anticipated following the successful completion of the Plan.

In his talk "Recollections" Cliff observed: "We were well into the Ten Year Plan, that critical Ten Year Plan which had to be successful so that the Universal House of Justice could be formed. It became particularly critical after the Guardian died, because if we were not successful, there would be no divinely infallible institution to guide humanity."[141] Following Shoghi Effendi's sudden passing, and the disappointing response to the Guardian's call to the Toronto Bahá'ís to disperse, the Huxtables decided to pioneer. The "push-pull" modus operandi that George Spendlove once described to them as an answer to prayer was working. They felt as if they were being "pushed" out of Toronto and "pulled" by the magnetic attraction of the pioneering field. Their decision was met with well-meaning attempts to discourage them by family and a few close friends. These concerns were understandable given the fragile state of Catherine's health, but in the end their misgivings did not weaken the Huxtables' resolve. They knew that given Catherine's condition, pioneering would be no easy task; a companion-helper would have to be found to fill those hours when Cliff was away working. Although it was not immediately clear just where they should go, and who their helper would be, they were determined to act. Their firm resolve and their prayers soon revealed the way.

-6-
REGINA, SASKATCHEWAN:
Pioneers Building Community (1957–1959)

Last Days in Toronto

Shoghi Effendi stressed in his letters to the Bahá'ís, and through his comments to pilgrims, that the answer to prayer can come only through direct action.[142] Once the decision to pioneer was made, the Huxtables did indeed take action, but their first tentative efforts produced no results. They looked into the possibility of pioneering to the Magdalen Islands, and also to Anticosti Island, but these destinations did not prove practicable. Anticosti Island, a goal first set by the Guardian in 1953, proved especially resistant to receiving and maintaining pioneers.

After the Canadian National Spiritual Assembly appealed to the Guardian to change the goal of Anticosti Island, in view of the difficulty of landing and maintaining a pioneer, the Guardian responded by asking them to recommend a substitute:

> He has decided that, in view of the fact that Anticosti is so extremely difficult to get into, the Canadian Assembly can choose some other goal as substitute for Anticosti. In other words, a territory or an island in the vicinity of Canada, which has never been opened to the Faith, may be opened in the place of Anticosti, and thus the goals of the Ten Year Plan will not be decreased. On the other hand, Anticosti should be maintained as an objective; and every effort be made to get a Bahá'í in there.[143]

Although Knight of Bahá'u'lláh, Mary Zabolotny (McCulloch) did in fact open Anticosti Island in 1956, for reasons unknown to this author, she left her post after only four months.[144] The NSA's substitute recommendation was the southern Gulf Islands off the west coast of British Columbia, a group of islands sandwiched between Vancouver and the east coast of Vancouver Island. Shoghi

6 ∞ Regina, Saskatchewan 83

Effendi reluctantly changed the goal to the Gulf Islands during the final days of his life, four years after he had announced Anticosti Island to the Canadian Baháʼí community during Riḍván at the inception of the Ten Year World Crusade (1953). When they left Toronto for Regina, the Huxtables could not have known that they themselves would later become the pioneers who would fulfill the final goal chosen by the Guardian during his ministry.

Following a pleasant summer 1957 motoring holiday at Ivry-sur-le-Lac in the Laurentian hills sixty miles (97 km.) north of Montreal, where they stayed for a week with Vera and Harry Raginsky, the Huxtables visited Winnifred Harvey in Ottawa on their return trip to Toronto. During a brief consultation in which they sought her advice on a possible destination, she challenged them to go and find their own goal. Winnifred's advice proved to be wise, and it was not long until the Huxtables found a location.

One Sunday afternoon, as they sat in their bed-sitting room, feeling very discouraged about their pioneering prospects, Cliff was leafing through a Toronto newspaper. On an impulse, Catherine suggested: "Let's say the Tablet of Ahmad together!" Each of them read one half of the prayer. Cliff takes up the storyline from there:

> And then I picked up the newspaper again, turned to the next page, and one advertisement jumped out at me. It was "Career Opportunity in Education in Regina." We knew that Regina had been a trouble spot because an assembly had fallen there. So I telephoned members of the National Assembly, learned what we could about the situation, and applied for the job. It was just one of those crazy things. I got the job, and we went out to Regina, along with Eileen White, Roger White's sister, who wanted a change and who came as our helper.[145]

When the Huxtables consulted some NSA members, they discouraged Cliff and Catherine from pioneering to Regina. There was no question that these friends had the Huxtables' best interests at heart, but they felt that the distant relocation would take a severe toll on the Huxtables' mental and physical health and perhaps on their marriage. The morale in the Regina community, moreover, was far from ideal now that it had fallen understrength. Their friends felt that the Huxtables would be severely tested by the challenging situation in which they would find themselves. In spite of the cautionary advice, Cliff applied for the job. He made a favorable impression on his prospective employer and was hired with a considerable increase in salary.[146]

Dinner with Eileen White Collins: Co-Pioneer, Companion-Helper

The circumstances that led Eileen White Collins to join forces with the Huxtables showed that when the need is sufficiently great, divine assistance becomes readily available. As the Bahá'í sacred writings amply attest, and as believers have experienced time and again over the generations, when Bahá'ís are moved to action, the way becomes plain. The service that Eileen White rendered the Huxtables, as Catherine's first independent caregiver, also indicates that service may be rendered to the Bahá'í Faith by those who are not yet registered Bahá'ís.[147]

Eileen met Cliff and Catherine through Cliff's sister Janet Huxtable when Eileen was nineteen or twenty years old. Eileen used to visit "Back Achers," the farm at Claremont, near Uxbridge, Ontario, owned by Cliff's parents. Eileen had learned originally about the Bahá'í Faith from her brother, Roger White (d. 1993), a religious poet who wrote in contemporary language, well-known to Bahá'í readers for his cogent reflections on profound spiritual themes, and his sometimes delightfully ironic and humorous portrayals that capture effectively the unique personalities of memorable Bahá'ís.[148] Although Eileen was intellectually curious about the Bahá'í Faith, she volunteered to this author that she was "not emotionally involved" before she moved to Regina. Eileen and Janet Huxtable had shared an apartment in the heart of Forest Hill Village (Toronto) with Pat Bennett and Anne Collins, the sister of Eileen's second husband, George Collins. The foursome hosted breakfasts during the Bahá'í Fast, even though Janet was the only Bahá'í. Among the visitors during the Fast were Michael Rochester, who later married Elizabeth Manser, and Don Dainty, who later became the husband of Diana Merrick. In addition to the Toronto and Uxbridge visits with Catherine and Cliff, Eileen also went to the occasional dinner at the Hewards' home.

One winter evening in 1957, Eileen invited Cliff and Catherine to dinner. Cliff carried Catherine up three flights of stairs to reach the apartment. It was a Herculean task he was to perform many times until Catherine's death. They had been talking about the Huxtables' upcoming move to Regina when Cliff said jokingly: "Eileen, you should pack up and move to Regina with us and look after Catherine while we get settled." When Cliff stepped out to purchase a bottle of ginger ale in one of the local shops, Catherine became pensive. Now Eileen observed that when Catherine was about to say something insightful, or to make a comment that required diplomacy, she would gracefully smooth out the material of her skirt. This was one of those moments. Catherine then asked quietly: "Would you seriously consider moving to Regina with us?" Eileen responded that she would give the proposal serious consideration. If it were meant to be, she would go—on condition of being able to dispose of her furniture and many books. It turned out that Eileen was able to dispose easily of these possessions; by Christmas the trio would be off to Regina.

In the Shadow of William Sutherland Maxwell: Apartment 1010 in Regina's Tower Gardens Apartments

On December 26 Mrs. Heward drove the Huxtables to Malton Airport (now Toronto's Pearson International Airport), where they said their goodbyes. Catherine and Cliff boarded a flight for Regina. Bound for Regina, Eileen had been visiting her parents for Christmas in Windsor, Ontario. She found the Huxtables already on board when the plane made a stopover there. When they landed in Regina, they were met at the airport by a group of friends, including Roberta "Bobbie" and Angus Cowan, who were key figures in the teaching work in Regina and in the reestablishment of the LSA. Before leaving Toronto, the Huxtables had not been able to secure advance accommodation, a situation that made the first week in their new location temporarily inconvenient. Cliff recalled that on New Year's Eve he spent the night with Angus Cowan "traipsing around the streets of Regina, knocking on door after door desperately seeking accommodation. It just wasn't to be had."[149]

But the situation soon changed. Through the man who became Cliff's director in Adult Education, a short-term stay was arranged for the threesome at his apartment in the Tower Gardens Apartments, 1100 Broadway Avenue. At the end of the week, the situation of the three pioneers suddenly turned favorable. They found a home in apartment 1010, the top floor of the same building. Catherine described the Tower Gardens as "the most sought after apartment building in Regina."[150]

Cliff had secured a job as one of three Adult Education supervisors hired by the Saskatchewan government. His task was to develop the pre-existing curriculum of Regina evening classes and to maximize the number of students enrolled. The varied programs offered everything from "leather-craft to basic English and farm accounting to international affairs."[151] He was also sent to weekend-long meetings with teachers, laborers and farmers at the Fort Qu'Appelle Conference Centre to facilitate discussions among the three groups regarding how their various needs could be met by the Adult Education curriculum. The Department of Adult Education was housed in the Provincial Parliament buildings in Regina that had been designed by Hand of the Cause of God, and noted Canadian architect, William Sutherland Maxwell (1874–1952). The evening classes were housed in the former residence of the Lieutenant-Governor who had moved to a hotel apartment.

Catherine's annual letter of December 1958 indicated that their first year in Regina was one of "great excitement, adjustment and change." Her first letter from Regina to the Daintys captured her fresh enthusiasm at being in new surroundings. Just as in the letters written to Michael Rochester, some six years earlier, the letters to the Daintys, written in dark green ink, and her mimeographed annual letters, reveal the same character traits of Catherine Huxtable's personality: affection coupled with frankness, easy humor, childlike enthusiasm, dedication to pioneering and devotion to teaching the Bahá'í Faith are evident throughout. Catherine's letter of January 25, 1958, to Don and Diana Dainty in St. Catharines, Ontario, expresses her elation at finding their first "home" with its wonderful view of Regina:

6 ∞ Regina, Saskatchewan

Dear Di & Don (Maw & Pa), Well! Here are Cliff and I spending a quiet evening at home— and when I say home I mean HOME—our very first! It still all seems like too great a miracle to be really true. We were expecting great tests and privations and, although the first week was hard, here God has put us in the most sought-after apartment building in Regina, and not only that, but on the top floor, where we have the best view in town! . . . We found this on the day we had to move out of Cliff's boss's apt., and only had to spend one night in a hotel while this was being painted. . . . There is this <u>view</u>— or rather 2 views, as we're on a corner facing north over the majority of the city and west facing the Parliament buildings designed by Sutherland Maxwell (it reminds me of the Shrine of the Báb every time I look at it) and the "lake" (an enlarged puddle, but very nice!)—and in this flat, flat country a view means a lot 'cause its [sic] hard to come by. The city is only seven miles across and so we can see the prairie beyond the city on both sides, plus 2 oil refineries, lots of trees nearby, and the airport in the distance. Immediately below us is a large playing ground and a skating rink which currently provides better entertainment than TV— and I can keep an eye on Cliff when he goes out to play!! (He bought some skates yesterday.) All this is rather nice since I don't get out much without a car of our own.

Catherine listed other advantages in her letter to the Daintys: fifteen foot "Vistavision" windows; peace and quiet because they were on the top floor; interesting neighbors to visit "without even getting my nose cold"; washer and dryer on every floor; ample storage space; three large rooms; abundant indoor heat: "I'm warmer than I was in Toronto!" Cliff's job required travel to nearby towns which could have potentially involved what was called then "Indian teaching." Catherine was hopeful: "There's a strong chance that he'll be brought into contact with Indians in his work—which of course is what we're praying for." Catherine was still under the illusion that being in a wheelchair would be an obstacle to teaching the Bahá'í Faith, but she used to cruise up and down the halls and take the elevator to meet other tenants. To make friends and to inform them of the Bahá'í teachings, she invited those whom she met to tea.[152]

Travel was made possible through the purchase of their first car, a 1946 Mercury, bought off a car lot for $125.00 in Estevan, Saskatchewan. It came complete with one white-walled tire and no back bumper! Cliff made extra income for the household with a brief, not so successful stint in buying and selling used cars. The Mercury was the first of four vehicles, the maximum number of cars allowed to be legally sold without a provincial license. An unexpected and generous monetary gift of $3000 from ninety-year-old Colonel Heward, shortly before his death on August 6, 1958, allowed Cliff to "trade up." With a trade-in of three cars, they were able to purchase a brand-new 1958 Mercedes-Benz 180 diesel, a car that would see them through the six years of their stay on Salt Spring Island, until their departure from the Gulf Islands in October, 1965.

Catherine's and Eileen's Frank Friendship: Tests Faced by Pioneers

The same newsy letter to the Daintys expresses Catherine's satisfaction that the relationship with Eileen White is working well:

> Eileen White is working out <u>ideally</u> as my helper-companion. There is still something holding her back from becoming a Bahá'í, but she definitely <u>intends</u> to become one, and she and I have wonderful discussions every day. She definitely feels she did the right thing in coming out here, and is happy in her work, although there have been some difficult adjustments to make.

Catherine reported to the Daintys that Eileen White arrived "like a breath of fresh air in this community." By her own testimony, Bobbie Cowan had been in a "spiritual slump" for some two years before the Huxtables arrived. Bobbie welcomed Eileen's coming because at last she found someone "that she

6 ∞ Regina, Saskatchewan

could <u>really</u> talk to." Catherine remarked that a few of the Bahá'ís in Regina had been a test to Bobbie—and, Catherine added, to the Huxtables also. Eileen White Collins diplomatically observed: "There were two characters, sincere in their intentions, who were a source of opportunities for our individual and community growth."[153] This is likely a veiled allusion to the anti-fluoridation controversy that had temporarily troubled the community. (See further two sections below).

In the same letter, Catherine went on to enlarge on the value of pioneering and the inevitable tests that come with it, tests that favor spiritual growth:

> We've all three found a new routine and getting established in a new community a considerable spiritual test—a test of our faith. Cliff and Eileen are still in a bit of a slump—and I was in a bad one for a week but Jamie and Gale Bond's visit last week snapped me out of it and I now feel able to give a talk in a week's time. We were conscious of all the spiritual props we had in Toronto until they were pulled out from under us, and it's been quite a challenge. But not a <u>surprising</u> one as we'd heard enough about others' pioneering experiences—and not an unwelcome one really as the opportunities for growth are great—and insistent and that's what I wanted back in Toronto. Not that there weren't lots of pressures in Toronto too, but here I feel we will suffer more usefully! And there is no refuge save God. It makes me wonder if a large part of the reason why 'Abdu'l-Bahá and Shoghi Effendi stressed the importance of the majority pioneering isn't this very fact—that uprooting one's body and planting it in a different part of the world is a spiritual cause of grow or die—and with all the bounties surrounding us this day, the chances of growth are much greater than the chances of death! And in this way the new race of men begins to emerge.

Reestablishing the LSA: Restoring Unity, Problem Solving Through Consultation

In pioneering to Regina, the Huxtables, like the Cowans, who had arrived two years earlier, intended to strengthen the Local Spiritual Assembly, first formed in 1944. Sociologist Will van den Hoonaard has pointed out that after the formation of the LSA, the Bahá'í community in Regina had difficulty in establishing a stable, solid core and in finding believers from Regina itself. People were frequently moving away; very few of them, with the exception of Mabel and Leslie Silversides, who pioneered in 1950 to a nearby First Nations' reserve, left to fill pioneering posts.[154] Some other factor, perhaps personality issues, must be suspected for the difficulties in Regina.

Although they were grateful for the accommodations Catherine's parents had provided at 7 Clarendon Crescent, the Huxtables were happy to have begun independent living. They missed their close friends in Toronto and southern Ontario, but they felt that leaving Ontario's capital for the pioneering field was precisely the right move. The Huxtables observed that certain tensions were rising to the surface in Toronto following the general inaction that had greeted the Guardian's call to disperse. The Huxtables soon found, however, that building and maintaining community unity are both the challenge and test of every Bahá'í community; Regina was no different. Bobbie Cowan's reticence to confide closely in any of the Bahá'í friends before the Huxtables and Eileen White arrived, indicated that the favorable climate necessary for heartfelt communication was lacking. However, once the newly invigorated group began to follow Shoghi Effendi's guideline of having "frank and loving consultation,"[155] problems were brought to the attention of the LSA, consulted upon and resolved.

In the handwritten post-scriptum of her letter of December 1958 to the Daintys, Catherine wrote: "There were tears at Feasts and all sorts of excitement!" One of the Regina Bahá'ís had taken a strong anti-fluoride stand and had successfully campaigned through the media to prevent fluoridation of the city's water supply.[156] While this believer was doubtless well-motivated, based on legitimate health concerns, the issue became political. Bahá'ís became known as the anti-fluoridation group, a label that necessarily associated the friends with a highly divisive issue that, in the judgment of the LSA, was turning seekers away from investigating the Faith. The individual voluntarily moved away "after stern measures being taken by our Assembly." Once unity was restored, enrolment grew, bringing hope and vitality to the community. Within four months of the arrival of the Huxtables and Eileen White, the LSA was reestablished on April 21, 1958. Following the reestablishment of the LSA, the creation of committees, formulating teaching plans, finding new "contacts," setting extension teaching goals, and doing "Indian teaching" all helped to give the community a forward-moving, positive orientation. Catherine wrote in her annual letter: "One of our reasons for coming to Regina was to help re-establish the Bahá'í Assembly here. We had the satisfaction of seeing this come about in April, and we greatly enjoy being part of this growing community."

The Letter from Rúhíyyih Khánum (1958)

Catherine had written Rúhíyyih Khánum earlier about their pioneering move to Regina. She received an answer in a letter written from Haifa dated April 13, 1958. It read:

> Dear Catherine: I was so happy to receive the good news your letter brought. It shows that when the spirit of love for the Faith is strong enough in the heart, all difficulties are surmounted and all doors opened. How wonderful that you can render our beloved Guardian this service so soon after his passing and that you have assured another Assembly's existence this year! Such things brought him great joy. I was also most happy to know dear John [Robarts] has visited you there. He is a wonderful soul, and I am sure his Canadian trip will be both a healing and an inspiration to the believers at this time. Please give my love to your husband and the friends there, and I hope the coming year holds much happiness and many victories for you all. With warmest Bahá'í love, Rúhíyyih[157]

The Huxtables, Eileen White and the rest of the community rarely felt lonely with the goodly share of visitors that came to Regina. Catherine recorded the names of the stream of visitors that year:

> Our Bahá'í friends were of great assistance and through our many activities we have met wonderful people from all over the province; pioneers, business men, writers, teachers, Indians, new Canadians, "Addled Educators" [a pun on Adult Educators], and ex-convicts. And our year has been highlighted by visits from relatives and old friends; Catherine's mother, Cliff's brother Wes with wife Mary and child David, the Fortnums from England, Cliff's cousin Shirley, the Cleathers [Toronto Bahá'ís Charles and Carol], Doug Appleton, John Robarts, Roger White, Kay White, Patricia Paice, Gale and Jamie Bond, Nancy Campbell and Peggy Ross.

Growing the Community and Other Positive Developments (1958–1959)

Four other notable events took place concurrently with the reestablishment of the LSA. (1) Summer vacation of 1958 took the Huxtables to Horseshoe Bay in West Vancouver to the home of friends Ann and Sven Kerr whom we met in chapter 2. Catherine was particularly intrigued by the view when they saw for the first time the Strait of Georgia and Salt Spring Island from a distance. (2) Eileen White became emotionally and spiritually, as well as intellectually engaged with the Bahá'í Faith. Through her association with the Huxtables and the effective teaching work of Angus and Bobbie Cowan, she "signed her card" the night before the Fast began, March 1, 1958. (3) Eileen married Albert Vail in the month of August, 1958—Vail was no relation to the early American believer of the same surname. (4) Eileen's marriage necessitated a change in helpers. Eileen was replaced for the summer by a seventeen-year-old aboriginal girl, Georgina Stevens. Following their summer holiday, Bernice "Birdie" Boulding, a seventeen-year-old orphanage runaway, whom the Huxtables "adopted," became their helper. Bernice would accompany the Huxtables to Salt Spring Island, become a Bahá'í, and remain with them until her marriage on December 30, 1961.

6 ∞ Regina, Saskatchewan

Catherine's 1958 description of their life in Regina seemed to indicate that they were going to settle down to life in the city for some time to come:

> We enjoy the wide open spaces, the tremendous expanse of sky with its vivid sunsets, northern lights and sun dogs, the wide variety of birds to be seen everywhere, and the clear dry air. There are quite a few trees in the city and Regina homes have lovely gardens in the summer. We were given flowers every week from May to September. . . . Life is busy here as it is anywhere, and we find it a satisfying place to live.[158]

Cliff's job, however, became the fly in the ointment of their marriage and pioneer life. His professional duties required him to travel on weekends and to work late three evenings a week. The Huxtables were beginning to feel like strangers. Cliff grew to realize that "by this time Catherine and I were not terribly happy."[159] But despite the temporary distance created by Cliff's job situation, the Huxtables were clearly heartened by the several bright spots that were casting a more cheerful light on the Bahá'í community of Regina. Spring of 1959 had been a banner season. As already mentioned, the LSA had been reestablished the previous year, and in March 1958, just after Eileen White's enrollment, Phil Schmalenberg joined the community, followed later by his wife Nona.

The blessings of the Fast produced five new believers in 1959: two married couples, Verne and Mabel Ennis and Tom and Sophie Anaquod, who had three and five children respectively, and Albert Vail, Eileen's husband. Catherine referred to the Anaquods as "two of Regina's 'leading' Indians."[160] "We are too thrilled for words," she wrote, sharing her joy with the Daintys in a letter of March 26, 1959. Because of the presence of such families as the Anaquods, Doug and Marian Crofford, Margaret and Gunter (Gordon) Schmitt, Verne and Mabel Ennis, Phil and Nona Schmalenberg,[161] the Regina Bahá'í community had grown to have about fifteen children and youth, a number sufficiently large to necessitate the childrens' class being divided up.[162] The temporary bumps that had initially greeted the Huxtables, when they moved into Regina at the end of the previous year, had been all smoothed out. By the middle of 1959, there was no longer a pressing need for the Huxtables to stay.

Angus and Roberta Cowan: Teaching the Faith in Regina and Legal Recognition of the Bahá'í Marriage Ceremony

At Cliff Huxtable's request, I should like to mention in passing the central role played by Angus and Bobbie Cowan, the dedicated couple who spirited the teaching work in Regina.[163] In "Restoring the Regina Assembly," chapter 8 of *Angus: From the Heart* (1999), Patricia Verge has outlined the Cowans' major contribution to the expansion and consolidation of the Bahá'í community in Regina. Since December, 1953, Angus had been serving on the National Spiritual Assembly of Canada.[164] He served on that body until 1957 and again from 1961 to 1970. The Cowans arrived in Regina in 1955 to help reform the Assembly when Angus was forty-one years old. While the Huxtables contributed their fair share to the reestablishment of the LSA, Angus and his wife, Bobbie, who always provided quiet, solid and effective background support, were the main generators of the teaching work in and around Regina. Inspired by the directive of Shoghi Effendi in his letter of September 2, 1957, to enlist Aboriginals and French Canadians within the Canadian Bahá'í community, the Cowans reached out both to First Nations and the general community.

The Cowans and the Huxtables were instrumental in assisting Tom and Sophie Anaquod, who belonged to the Saulteaux nation, to become Bahá'ís. Angus had met Tom at a conference at Saskatchewan House in Regina that aimed to assist Aboriginals with problems of adjustment to life in urban environments. The conference was also attended by Cliff Huxtable and Don MacLaren.[165] Angus announced to Tom immediately that he was a Bahá'í, and introduced Cliff Huxtable also as a Bahá'í. Cliff and Catherine had met Tom and Sophie Anaquod at the YMCA friendship group that Angus had requested that they attend, but they had not told Tom at that time that they were Bahá'ís.[166] At the Saskatchewan House conference, Angus gave Tom a pamphlet with some verses from the sacred writings that penetrated his heart.[167]

Angus Cowan was by nature a gregarious individual. From the time he was a young man, he had volunteered with church and community service organizations, and worked with disadvantaged and troubled youth as a member of "the Big Brothers Association, president of the John Howard Society, and the representative from Saskatchewan on the national committee of the Canadian Corrections Association."[168] As a former alcoholic who had been spiritually transformed and who had successfully overcome his addiction, he was anxious to impart the remedy he had found in the Bahá'í teachings to all those who aspired to moral, spiritual and social transformation.

Assisted by Cliff, Angus also facilitated legal recognition of the Bahá'í marriage ceremony in Saskatchewan. Angus one day spontaneously invited Cliff, a Saskatchewan civil servant, to accompany him to an appointment he had made with a government official. Although Angus and Cliff were courteously received, the interview met a stumbling block when they explained that the organization of the Bahá'í Faith had been structured without clergy. However, the department of Vital Statistics required the name of the cleric who would perform the marriage to be recorded in its Registry. After a brief discussion, the official agreed to accept the name of the chair of the Local Spiritual Assembly, even though he understood that the chair could change after every annual election. Angus and Cliff left the official's office within fifteen minutes with the assurance that the Bahá'í marriage ceremony would be granted legal recognition throughout the province of Saskatchewan.[169]

By providing loving but firm guidance, Angus and Bobbie assisted the Huxtables in stabilizing the life of the runaway teenager, Bernice Boulding, who became the Huxtables' helper in the summer of 1958 for the period of the next three years. Angus's great love of people, his humility, simplicity, honesty, reliance on prayer, his warm and ready smile, illumined every gathering and put seekers in a receptive mood to hear about the Bahá'í teachings. The entire Regina Bahá'í community supported the teaching initiatives undertaken by the Cowans, initiatives that bore fruit in the enrollments of 1958–1959.

The Power of Example: Aboriginal Believer Tom Anaquod Seals the Purchase on the Huxtables' First Home (1959)

Included in the positive developments of 1958–1959 was the purchase of the Huxtables' first home. Catherine and Cliff decided to make a down-payment on a yellow brick bungalow in the Regina suburbs that was more suited to their special needs. The purchase of their home in suburban Regina is worth noting because it informs us that living the Bahá'í life, free of racial or ethnic prejudice, actually became a factor in its successful purchase. While Cliff was on his way downtown to submit a bid to the developer, he ran into Tom Anaquod, mentioned above (d. 2006), who later became the first Aboriginal to serve on the Canadian National Spiritual Assembly. Tom had just become a Bahá'í that past spring. On the spur of the moment, Cliff invited Tom to accompany him to the real estate office. When Cliff later became friends with the developer, he volunteered that he sold the house to the Huxtables, despite the other offers that he had received, because Cliff had come to the appointment accompanied by an "Indian friend."[170] On January 1, 1959, in the dead cold of the Regina winter, the Huxtables moved to 1837 Grant Drive, in the newly completed subdivision of Whitmore Park.

Taking Leave of Regina (1959)

Although they had purchased their first home only months before, the call to pioneer again impelled Cliff and Catherine to begin making plans to move further west. The Huxtables had not forgotten the intriguing Gulf Islands that they had seen from the Kerr's home in West Vancouver during their summer vacation of 1958. Catherine was particularly keen on settling on Salt Spring Island. The one remaining obstacle to the next stage in pioneering was the sale of their recently purchased house. Now Cliff had taken a $1800 lien on the Mercedes to make a down payment on the house, and the house had to be sold to pay back the lien before he was allowed by law to leave the province. Help came through their friend, Richard "Dick" Stanton, Knight of Bahá'u'lláh for the northern District of Keewatin,[171] in today's Kivalliq region of Nunavut. During an invitation to dinner, Dick told the Huxtables that he had a friend who was a real estate agent.

He proposed to invite her for a house inspection and consultation. She came and suggested that a more positive first impression would be made on prospective buyers by upgrading interior finishing touches with luxury towel rails and other quality items. The agent soon bought the house for resale herself, after replacing the Huxtables' economy fittings, freeing them to depart, two days before the September deadline they had set for themselves. In her annual letter of December 1959, written from Salt Spring Island, Catherine reflected that at the time of their departure, the Regina community "had doubled in numbers and had become strong, united and active."[172]

Eileen White Collins Remembers Catherine Huxtable

Eileen had been Catherine's companion-helper for a period of eight months, until her marriage in August 1958 to Albert Vail. Eileen remembered that Catherine generally awoke in low spirits. Despite the dystrophic condition that rendered her immobile, she did not like to be dependent on others. While they were living in Regina, Catherine allowed only Cliff and Albert Vail to lift her, although that favor was also enjoyed by Michael Rochester in Toronto. After her morning devotions, with her spirits refreshed, she would call out to Eileen in a cheery voice—"Ready!" Eileen managed the daily morning routine of transferring Catherine into her wheelchair, a procedure that was accomplished by a hydraulic Hoyer patient-lift. After the transfer was complete, Catherine would have breakfast. It took until eleven a.m. to complete the morning routine.

Catherine always began her day with prayer and meditation, a spiritual practice that greatly assisted in raising her spirits. The depth and strength of her prayers became the foundation of her spiritual life. Eileen recounted that Cliff was making bookcases in apartment 1010, when an earthquake tremor occurred. He paused, smiled and quipped: "Catherine, stop saying the Tablet of Ahmad!" His wife's prayers were powerfully imbued with a spirit of sincerity, purity and devotion.

In her response to my request to describe Catherine's character, Eileen repeated some of the same attributes I had heard mentioned by others of her generation. She remembered the smiling face, the radiance that could light up a room.

The frankness that appears in her letters was confirmed by Eileen: "She was very honest in her relationship with Cliff," she indicated. She was also honest in her conversations with Eileen, an honesty that Eileen reciprocated. Their exchanges created a climate of mutual confidence: "We could talk about things and be forthright with one another," she said. But, as I have mentioned elsewhere, and as both Eileen and Cliff confirmed, it was an honesty that was always courteous, although it could be blunt if the occasion required. Eileen never saw Catherine angry, but it is my observation, after carefully studying the letters that came into my hands, that Catherine revealed more of her true feelings in writing than in speech.

Just as Bernice Boulding Crooks, her next companion-helper, testified to Catherine's great courage, Eileen also recalled Catherine's "tremendous [moral and spiritual] strength." Eileen recalled that Cliff used to joke with his wife: "God put you in that wheelchair to protect the human race." Because Catherine still had the mistaken impression, at least while they were living in Regina, that being a person managing a physical disability presented a barrier to teaching the Bahá'í Faith, it must have taken courage to reach out to the other tenants in the Tower Gardens Apartments, whom she met while she cruised the halls for recreation. Roger White's eloquent, sensitive pen-portrait of Catherine's spirituality makes no mention of courage, but highlights instead her serenity, nobility, radiance, saintliness, gentility, refinement and subtle ethereal qualities, as well as her balanced humanity. No doubt courage is also assumed by the poet when he mentions their pioneering to "the lonely, volcanic island of St. Helena, final prison and resting place of Napoleon Bonaparte."[173]

Catherine was also tolerant of the foibles of others. "She put up with my inadequacies," Eileen confided. She also alluded to Catherine's sense of humor, but she smiled more than she laughed because the weakness produced by muscular dystrophy would not allow her to enjoy a vigorous "belly laugh." Instead, the air from her lungs would vibrate her vocal cords, creating a thinner, weaker laughter. When I asked Eileen the more awkward question as to whether or not she thought Catherine was a saint, she responded that she heard Hand of the Cause of God, John Robarts, say that she was a saint, a view that Cliff also affirmed. Cliff did not shy away from writing after Catherine's death, that Mr. Robarts had been proclaiming her as one of the saints and heroines of the Bahá'í dispensation. Hand of the Cause Zikrullah Khádem placed Catherine "next" to the distinguished Canadian pioneer Marion Jack regarding courage and detachment. (See chapter 11 for further details.)

But Eileen, who saw Catherine struggle daily with muscular dystrophy in the mundane, domestic circumstances of her life with Cliff, was not inclined to speculate on Catherine's saintliness. She offered, instead, the more down-to-earth view that she was "an admirable human being," and "a normal person dealing with physical challenges." This assessment is no doubt closer to the way that Catherine wanted others to perceive her. But again, how Catherine wished to be perceived, in her humble desire to be viewed just like everyone else, and what she actually achieved in living the Bahá'í life, are two different things.

The Question of a Saintly Life

I should point out here that Bahá'ís, unlike Catholic Christians, have no official methodology for determining who is a saint, nor has any call ever been raised to elaborate a canon of Bahá'í saints. This does not mean, however, that the Bahá'í sacred writings do not recognize the existence of saints, both within and without the Bahá'í Faith. On the contrary. To cite just one reference from 'Abdu'l-Bahá: "The word [saint] has a very real meaning. A saint is one who leads a life of purity, one who has freed himself from all human weaknesses and imperfections." One of His talks, given on All Saints' Day, November 1, 1912, in Paris is devoted to that very topic.[174] We shall soon realize that even a cursory examination of the sacred writings of the Báb, Bahá'u'lláh, and 'Abdu'l-Bahá, and the historical writings of Shoghi Effendi, as well as his moral exhortations, attach great importance to living a saintly life. These writings all recognize the existence of saints in the Bahá'í dispensation, and their spiritual companions, heroes and martyrs, particularly—but not exclusively—during the early and tumultuous "Heroic/Apostolic Age" of the Faith (1844–1921). Closer to our time, Shoghi Effendi referred, for example, to two Hands of the Cause, Martha Root (1872–1939) and William Sutherland Maxwell (1874–1952), respectively as a "saintly soul"[175] and as one who had led a "saintly life."[176] Aside from the considered opinions of those who knew Catherine well, and outside any specific qualification of persons mentioned as saints in the Bahá'í writings, sainthood, like beauty, remains in the eye of the beholder.

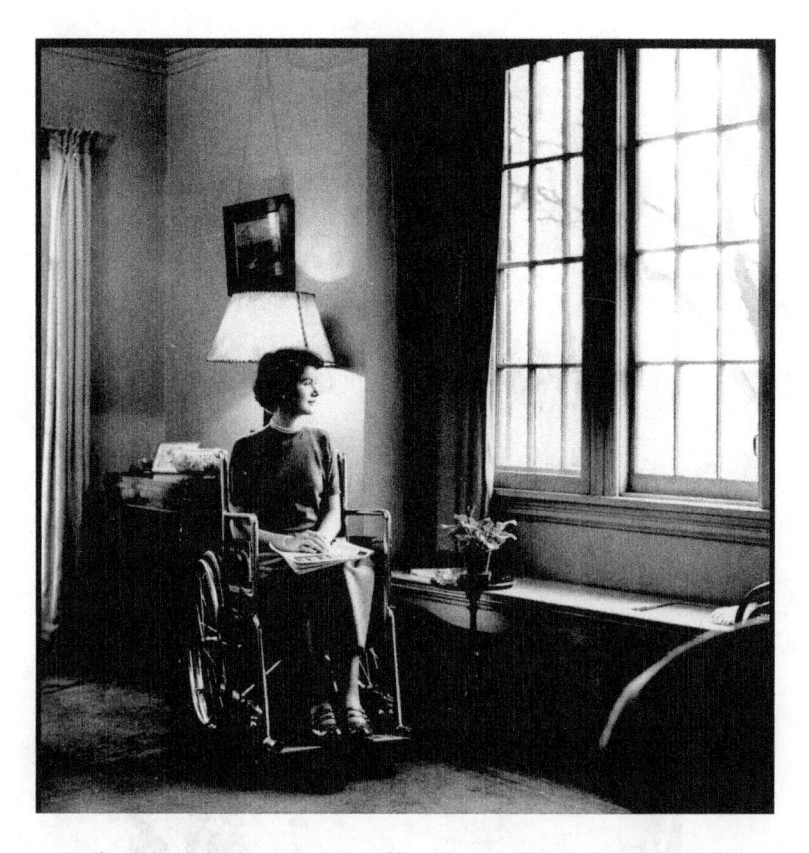

Catherine in the living room of her parents' home at 7 Clarendon Crescent, Toronto, early 1950's.

Above: Catherine's older sister Julia, their mother Helen Bury Heward, and 5-year-old Catherine. Photo taken c. 1937 in Charlwood, Surrey, England.

Below: Catherine during a sea-voyage to England in 1949 when she was 17 years old.

Catherine doing needlepoint at home at 7 Clarendon Crescent, Toronto.

Catherine and Cliff at Edinswold, c1952.

Cliff at the Bahá'í House of Worship in Wilmette, Illinois, during the Huxtables' honeymoon, May 1955.

Above: The Huxtables' first house on Lees Hill, Salt Spring Island, British Columbia, November 1959.
Below: Catherine with companion-helper Bernice Boulding, later Crooks, at their first house in Lees Hill, 1959.

Above: Catherine with close friend Michael Rochester, who was taught the Bahá'í Faith by Cliff.

Left: Rúhíyyih Khánum, visiting some Bahá'í friends, at the home of Ann and Sven Kerr, West Vancouver, 1960. While Rúhíyyih Khánum conversed with Catherine, artist Joyce Devlin painted Rúhíyyih Khánum's portrait.

Above, left: Fletcher and Elinor Bennett, early Bahá'ís on Salt Spring Island, 1964. The Bennetts were taught the Bahá'í Faith by Catherine and Cliff Huxtable.

Above, right: The Huxtables' third and last home on Beddis Road, Salt Spring Island, British Columbia.

Catherine with a group of Toronto Bahá'ís, c1956.

The first Local Spiritual Assembly of the Gulf Islands (Salt Spring Island), British Columbia, April 21, 1964.

Left to right, front row: Elinor Bennett, Catherine Huxtable, Cliff Huxtable. Back row: Edna Moen, Fletcher Bennett, Bernice Boulding Crooks, Kate Saunders, Walter Luth, photographer and LSA member Lisa Luth absent from photo.

Last photo of Catherine taken on St. Helena Island, South Atlantic, December 1966.

-7-
WEST TO THE GULF ISLANDS:
The Joys And Trials Of Knighthood (1959–1966)

The Anachronism of the Chapter Title

Regarding the chapter title, I should alert the reader to the following anachronism. Shoghi Effendi did not name the Huxtables Knights of Bahá'u'lláh: they arrived on Salt Spring Island in 1959, two years after the Guardian's passing. They were not officially named Knights of Bahá'u'lláh by the Universal House of Justice until September 14, 1969, two years after Catherine's death. Nonetheless, because this act of service eventually merited the title of Knights of Bahá'u'lláh, I have used it for the purposes of this chapter.

It is important to clarify the following points regarding the Huxtables' motivation in pioneering to the Gulf Islands. Catherine and Cliff knew, of course, that the Gulf Islands had replaced Anticosti Island as an unopened territory, and that the Gulf Islands had not yet received any pioneer when they left Regina in September, 1959. But they thought that the Guardian's bestowed title, "Knight of Bahá'u'lláh," was time-limited and had expired following his passing. The reward of knighthood was, consequently, never in their minds as an inducement to pioneer. Cliff Huxtable was indeed pleasantly surprised, when two years after Catherine's passing, Hand of the Cause John Robarts informed him that they had been named Knights by the Universal House of Justice.[177] (See Appendix 2 for further details.)

A Virgin Territory of the Ten Year World Crusade/Plan (1953–1963)

I shall review briefly here how the Gulf Islands came to be chosen as a goal of the Ten Year World Crusade/Plan. Shoghi Effendi's world-embracing vision of the global expansion of the Bahá'í Faith included settling Bahá'ís in islands, territories and dependencies in some of the remotest, most sparsely populated areas of the world. In 1957, just a short time before his passing, the Guardian approved the Gulf Islands, British Columbia, on the recommendation of the Canadian NSA, as a substitute for Anticosti Island which was privately owned by the Abitibi Pulp and Paper Company. Mary Zabolotny (later McCulloch) of Verdun, Quebec, had in fact opened Anticosti Island to the Bahá'í Faith in April of 1956, an act for which she received the title of Knight of Bahá'u'lláh, but she stayed, as was mentioned above, for only four months.[178] This goal had to be eventually abandoned because the task of settling a pioneer on Anticosti proved unfeasible. In the year 2015 CE, Anticosti Island, with a population of approximately 300 people, still has no Bahá'í inhabitant.[179]

Fascinating Salt Spring Island: Today's California of the North

With the confidence born of the success of their two-year stay in Regina, the Huxtables and companion-helper Bernice Boulding, took the road west on September 8, 1959. The threesome set out, with all their worldly goods in tow, mounted on "a rickety wooden trailer made out of the back end of the frame of a 1929 Chrysler car with two aged wooden-spoked wheels and one spare rim and tire . . ." Once settled on Salt Spring, Catherine wrote to their friends in central Canada some six weeks later to inform them of their new situation. The letter described the stormy beginning of that journey: "Into the teeth of a terrible gale we headed our trusty car westward on September eighth."[180] It was an inauspicious start. In the middle of a "powerful head wind, black, driving rain"[181] a trailer-tire went flat. Cliff had to change both tire and rim in a ferocious storm that practically bowled him over. With the task completed, the threesome chugged along through the Rocky Mountains, arriving again at the Kerrs' home where they put up for a month.

Catherine's fascination with Salt Spring Island has been shared by many who have become residents. For some, Salt Spring Island becomes home and the center of their universe; for others, it is a transition point between chapters in their life journey. Today's Salt Spring Island is sometimes described as "the California of the North." It has a colorful assortment of characters, a vibrant community devoted to the arts, an ecologically alert, organically aware population ready to safeguard the natural heritage of the island in its resistance to what seems like a losing battle to ongoing "development." Despite its folksy atmosphere, Salt Spring's population has its fair share of millionaires, a comfortable middle class

7 ∞ West to the Gulf Islands

and relatively few transients and homeless. At twenty-seven miles in length, Salt Spring is hilly and beautiful. Lovely vistas of the Strait of Georgia, with its bracing, salty sea air and fluctuating tides, are highly prized and never far away. The climate is "cool Mediterranean," consisting of warm summers and mild, rainy winters, with winter temperatures averaging a few degrees above thirty-two degrees Fahrenheit (0 degrees Celsius). The recent effects of global warming seem to be brightening the normally grey skies of winter.

At the time of the Huxtables' arrival in 1959, the character of the island was simpler and more rural, much less marked by today's artistic trends, tourist desirability, folksy atmosphere and environmental concerns. It had a population of 1500 souls that swelled during the summer.[182] Today's population is approximately 10,000 people, swelling to several thousand more in summer. Catherine remarked on its "wide variety of friendly inhabitants." Rental properties were considerably cheaper than in Regina. Salt Spring Island seemed like the perfect place to settle down. But neither Cliff nor Catherine could have foreseen that within the next six years, Cliff's health and well-being would be brought to the breaking point, shattering their idyllic dream of island pioneering.

Assistance from Salt Spring Islanders: The Little White House on Lees Hill

Tests and difficulties become the unavoidable lot of those who open far-away places to the Faith of Bahá'u'lláh, but as the pioneering experience has proven time and again, the emphatic promises of divine assistance become realized to aid the pioneer. Although this assistance manifests itself in mysterious ways, it is usually forthcoming from helpful souls in the day-to-day experience. Now Cliff had ferried over first to attend to the most pressing need: finding accommodation. He arrived on Salt Spring with about $240 in his pocket, a year-old car and a monthly income from Colonel Heward's estate to provide for Catherine's medical expenses.[183]

Cliff's first helper on the island was a kindly man named Gil Humphreys, who jokingly called himself "comfy Humphreys." He worked for Salt Spring Lands as a real estate agent. Cliff explained to Gil that he needed to find accommodation for "next to nothing." Although the bulk of Gil's income came from the sale of expensive properties, not low-income rentals, he spent an entire day with Cliff showing him around the island. The very same day, he found the Huxtables a charming white clapboard two-bedroom cottage, with pale-green trim, part way down Lees Hill, just minutes drive away from Fulford Harbor at the southern end of the island. The house had just been bought by a Mr. and Mrs. Campbell, but they were not prepared to take immediate possession. The rent was only $27.50 a month.

Six years later, after the Huxtables had left Salt Spring Island and had arrived on St. Helena Island, Cliff wrote to Gil Humphreys to remember his kindness in helping them to find their first home on Salt Spring and to bring him up-to-date on their journey since leaving the Gulf Islands. His affection for Gil was clearly expressed in his letter of September 12, 1966, written from Jamestown, St. Helena: "Dear Gil, You came to mind last night and in the odd quiet moment during today I found my thoughts turning towards you again and again. I wonder how you are and Nonie and the children."

For much less than the cost of municipal taxes on their suburban Regina home, Cliff was able to sign a nine-month lease on a house and property that included a spring water source, an acre of apple orchard, vegetable and strawberry patches, a few rose bushes and a lovely view that included fields, forests, mountains, and passing deer.[184] The threesome arrived on October 13, 1959. In a mimeographed letter dated December, 1959 (no day), Catherine captured the marked contrast between their modern, suburban home in Regina and their new rural setting on Salt Spring Island: "From a modern brick house in a city suburb to a little clapboard cottage in the country. From the dry, treeless plains and extreme weather of Regina, to the forested mountains and balmy sea air of a West coast island. From an automatic gas furnace to a wood-burning range; from secure and well-paid work in adult education to the uncertainties and low pay of unskilled manual labour. From meetings and entertaining nearly every night of the week to being home alone together most evenings."

7 ∞ West to the Gulf Islands

Cliff's First Jobs as Self-Employed Laborer

Cliff left a secure a job as a representative in Adult Education in Regina to arrive on Salt Spring Island without prospects. But the bright twenty-seven-year-old former teacher was about to become a self-employed manual laborer. The spirit of alacrity with which Cliff took on these jobs, the only work that he was able to secure during the first six months on Salt Spring Island, shows that he did not consider any job beneath his dignity. The urgent financial responsibility for Catherine and helper Bernice Boulding fell directly on Cliff's shoulders.

Since Cliff had been successful with the local real estate company in finding a first home, he returned there for help with employment. Fortune smiled again. This time Charles "Charlie" Horel (d. 1998), a descendant of early Salt Spring pioneers, and senior salesperson with Salt Spring Lands, hired Cliff to dig ditches near Long Harbor, the ferry terminal on the north-east coast of the island. He rolled up to the job site in his Mercedes with pick and shovel in hand and began to dig. His next job was deceptively simple. Although starting a fire seemed like an easy enough task, when Cliff arrived at the newly excavated Mount Baker subdivision, just above downtown Ganges, he discovered that it was not a simple case of brush-burning. He found himself standing before an enormous pile of uprooted trees, the size of a three-story house, all bulldozed together, so high that he could walk into it! The job had to be abandoned when his employer determined that a chainsaw would be required to light the fire.

Cliff thought he would be sacked because he had no experience handling a chainsaw, but instead he was sent back to the Mount Baker subdivision, where he continued to dig ditches. As Catherine wrote in her annual 1959 letter, "ditches and more ditches." One of them happened to be located in front of the white paneled bungalow at 131 Mount Baker Crescent, the house that became my parents' retirement home in August 1978. Cliff dug ditches "all across the top of the subdivision." Ditch-digging in the Mount Baker subdivision was bone-jarring labor. The hardpan was so solid that Cliff could hardly penetrate it with a pickaxe. He found employment later in Vesuvius, on the northwest side of the island, helping a fireguard to build his house by doing form and concrete work. He found other work digging out silted-up septic tile beds and cleaning out the sludge. He found another job doing rough carpentry when a retired woodworking teacher hired him to help build a house on Grace Point in downtown Ganges.

A Benefactor is Found: The Island "Baron" Gavin Mouat Employs Cliff

A few months after Cliff had completed his first series of jobs, a benefactor entered the Huxtables' life. Gavin Colvin Mouat (d. 1961), was the ninth of eleven children of pioneer Shetland Islanders, Thomas and Jane Mouat, who landed on Salt Spring Island in 1885. The year 2007 marked the centenary of the founding of Mouat's Trading Company on Salt Spring Island. The Mouat name is well-known and synonymous with economic and social development on the island. The annual revenues of their business interests run into the millions. Mouat's Trading Company and Mouat's Home Hardware in downtown Ganges are longstanding, familiar landmarks to all Salt Spring islanders.[185]

At the time that Cliff met Gavin Mouat through Charlie Horel in 1960, Mr. Mouat had long been prosperous, but he was nearing the end of his lifespan. He had organized and was president of the Gulf Islands Ferry Company. Some other commercial enterprises included: president of the Water Works; general manager of the Salt Spring Lands and Investment Company; owner of rental properties, including the post office, telephone company, garage, Royal Canadian Mounted Police station, Bank of Montreal, barber shop, taxi stand and Centennial Library.[186]

In his business persona, Mr. Mouat was a direct, sometimes gruff man. As a local corporate boss, he directly controlled a substantial portion of the economic life of the island, and his employees' livelihood with it, but the Huxtables were the recipients of his kindness and generosity. Catherine wrote in her letter of December 1959, that Gavin Mouat had taken "a benevolent interest in us." Cliff was close enough in his interactions with the man who was to become his employer to sense his admiration for Catherine's courage and "class." As was typical for the taciturn men of Gavin Mouat's generation, this appreciation was unspoken, but it became apparent in his demeanor. Catherine and Gavin became better acquainted when they were both hospitalized at the same time in February 1961, in the Lady Minto Hospital in Ganges. Gavin would die only nine months later, on

7 ∞ West to the Gulf Islands 107

November 26, of an undisclosed illness.

Gavin Mouat provided Cliff with his longest stretch of employment to that point, when he hired him to work as a farmhand on the Mouat family farm in the winter and spring of 1959–1960. The ranch style house was located on Sunset Boulevard, just beyond Vesuvius. He dug fence-post holes and cleared patches of land, but Cliff Huxtable was no farm boy at heart. His least favorite job was holding sheep while they were being neutered. Cliff's tasks included cutting down saplings using an axe. The first morning on the job, Gavin Mouat himself demonstrated the technique by pacing Cliff. Although the older man was sixty-seven years old, and only as tall as Cliff's shoulder, the twenty-eight-year-old quickly reached the point of exhaustion, bent over and vomited. Gavin looked at Cliff blankly and walked off. Cliff thought he would be fired. "He was like a machine," Cliff remembered. "I just couldn't keep up with him."[187]

Gavin Mouat rendered the Huxtables another important service: he provided them with a mortgage at the rate of five percent per annum on the purchase of their second house on Sharp Road in May 1960. Gavin's offer was timely. The Campbells wanted to take possession of the little house on Lees Hill, and to the three adults, the two-bedroom cottage was starting to feel cramped. Gavin advised Cliff to submit an offer of $5000, a price well below market value, but the offer was immediately accepted. No money actually changed hands because the owner was indebted to Mr. Mouat for the price of the mortgage.

When Gavin called Cliff in to sign the contract, Cliff informed him that his irregular income would not allow him to pay off the mortgage. Mr. Mouat told Cliff not to worry; he would find him work. But at the end of the winter-spring season, Gavin announced that he was terminating Cliff's job and would pay him off on the upcoming Friday. It was not welcome news. Now that he had a mortgage, Cliff was facing unemployment again, after Gavin had assured him that he would provide Cliff with a job. When the following Friday afternoon rolled around, Cliff wanted to remind Gavin of his commitment, but instead he said nothing, remembering the kindness that his employer had already shown. Instead, Cliff thanked Gavin for his help. Gavin at first thought that Cliff was being ironic or insincere in his expression of thanks, but he quickly realized that Cliff's gratitude was genuine. Within a matter of hours, Cliff's sincerity would pay off.

From Deckhand on the Delta Queen to School Principal on Saturna Island (1960–1961)

"I hardly got in the house, when the telephone rang," Cliff recalled. Gavin Mouat went straight to the point in his usual direct manner, foregoing formalities: 'Do you want a job on the ferry?' he asked. After the previous seven months of manual labor, Cliff was simply elated at this offer. He loved the scenic beauty of British Columbia and he loved the sea. He had a homecoming feeling the minute he had driven across the Alberta-British Columbia border on their summer vacation of 1958. Deckhand was the one job on the island that he had longed for, although, as an outsider, he appeared to be an unlikely successful candidate because of the long preferred list of islanders who had already applied.

Cliff began the very next day. His Saturday shift started at 6:15 a.m. He worked right through the weekend. His duties included directing vehicle traffic, polishing brass, washing windows, cleaning the toilets and steering the boat while the captain had tea. Cliff worked weekdays on the Delta Queen on the Fulford-Swartz Bay run (Salt Spring to Victoria) and some weekends on the Vesuvius-Crofton run.

The job unfolded nicely from May to December. Cliff was thriving, but unbeknownst to him, Gavin Mouat had been formulating another plan for the Bahá'í pioneer. His employer chose an opportune moment to declare his intention. Now Gavin knew that Cliff was a Bahá'í. Assuming that he would not object to foregoing his Christmas day holiday, Gavin asked Cliff to work on December 25 to allow the regular deckhand to spend Christmas at home. Cliff replaced the deckhand and Gavin replaced the higher-ranking mate of the "Motor Princess," the wooden, forty-vehicle vessel that in those days ran from Ganges to the outer islands.

Gavin invited Cliff to Christmas dinner in the ship's restaurant where he broached the subject. Having established that Cliff had a university degree, Gavin asked him if he had ever done any teaching. His employer wanted him to apply for the vacant post of principal at the two-room elementary school on Saturna

7 ∞ West to the Gulf Islands

Island, a sparsely populated, mountainous island, twenty-five miles (41 km.) east of Salt Spring Island, a two-hour ferry ride away, and mere miles from the Canada-U.S. nautical border. Cliff replied that he had some teaching experience, but this time he balked at Gavin's proposal. Being a deckhand was a job Cliff loved. Besides, he had not yet completed the courses required to obtain a teaching license, and Cliff had no inclination to move Catherine from Salt Spring where the Lady Minto Hospital was located in Ganges. When Cliff said no, Gavin struck back. He informed Cliff that they were cutting back on their winter schedule as of January 1, 1961; he could not guarantee a job: 'I think we might find it very hard to find a place for you,' Gavin threatened. Cliff was annoyed. He was being bullied by a man who was used to having his own way, but because Gavin had been like a father to him, Cliff decided that he was going to put up with it. It was to be one of the great lessons of pioneering. Pioneers had to endure all kinds of things—that is, up to a point, as Cliff would have to learn later at the hands of an abusive neighbor. Gavin directed Cliff to apply for the job of principal at the elementary school on Saturna. Reluctantly, Cliff agreed.

Cliff later understood that Gavin had an ulterior motive. His real interest in having him take on the direction of the Saturna school was in part political. In keeping with Gavin's keen interest in running school affairs, just one of several key areas followed by the "baron," Gavin and the School District Superintendent, Art Jones, wanted Cliff to run the school successfully in order to help win the third referendum for a consolidated high school in Ganges. The outer islands had voted against locating the high school on Salt Spring Island because it would mean ferry-travel for those students who did not live on the larger island. Cliff met the superintendent, secured the job, and served as principal of the two-room schoolhouse from January until June 1961. With the help of a female teacher on Saturna, through good teaching and effective discipline, Cliff and his colleague created a favorable reputation for the school and for himself. Although Cliff did not actively campaign in favor of the central high school, the proposal received a majority number of votes on the third referendum. Gavin's plan had worked.

Cliff moved first onto the small island of 140 people, but not long after Catherine and companion-helper Bernice arrived, Catherine contracted red measles. As a precaution, because of her already weakened condition, Dr. Jansch shipped Catherine back to the Lady Minto Hospital in Ganges, a move that infuriated the head-nurse because red measles is highly contagious. Catherine's recovery was normal, despite her muscular dystrophy. She was soon able to rejoin Cliff on Saturna for the rest of his six-month tenure.

Meeting Rúhíyyih Khánum in Vancouver (1960)

Before the Huxtables met Rúhíyyih Khánum in Vancouver, Catherine had corresponded with the Montrealer who became the Guardian's wife, secretary, confidant, Hand of the Cause, and leading world ambassadress of the Bahá'í Faith until her death in Haifa on January 19, 2000. Rúhíyyih Khánum had answered one letter to Catherine in 1953, written on behalf of the Guardian. Catherine had solicited Shoghi Effendi's advice as to how she could best serve the Faith when she was barely coping with muscular dystrophy. The letter advised Catherine that she could transcribe the Bahá'í writings into Braille and record them for the blind.[188] (See chapter 8 for further details.) The two women continued to correspond. Rúhíyyih Khánum exchanged friendly letters with Catherine in 1955, 1958, 1963 and 1966.[189]

Rúhíyyih Khánum's Canadian visit to Vancouver took place in the early spring of 1960. The Huxtables ferried over from Salt Spring Island to West Vancouver to attend the more intimate meetings with the former Mary Maxwell that were held at Ann and Sven Kerrs' home, overlooking Larson Bay. Rúhíyyih Khánum had requested that Cliff pick her up each morning at her Vancouver hotel and bring her to the Kerrs' home, where she would meet informally with some of the friends and sit for a portrait painted by Joyce Frances Devlin, while she conversed with Catherine. During our 2013 interview in her beautiful studio-home in Burritts Rapids, Ontario, Joyce Devlin remembered Catherine. Even in Catherine's wheelchair, Joyce remembered that she manifested a spirit of independence: "She was so beautiful, you didn't really notice that she was in a wheelchair," she recalled. "She was so sweet," Joyce continued. "I just loved them. I thought Catherine was heroic, and I thought Cliff was charming and sensitive."

7 ∞ West to the Gulf Islands

The Final Goal of the Ten Year Plan Approved by Shoghi Effendi

Madame Rabbaní took a special interest in the Huxtables. It was a personal consolation to Rúhíyyih Khánum to know that the goal of the Gulf Islands had been filled by our pioneers. That they were able to meet in Vancouver was a special consolation to all three. The opening of the Gulf Islands gave the islands a particular status because they were the very last goal approved by Shoghi Effendi. At one gathering at the Kerrs', Madame Rabbaní produced a small piece of paper that she had found affixed to Shoghi Effendi's world map that was in his hotel room in Knightsbridge, London, when he died. On it he had notated "indicates Gulf Is." He had drawn an arrow pointing toward a small dot.

In his 2014 anecdote, *Shoghi Effendi and the Gulf Islands: A Few Little Miracles*, Steve Fletcher, former Canadian pioneer to Swaziland, who became a Bahá'í on Salt Spring Island on August 2, 1970, recalled the circumstances in which he saw the original artifact for the first time. He arrived in Swaziland as a pioneer on August 31, 1972, and met Rúhíyyih Khánum there when she and Violette Nakhjavani were on the "Great African Safari" (1969–1973). Steve Fletcher met her in Tshaneni, northern Swaziland in early September, 1972, within days of his arrival. When Rúhíyyih Khánum learned that he was from the Gulf Islands, she asked him to approach:

> She then told me to come closer, that she had something I would be interested in. She opened her purse, took out a scarf, untied it and inside was another scarf. She opened that second scarf and pulled out a small paper that was a torn off corner of an airmail envelope. She said that the Guardian had left this paper on the world map in his hotel room in London when he had died. . . . She said this is how the Gulf Islands were added to the Ten Year World Crusade. [192]

Steve added the following reflection: "How she was inspired to pack this when she left Haifa, only God knows. Why did she have it in her purse that day? To me this is nothing short of a miracle." She gave Steve a photocopy of the artifact and a prayer book in which she wrote a dedication that contained the lines, 'this additional goal of his Crusade [was] made in the very last days of his life.'"

Teaching the Bahá'í Faith: Early Caution Followed by More Direct Teaching

After their arrival on Salt Spring Island, the Huxtables at first decided to be cautious in teaching their religion. Catherine wrote to the Daintys on November 10, 1959, only a month after their arrival: "It's hard to keep our religion secret in a place like this—three people have forced it out of us already—hope it isn't too soon." But at this early stage, no serious conversations took place with non-Bahá'ís. People were too polite or uninterested to ask, although helper Bernice Boulding's teenaged friends asked "lots of frank questions." [underlining in original]. These "frank questions" probably related to personal morality. In the same letter, Catherine relayed Rowland Estall's view that Salt Spring islanders were too ruggedly individualistic to want to conform to anything at all, including religion. (By contrast, religion and spirituality are thriving today on Salt Spring.)

Their initial hesitation to teach their religion came from the understanding that the Guardian advised pioneers to go very slowly, but Catherine, in her usual enthusiasm, felt that "Times have changed, and the needs are more urgent." Within just a few months, Catherine had grown impatient. She later wrote to the Daintys on March 7, 1960, that she was "just itching to do direct teaching again." From that point on, they started teaching informally, and by November 1960, they had hosted at least three impromptu firesides.[193] Catherine also shared the viewpoint, based on the experience and advice of Joan and Ted Anderson, Knights of Bahá'u'lláh for the Yukon Territory, that some opposition provided fertile ground for teaching. That opposition did eventually come within a few years, but it did not take the form of adversaries to their religion, but in the mental tests for westerners foretold by 'Abdu'l-Bahá—especially for Cliff. These severe tests all but completely broke his health. But in those early days in the little white house on Lees Hill, Catherine felt that the situation was just "skookum," an island expression, originating in the Chinook language, meaning very good, strong or solid.

7 ∞ West to the Gulf Islands

The presence of our pioneers did not go unnoticed on Salt Spring Island. In the last of our three telephone interviews, just two weeks before she passed away, Elinor Bennett recalled: "They were amazing. They knew everyone on Salt Spring and everyone knew them. People were interested in Catherine. They were friendly and helpful neighbors, and they invited people to tea. If someone dropped in, they were invited to dinner. Friends were always dropping by."[194]

Not long after their arrival on Salt Spring, Catherine had reversed her earlier attitude that her wheelchair status hindered the formation of friendships. She now indicated to the Daintys that the presence of her wheelchair "automatically predisposed" acquaintances and friends in her favor, "before they've even bothered to look at what is in the chair, or speak to one, and they make allowances for any 'peculiarities' they may discover later!"

Bernice "Birdie" Boulding: The First Bahá'í to Enroll in the Gulf Islands (1960)

We have seen above that Bernice Boulding, whom the Huxtables considered to be their "daughter," joined them after their friend Eileen White, their first companion-helper in Regina, married Albert Vail in August 1958.[195] Bernice's life story tells of the positive, life-changing influence mediated by the Huxtables, following her troubled childhood and youth. She was born in Jameson, Saskatchewan, one of thirteen children. Her mother died when she was seven years old. Her alcoholic father was unable to satisfactorily care for his children, and her grandfather removed the children to the Orange Home, an orphanage run by the Protestant Orange Lodge in Indian Head, Saskatchewan. Bernice was unhappy there, and after she ran away from the orphanage with two other girls, they were caught and returned by the police. The school administrators interviewed Bernice, and questioned her about a possible future career. She deliberately concocted the idea of becoming a nun, in the full realization that her pretense to convert to Catholicism would provoke the strong anti-Catholic prejudice of the Orange Order. Her tactic produced the desired effect. At age sixteen, she was summarily expelled. Bernice moved to Regina to live with her sister.

Bernice met the Huxtables when she answered a want-ad that they had placed in a Regina newspaper, soliciting care for a woman in a wheelchair, with the added inducement of travel to the Gulf Islands. About a dozen young women answered the advertisement. Now Bernice knew how to operate a wheelchair. When she lived in the orphanage, she used to wheel the seamstress, who needed a wheelchair and who mended all the clothes in the residence, from the girls' to the boys' building, where the meals were taken. The prospect of travel to the Gulf Islands also appealed to the adventurous young woman, but Bernice told this author that she had no idea where the Gulf Islands actually were. Most of the dozen respondents were unsuitable, but Bernice was a very good fit. She joined the Huxtables following their summer holiday of 1958.

Cliff described Bernice as a "bluff, bonny, 'skookum' lass,"[196] a regular diamond-in-the-rough.[197] The Huxtables were not aware that Bernice had run away from the Orange Home. When the Child Welfare agents came investigating, they were satisfied that Bernice had landed in a healthy environment; they wisely left Bernice in the Huxtables' care. But during the early days of her two-year stay with Catherine and Cliff, Bernice fell in with the wrong crowd. For her own safety, the Huxtables set a curfew. They introduced Bernice to Roberta and Angus Cowan. Angus was well-qualified, as we have seen in chapter 6, to work with troubled youth. With the love and guidance of the Huxtables, and the Cowans' positive but firm hand, Bernice's attitude and behavior improved. Catherine wrote later: "She has worked out so perfectly we can hardly believe it."[198] The Huxtables were not at first sure whether Bernice would want to accompany them to the Gulf Islands, but she requested to join them, even though Cliff was not able to pay her until he had found gainful employment.

Bernice readily acknowledged her gratitude to the Huxtables: "They were my saviors," she declared matter-of-factly. "I would not be the woman I am today without them." After leaving Regina in September 1959, by the time the Huxtables had reached West Vancouver in October, Bernice had already expressed her intention to become a Bahá'í,[199] but it was not until they reached Salt Spring Island that she acted upon her intention. The time came, as it had for Michael Rochester, and as it does for many of those who become Bahá'ís, in a memorable moment of clarity. Bernice was chopping wood under open skies beside the little white house on the slope of Lees Hill. "I just felt very light and happy," she said. "I didn't know exactly what it was that was happening to me, but I was very happy and excited to be in such a place." Early in 1960, Bernice became the first believer to enroll on Salt Spring Island.

The House on Sharp Road: Bernice Boulding Marries and Moves to Saturna Island

Before their nine month lease was up, on May 9, 1960, the Huxtables moved into their second home on Sharp Road, a house they occupied until 1964, except for the six months they spent on Saturna Island during the first half of 1961. The house on Sharp Road was just minutes away by car from the main town of Ganges. The undulating terrain featured a wooded field, orchard, spring water, level ground for a garden, and fenced-in pasture. The seven sheds on the property once formed part of a Japanese market-garden home, until it was confiscated by the Canadian government, under the War Measures Act during World War Two. After the Japanese attack on Pearl Harbor in 1941, and despite the fact that the vast majority of the 22,000 strong Japanese population on the British Columbia coast had been born in Canada, they were deemed "enemy aliens." Their properties were confiscated, and they were sent to internment camps in the interior of British Columbia and Alberta for the duration of the war.[200]

It was while she lived in the house on Sharp Road that Bernice married a logger, Barry Crooks, a resident of Saturna Island. Bernice met Barry in 1961 on Saturna, after Cliff became teacher-principal there in the month of January. The marriage took place on December 30, 1961. According to Bernice, it was the first wedding performed after the Bahá'í marriage ceremony had gained legal status in the province of British Columbia in 1958. Kay Cronan came from Vancouver to serve as marriage officer. The ceremony was followed by an Anglican wedding. The Huxtables planned the wedding and purchased Bernice's bridal dress. "Catherine wanted to make sure I looked properly," Bernice recalled. After the wedding, Bernice moved to Saturna Island where the Crooks raised a family of four children, Sam, Sandra, Shelly, and Clifford. Barry was opposed to Bernice's participation in Bahá'í activities, and he forced her to choose between the Bahá'í Faith and her children. The Boulding-Crooks eventually divorced, but Bernice remained on Saturna Island as an isolated believer until the time of her death on June 16, 2014.

In her letter of March 25, 1963, to Diana Dainty, Catherine reflected on the satisfaction that she and Cliff enjoyed from observing the positive transformation in Bernice's life: "Having watched Bernice grow from a highly disturbed orphan adolescent that [sic] verged on a being a juvenile delinquent to the present radiant, poised, calm, lovely young wife and mother has been one of our most cherished experiences. Seldom have we seen stronger evidence of the power of the Faith." Of course, the power of the Faith was working through the Huxtables, and especially through Catherine's prayers. "I always knew when she was praying," Bernice remembered. Bernice also commented on Catherine's courage, the same quality that had been mentioned by Eileen Collins during their stay in Regina: "She had so much courage," Bernice said. "It amazed me the courage she had. I would think she was a saint."[201]

Dr. Robert Bourdillon and "Nought to Six": Connecting the Huxables to Fletcher and Elinor Bennett

I mentioned above that when no other Baháʼís are present to assist newly arrived pioneers, helpers will appear from among the local population to smooth the way. Robert Benedict Bourdillon (1889–1971) was one of the local helpers whose name has to be added to those of Gavin Mouat, Gil Humphreys, and Charlie Horel. Catherine Huxtable and Elinor Bennett met in an early childhood education group led by Dr. Bourdillon, an Oxford chemistry don, founder of the Oxford University Mountaineering Club (1909), and medical doctor. His eldest son, Tom, tragically killed in a fall in the Bernese Oberland (1956), was a member of the successful 1953 British Mt. Everest expedition.

"Nought to Six" is an association dedicated to early childhood learning and positive communication between parent and child, a subject that interested both Elinor and Catherine. Cliff remembered that "Dr. Bourdillon was very keen on interesting the mothers in teaching their children to read before getting to school."[202] The doctor was perceptive and caring enough to realize that the Huxtables, with their belief in the Baháʼí teachings, would be good company for, and

7 ∞ West to the Gulf Islands 117

have a positive influence on, the Bennetts—particularly for Fletcher, who was going through a psychological crisis. The crisis was serious enough that it had necessitated consultations between Elinor, Fletcher and Dr. Bourdillon before the Huxtables joined Nought to Six. The doctor was a friend of the Faith; he could see merit in the religion, but he was not inclined to join himself. During a 1998 talk at my parents' home on Salt Spring Island, Cliff observed on a note of subtle humor: "He was one of those who thought that the Bahá'í Faith was good for others but not for him."[203]

But as was mentioned above, early in 1961, the Huxtables moved to Saturna Island, where Cliff had assumed the principalship of its small elementary school. Distance was no object, however, because Fletcher piloted his own small plane. Dr. Bourdillon arranged for Fletcher and Elinor to fly to Saturna Island to facilitate the Bennetts' friendship with the Huxtables. During their visits, Catherine took the opportunity to offer Bahá'í literature to the Bennetts. Elinor accepted it, but she did not read it seriously at that point. She was, in fact, quite content to remain a Christian.[204]

"My calamity is My providence": Fletcher Bennett is Touched by Divine Love

In chapter 2, I exemplified the truth of Bahá'u'lláh's statement that "My calamity is My providence" by retracing the circumstances that led to the meeting of Catherine Heward and Cliff Huxtable. This same truth applies to the early spiritual search of Fletcher Bennett. In the dark days of Fletcher's breakdown, he received a consoling, mystical visitation that put him on the path of search that led to his discovery of the Bahá'í Faith. In the midst of his depression, Fletcher was suddenly and mysteriously surrounded with a moment of "all-embracing love."[205] This loving illumination was strong enough to break through the cloud that surrounded him and touch his soul, that divine reality that cannot be impaired by any mental dysfunction. Elinor confirmed that this singular experience was the starting-point for Fletcher's spiritual search: "After this experience, he kept on looking for this divine love,"[206] she said. Fletcher had been born a Methodist, but he investigated, among other religions, Christian Science and the Seventh

Day Adventists. A man of great generosity, Fletcher came from a family that had acquired wealth through the rich iron ore deposits of the Mesabi Range in Minnesota. He had once donated a plane to the Wycliffe World Missions in South America, whose mission it was to bring the Bible to indigenous peoples in their own language.

The Fireside Surprise: The Talk by Husayn Banani and Elinor Bennett's Reaction (1961)

The fact that Salt Spring Island was situated on the west coast of Canada did not prevent it from receiving Bahá'í visitors roughly every two months. They came from Victoria and Vancouver, central Canada, the United States and abroad. In May of 2014, I received by mail a list of sixty-six names Elinor Bennett had compiled of travelling teachers who had journeyed to Salt Spring Island between the years 1961–1970. They included two Hands of the Cause, William Sears and John Robarts, Auxiliary Board Members, and nine members of the NSA of Canada, who were then serving that institution or who became former or future members.[207]

Included in the list of names was Husayn Banani, the son of the Hand of the Cause, Musa Banani (1886–1971), proclaimed by Shoghi Effendi as the "spiritual conqueror" of the African continent. Mr. Banani led the wave of pioneers who established thriving Bahá'í communities in Uganda and other African countries between 1950 and 1971. Husayn is also the brother of the late distinguished Iranian studies scholar, Amin Banani (d. 2013). Husayn Banani served the Canadian Bahá'í community in his role as member of the National Spiritual Assembly for no less than forty-four years (1962–2006). But during his early service to the National Spiritual Assembly, he also contributed to the growth of fireside, youth and deepening activities in the Toronto area during the 1960s and beyond. (On a more personal note, my sister, Mary Lou McLean, considers Husayn Banani to be her spiritual mentor for the knowledge of the Bahá'í teachings that he imparted to her during youth classes, and for the depth, reverence and integrity with which he taught the youth of her day.)

7 ∞ West to the Gulf Islands

In August of 1961, Toronto Baháʼís Husayn Banani and Marjorie Merrick[208], travelled west from the Banff Summer School to visit the Huxtables, who had left Saturna Island at the end of the school year. During their brief visit, the Huxtables organized an impromptu fireside in their house on Sharp Road that was attended by Elinor and Fletcher Bennett. While Catherine sat in her wheelchair saying prayers, Husayn gave an introductory talk during which he mentioned the meaning of Baháʼí and Baháʼuʼlláh as denoting "light" or "glory." As Husayn continued to disclose the Baháʼí teachings, it struck Fletcher that this was the very religion that manifested the divine love that had illumined his darkest moment. There and then, Fletcher decided to become a Baháʼí!

Fletcher's sudden declaration of faith came as a shock to Elinor. It seemed like a hasty, spur-of-the-moment decision during a troubled time in her husband's life. In embracing the Baháʼí Faith, Fletcher had spontaneously followed his heart: he knew very little about the religion he had just joined. Elinor knew no more than her husband. Always the perceptive one who was attuned to her surroundings, Catherine sensed what was happening. She turned to Elinor and said: "I know how you must feel." Elinor said nothing, but fifty-three years later, she let this author know that "Catherine had no idea how I felt."

Discouraged, Elinor turned to Dr. Bourdillon for advice and consolation. The doctor quickly assessed the situation as just another passing phase in Fletcher's search for the stability provided by religion: "Don't worry. He'll outgrow it," Dr. Bourdillon reassured Elinor. Dispensing a dose of the it-could-have-been-worse-philosophy, he added: "He could have become a Jesuit!"[209] Dr. Bourdillon's hasty judgment turned out, of course, to be wrong. For Fletcher, there was no outgrowing the religion he had just joined. Fletcher's calamity became his providence. He remained under the Faith's guidance until his death on July 28, 2013. Cliff Huxtable attended Fletcher's "dignified and moving" funeral on Salt Spring Island, and reflected later on the spiritual battles that Fletcher had fought and won: "Turning to the Faith as a gentle and emotionally fragile man with a depressing prognosis, and with Elinor's stabilizing love, Fletcher became a champion of the Cause and brought his entire family with him, all of whom became pioneers."[21]

Parenthood: The Birth of Gavin Clifford Huxtable (June 27, 1962)

During their four-year stay in the house on Sharp Road, Gavin Clifford Huxtable, their only child, named after Gavin Mouat, who had died seven months earlier, was born on June 27, 1962, at 5:31 a.m. in the Royal Jubilee Hospital in Victoria. Six months later in December 1962, Catherine wrote in her annual letter: "Dear Friends, This has been a year of joyous fulfillment for us. The healthy baby boy that we longed for arrived safely in June, ending the trying months of anxiety and discomfort and starting us on the greatest adventure of our lives. . . . A more healthy, strong, adorable, wriggly, giggly little bundle no one could ask for!"

Although baby Gavin had been lovingly welcomed, his birth had been unplanned. Her letter does not say that behind the scenes, Catherine's pregnancy produced an emotional and moral crisis. Because the doctors feared that the labor and stress of pregnancy and childbirth might cause her death, they strongly recommended abortion, a recommendation that caused Catherine and Cliff much anxiety. Cliff, of course, wanted a child, as did Catherine, but he naturally did not want his wife to risk death in childbirth. Cliff knew that if need be Catherine would sacrifice her life for her baby, and he could not imagine his life without her. In a candid email of December 1, 2013, he informed me: "One night in bed, Catherine, under strong medical pressure to abort, was crying and said she thought she could depend on me for support for what she wanted so badly. Then I let her know I was in full support. I was never reluctant."

Women who suffer from muscular dystrophy usually do not live long enough to bear a child. Here again, Catherine found herself in select company. The delivery was normal after four and a half hours of labor. (The uterine muscles that control childbirth are directed by the involuntary nervous system, and they remain unaffected by muscular dystrophy). The birth had no deleterious effect on Catherine's muscles, and despite the fact that childbirth worsens the disease in some women, the beneficial hormonal release produced by childbirth probably extended her lifespan. Following Gavin's birth, some of the neighbors on Sharp Road lined up at the Fulford Harbor ferry terminal to welcome Catherine home from Victoria, an indication of the love, respect and affection that she had

7 ∞ West to the Gulf Islands

inspired in having the courage to bear a child against medical advice. In the same 1962 annual letter, Catherine wrote: "Parenthood has come more easily than we expected, and so far, our task has been sheer pleasure." The Huxtables were overjoyed with Gavin's birth, and although Catherine was no doubt challenged by maternity, in the summer of 1962, they acquired the services of Edna Moen, "a mature, middle-aged woman and her delightful twelve-year-old daughter, Patty," to assist with caring for Gavin. Edna Moen was a reliable woman with a strong social conscience, who had earned Catherine's high praise. In her annual letter of 1963, Catherine wrote: "Edna continues to serve us nobly, above and beyond the call of duty."[211]

Elinor Bennett Joins the Bahá'í Faith (1963)

Fletcher and Elinor Bennett had in fact heard of the Bahá'í Faith before they ever moved to Salt Spring Island.[212] During the time they lived on a ranch in Pincher Creek, a town tucked into the southwest corner of Alberta, sixty-three miles (101 km.) west of Lethbridge, a local television program first informed them of the religion they would eventually join. In 1959, Elinor's sister and TV host, Kay MacLeod, had read comparative religionist Marcus Bach's *The Circle of Faith*, which included face-to-face interviews with five world religious figures who in his view exemplified the teachings of Christ: Helen Keller, Pope Pius XII, Albert Schweitzer, Therese Neumann, mystic and stigmatic, and Shoghi Effendi, the Guardian of the Bahá'í Faith. Kay was interviewing Peggy Ross, who served on the NSA (1953–1963) and on the Auxiliary Board between 1957 and 1986.

Although Elinor was impressed that the Bahá'ís did not pressure Fletcher to contribute money to their fund, she was not going to be rushed into joining the Bahá'í Faith. During the next two years she watched and waited, read the literature, and attended firesides to hear the excellent talks given by the steady stream of travel teachers who visited the island: "The list of people who spoke in the community was amazing," she remembered. "All the NSA members came here." Attendance at a summer school in Banff, Alberta, during which Beth McKenty was one of the speakers, had a profound impact on Elinor. "Beth McKenty changed my life," she said without hesitation. In November 1963, Peggy Ross, the woman Elinor had seen on television four years earlier, visited Salt Spring Island. Elinor had volunteered to pick up Peggy on her arrival. Peggy's visit to the island was opportune; it moved Elinor to make a decision: "Peggy Ross was very dedicated and down-to-earth. I realized that since she was right there in front of me, I had to get off the fence," she said. Elinor's description of Peggy as "dedicated" and "down-to-earth" turned out to be an accurate description of Elinor herself.

Formation of the First Local Spiritual Assembly of the Gulf Islands (April 21, 1964)

The second birth the Huxtables witnessed was that of the Local Spiritual Assembly, on April 21, 1964. Fireside teaching continued, and in the evening of May 18, 1963, they decided to hold the first public meeting that took place at Central Hall. The speaker was Helen Wilks from Issaquah, Washington, who had recently returned from the Bahá'í World Congress, held in Royal Albert Hall in central London, England. Her topic was "One Universal Faith." The World Congress not only celebrated the completion of the Ten Year Plan, but it also marked the centennial of the inception of the Bahá'í Faith that occurred with the declaration of Bahá'u'lláh's mission on April 21, 1863, to a few followers in the Najíbíyyih Garden or Garden of "Riḍván" (Ar.=Paradise) in Baghdad. The rose-garden was located among palm trees on the eastern bank of the Tigris, north of the city walls. It consisted of four avenues leading to a circular area. It had once belonged to the former Governor of Baghdad (1842–1849), Muhammad Najíb Páshá. Today the Royal Hospital covers the site.[213] Námiq Páshá, the Governor of Baghdad (1861–1867), a fervent admirer of Bahá'u'lláh, allowed Him to use the garden to prepare for His upcoming exile to Constantinople/Istanbul.[214]

The nucleus of five believers—the Huxtables, Bernice Boulding Crooks, the Bennetts—would grow to form, within the next six months, the first Local Spiritual Assembly of the Gulf Islands. Following the enrollments of Bernice, Fletcher and Elinor, three others occurred: Germans Walter and Lisa Luth joined the community, as did the Huxtable's reliable helper Edna Moen. The ninth member of the Assembly was home-front pioneer Kate Saunders, who moved to the island from the Okanagan Valley in the southern interior of British Columbia.[215]

7 ∞ West to the Gulf Islands

The first Local Spiritual Assembly of the Baháʼís of the Gulf Islands was formed four-and-a-half years after the Huxtables arrived. A black-and-white photo taken on the night of the formation shows the following eight individuals: Clifford Huxtable, Catherine Huxtable, Elinor Bennett, Fletcher Bennett, Walter Luth, Edna Moen, Kate Saunders, Bernice Boulding Crooks. The ninth member, Lisa Luth, was the photographer. Catherine was elected chairperson. Beaming a broad smile, she is seated at the center of the photo, holding a framed picture of ʻAbduʼl-Bahá. When the NSA announced, at the beginning of the Nine Year Plan (1964–1973), that it had set the formation of an LSA as a goal for the Gulf Islands, the Salt Spring Island Baháʼís, and Bernice Boulding Crooks, who lived on Saturna Island, were delighted to realize that the goal had already been won.

Tests and Difficulties

"O SON OF MAN! For everything there is a sign. The sign of love is fortitude under My decree and patience under My trials." —Baháʼuʼlláh

Cliff's Declining Health, Road Accidents, Fatherhood, Finding Helpers (1961–1964)

Hardship is an essential characteristic of human life, but the Huxtables' cup of trials during this period was becoming increasingly full.[216] Cliff's first jobs as a self-employed laborer were physically exhausting. He was often tired and frequently sick. Because he kept his problems to himself, the Baháʼís on Salt Spring Island could not have been aware that he had been experiencing a gradual but steady increase of physical and psychological distress.

During their 1961 summer vacation at Mrs. Heward's in Toronto, about a week after their arrival, Cliff's father, Reuben, to whom Cliff was deeply attached, was suddenly killed in a car crash. Then, in the late spring of 1962, Cliff had his own auto accident. One Sunday afternoon, after spending too long at home, before returning to the University of Victoria, where he was taking his education degree, Cliff was speeding along the Fulford-Ganges Road intent on catching a departing ferry from Fulford Harbor. He found himself trapped behind a slower moving Austin. He buckled his seatbelt and pulled out to pass on a roller-coaster section of the road.

Cliff saw nothing coming, but when he got to the top of the hill, he was suddenly facing an eight-cylinder Pontiac sedan. He swerved at the last second, avoiding a head-on collision, and just touched the back bumper of the Austin ahead of him. The passengers in the Austin were not injured and kept going, but Cliff could not avoid the Pontiac. The impact knocked both vehicles off the road. The accident could have proved fatal, but fortunately the two elderly ladies in the Pontiac were only shaken up. Although the repairs to his Mercedes amounted to a costly $1,400, Cliff's only injury was a sore chest for weeks afterward. When later he appeared in court, the English magistrate fined Cliff $50.00 with the remark: "I don't think you'll be doing that again."

Even though she had help, Catherine, for her part, struggled to find the strength to deal with her daily tasks, grown more demanding since the birth of Gavin. After their son was born, Catherine's mother arranged for Hildur, Mrs. Heward's Toronto housekeeper, to come west and assist for a month after the homecoming of Gavin. After Hildur returned to Toronto, she was followed by Edna Moen's welcome arrival. Catherine wrote in her annual letter of December 1963, that Gavin "is the joy of our life and also our major trial, as it is hard to cope with such a bundle of energy when tired or not well." A sterilization operation the previous winter left Catherine "tired for a long time."

Following Gavin's birth, along with providing for the needs of the household, Cliff now had the added responsibility of fatherhood. He was also plagued by inexplicable low energy and mood-swings, until Dr. Bourdillon correctly diagnosed that he was suffering from an under-active thyroid. Medication brought new life and energy, but Cliff's professional responsibilities added to his burdens. He had by this time become joint vice-principal of the Ganges high school. He was also naturally preoccupied by the constant worry of Catherine's declining health with its inevitable outcome.

Cliff's Growing Professional Responsibilities as Joint Vice-Principal of the Salt Spring Island High School (1961–1964)

While he commuted to Salt Spring Island on weekends, between the fall

7 ∞ West to the Gulf Islands

of 1961 and the first half of 1962, Cliff completed "with high honors" his teacher training degree at the Faculty of Education, University of Victoria. The Salt Spring Island School Board, encouraged by District Superintendent Art Jones, had provided Cliff with an interest-free $3000 loan to complete his post-graduate teacher qualification. The school board granted the loan on the understanding that Cliff would return to teach in the Gulf Islands for three years following graduation.[217] The Board wanted him to move to Galiano Island, a long finger-like island just northeast of Salt Spring, but Cliff refused on the grounds that the island was lacking the medical services that Catherine needed. Based on their Saturna experience, when Catherine had to be ferried over to Salt Spring to be treated for red measles, Cliff insisted that the only option that could meet his wife's health requirements was to teach on the same island where the Lady Minto hospital was located; the school board agreed.

In 1962, Cliff began teaching a full load at the high school, with two grade levels of mathematics, a survey course in modern world history, and a junior science class. The marking and preparation demanded by his workload kept him fully occupied. In 1964, at the age of thirty-two, Cliff was promoted from subject teacher to the half-time position of joint vice-principal with Florence Hepburn, an effective and respected older staff member. These duties were additional to his teaching load. Although Cliff enjoyed teaching, dealing with the disciplinary issues of high school students produced additional emotional strain since he was required not only to work after school hours, but to mete out punishment. The man who hired Cliff was the congenial principal, Jack Evans. Jack related that Cliff had favorably impressed him when Cliff was still working as a deckhand. Whenever the principal rode the Delta Queen, he always knew when Cliff was steering: the crossing was on course and stable. "A man who would pay attention to that kind of job would pay attention to any job," Jack later volunteered to Cliff. [218]

For the discipline cases he had to settle, Cliff would have benefited from the advice and support of the experienced Jack Evans, but the principal, immersed in his own duties and the planning of the new high school, left his new vice-principal to sort out the rebellious students himself: "Sink or swim, you're in charge of discipline." With that remark, Jack launched Cliff on his new career. Cliff later remarked in an honest self-evaluation: "I was too young. I was carrying too much at home. I was too inexperienced."[219] Cliff overreacted when three laggard students stepped out-of-line. He expelled all three. Although Cliff regretted the decision, it turned out that the expulsion in no way hindered their employment opportunities. The students moved on to work at the nearby Crofton pulp mill, a change that fully suited their career aspirations. However, some of the teaching staff viewed Cliff as an upstart. They did not favor two part-time vice-principals, and they did not agree with what they viewed as his harsh approach to discipline. "There were teachers who had a very different view about keeping order," he recalled.

The Last House off Beddis Road and Other Strains on Cliff's Health (1964–1965)

Catherine could not bear a fourth winter in the house on Sharp Road. Their house was not fully winterized, and Salt Spring winters are damp and gloomy. In early 1964, the Huxtables purchased what was to be their last home on Salt Spring Island. The house was located at the end of a secondary road that turned off Beddis Road, south of the town of Ganges, and sat near the water overlooking a sand-spit. It had been purchased for $17,500 with a ninety percent mortgage loan from the British Columbia Teachers' Federation. The Huxtables put every available dollar into renewing the interior of the house. Cliff rebuilt the kitchen units. Some of the furniture was professionally refurbished, and other accessories were purchased to make the interior of the home as attractive as possible for Catherine who spent most of her waking hours there. Cliff decided to build an additional bedroom in the basement, but sewer rats invaded the house through the opening that he had breached in the wall to admit services. One night the menacing rodents raced frantically throughout the house creating chaos, even running into the bathroom while Cliff was there!

Catherine wrote in her 1962 annual letter: "Finding an ideal housekeeper solves one of our most ticklish problems." But not all housekeepers were ideal. Hiring and if necessary letting go unsuitable care-workers added to the Huxtables'

7 ∞ West to the Gulf Islands

stress. After Bernice Boulding married Barry Crooks in 1961, the Huxtables hired Geraldine Johnny, a young mother from the Cowichan First Nations Reserve in Duncan, British Columbia. Geraldine herself was quite satisfactory, but the involvement of her parents, who were also living in a cottage on the grounds of the house, soon developed into a complicated, abusive scenario instigated by her father. Although the police could have been involved, Cliff was able to resolve the situation peaceably. After several serious conversations with Cliff, Geraldine's father agreed to leave the island, a move that restored a peaceful environment to all concerned.

The strains on Cliff's health eventually spilt over onto the Bahá'ís, who had remained oblivious to the burdens he had been silently shouldering. The responsibilities of LSA meetings, although they were infrequent, coupled with family and professional life, finally became unbearable. Despite himself, with all that had been weighing him down, Cliff became "jaundiced in his attitude toward the friends."[220] His mounting difficulties also placed a heavy strain on Catherine who had to deal, not only with her own personal medical challenges, but also with the need to fulfill the demanding tasks of a mother with a toddler. Although Fletcher Bennett's fragile emotional health had benefited from Elinor's loving-kindness, patience, and understanding, Cliff also felt responsible for the well-being of the friend to whom he had introduced the Bahá'í Faith.

Cliff's emotional reserves were by then fully exhausted. He cracked one night at the Nineteen Day Feast. Cliff's sudden display of emotion was in reality a cry for help. With breaking voice, completely exhausted and frustrated, Cliff told the friends that he was fed up with them, that he did not care about them anymore. His emotional outburst elicited a sympathetic response from Elinor. Bursting into tears, she said: "Cliff, it never occurred to us that you would find it hard, that you would find *anything* hard."[221] Soon after that meeting, the Huxtables' septic field backed up, but this time his friends were more aware of the situation. Fletcher Bennett showed up with pick and shovel; he dug up, cleaned out, and returned the field to functionality.

A Bright Spot for Catherine: The Visit of Pamela Webster (August, 1965)

We have seen in chapters 2 and 3 that Catherine and Pamela Webster spiritually companioned one another during their late teenaged years. Pamela companioned Catherine in her investigation of Unitarianism; Catherine companioned Pamela in her investigation of the Bahá'í Faith. Pamela and Catherine continued to correspond regularly after Pamela left Toronto to study at Wellesley College in Boston in the Fall of 1950. Intermittent visits took place whenever Pamela returned to Toronto, until the Huxtables left for Regina in December, 1957. Pamela made one afternoon visit to the house on Beddis Road in August of 1965. She and her husband, Arthur "Pat" Webster, and their five young children, were making a cross-Canada tour, on their way to Stanford University in California, when their car struck cattle on Friday, August 13 in Strathcona, Alberta, just east of Calgary. With a badly broken leg that required two casts, one on her foot and another on her leg, and after leaving Pat and the children behind in West Vancouver, Pamela visited Catherine on Salt Spring Island, hobbling on crutches.

Although she was astonished that the Huxtables would have volunteered to settle in such a remote location, "the visit was celebratory and effervescent. She was so happy to see me," Pamela clearly recalled. She reflected on their close understanding and the spiritual compatibility they shared in the Bahá'í Faith. "We were in the same space," she said.[222] That afternoon turned out to be the last time Pamela would see Catherine alive, but Pamela's voluminous correspondence with Catherine continued to be a source of delight for both women. "I probably wrote more letters to Catherine than to anyone," she wrote.[223] The correspondence was frequent and regular; their deep conversations of earlier days continued uninterrupted. Pamela mentioned one thirty-page letter she had received from Catherine.[224] Responding to my questions about their correspondence, she wrote:

> She was a devoted correspondent and I was so interested to hear about the people we had met at the Unitarian Church because I wanted her to have a more active social life than was available to her at Clarendon Crescent. . . . It was intense,

emotional and an exchange only possible by very young adults who are thoughtful and articulate. . . . I do believe she trusted and loved me. . . . We were fortunate to know each other, blessed I would say by the Holy Spirit, which 'Abdu'l-Bahá said was God's love for mankind, if I am remembering correctly![225]

Breaking Point: Threats of Violence and Harassment from a Jealous and Mentally Disturbed Neighbor (1964–1965)

Following the move to the house off Beddis Road, a property line irregularity that should have been a non-issue suddenly exploded into ongoing threats and harassment from an elderly, mentally deranged and jealous neighbor. It was to make of the Huxtables' life a living-hell for most of their last year on Salt Spring Island; it became in fact one of the major factors in precipitating their departure from the island, an urgent but necessary move to ensure their physical and mental survival.

At first view, the neighbor appeared benign. The head of white hair suggested the wisdom of old age. The old man actually reminded Cliff of Moses[226], but paradoxically, his conduct was anything but saintly. Their neighbor had once been traumatized by some teenagers in Vancouver, with the result that if young people came anywhere near him, he became abusive because he was fearful to the point of paranoia. Whether the incident sent him over the edge, or whether he was constitutionally predisposed to mental aberration, one thing is sure: the neighbor's actions were definitely far beyond those of a sane individual.

Some "island bloods," once they had discovered the senior's predictable tendency to explosive behavior, responded in kind, and they began to torment him. In one incident, unknown to the Huxtables, they drove down Beddis Road at two o'clock in the morning, backed their cars up against the neighbor's house, spun the wheels and sprayed his house with gravel, producing a machine-gun-like rattle that jolted him out of his sleep. In his paranoid state of mind, he thought that Cliff Huxtable, the young vice-principal, had put them up to it. Cliff's whole purpose in moving into the house on Beddis Road, he was convinced, had been "just to make a monkey of him!"[227] He decided that he was going to show Cliff a thing or two! Because their friends visited the Huxtables regularly, the neighbor imagined that Cliff enjoyed great popularity. He had grown insanely jealous. The old man was going to get even with the Huxtables for the life he did not have. In his deluded mental state, the property boundary provided the pretext for retaliation.

Much Ado Over a Right-of-Way: His Neighbor Threatens Cliff with a Gun

The Huxtables had a right-of-way along a road that gave access to their property. The right-of-way was on the neighbor's land, along the edge of the Huxtable's property, and curved across in front of the senior's home. Although the Huxtables were fully within their rights to use the right-of-way, the neighbor discovered later that the lawyers who drew up the contract had mistakenly left the allowance about a foot (30 cm.) short of the Huxtables' property line. The Huxtables had to "trespass" on the adjoining property to reach home. One evening, after working late again, Cliff found the entrance to his home blocked by a huge pile of dirt. Flummoxed, Cliff suddenly remembered that his neighbor owned a bulldozer. A three-and-a-half hour "conversation" ensued at the neighbor's house, during which Cliff tried to disabuse him of the delusions that had sparked his provocative action. As Cliff attempted to reason with his neighbor, he went into a volatile rant and suddenly threatened Cliff:

> And when he was explaining about the young people in Vancouver, the ones who had terrified him, he started shouting about what he was going to do with them. I was sitting on the sofa and he was sitting on the chair. He picked up his gun and grabbed me by the throat and pushed my head back on the sofa, waving the gun about what he was going to do, and ranting about this.[228]

Under threat of violence, Cliff had an instinctive reaction: he laughed out loud! Risky though it was, his spontaneity deescalated the tense situation. After

7 ∞ West to the Gulf Islands

the neighbor simmered down, Cliff was able to convince him to use his bulldozer to remove the earth. Catherine and Bernice Boulding Crooks, who had been visiting from Saturna Island, had seen Cliff's car next door. By the time Cliff came home, it was close to midnight. Catherine was by then worried sick. When Cliff finally opened the door, he sat down to his evening meal and explained what had just happened. Judging the situation to be serious, Catherine urged Cliff to phone Dr. Jansch. The doctor was sufficiently alarmed that he asked Cliff to report the incident to the police the first thing next morning. Cliff drove as directed to the one-man Royal Canadian Mounted Police station the following morning. Dr. Jansch appeared at the same time to corroborate Cliff's story. The corporal asked Cliff if he owned a firearm. Cliff replied that he had a Browning automatic that Colonel Heward carried during the First World War, even though he was not even sure if the pistol was functional. The corporal advised him to sleep with the pistol under his pillow, and to shoot if any intruder entered the house during the night. Cliff found some bullets and loaded the gun. He slept with the Browning automatic under his pillow for nine months.

Dr. Jansch was willing to certify the neighbor as being dangerous to others. Perhaps because the neighbor's wife was a local nurse, no other doctor could be relied upon to give the second opinion necessary to authorize psychiatric restraint. Despite the neighbor's momentary conciliatory attitude, his crazy antics continued. The old man had grown impatient for a settlement to the property line dispute that dragged on because the British Columbia Law Society had not been willing initially to accept responsibility for its lawyer's mistake. They refused at first to provide the funds to build the road down the Huxtables' panhandle that Cliff had demanded, a solution that would have solved the problem. His neighbor continued to view Cliff as a trespasser. On some nights during the winter, Cliff would return home from school to catch a shadowy glimpse of his neighbor popping up from behind the trees to follow him with his gun sights trained on Cliff's car. Except for the Baháʼís, and a well-off woman named Barbara Hastings, who "drove around in an angular Jaguar with a Great Dane sitting beside her in the passenger's seat," most of their friends stopped visiting. Cliff admired Barbara's courage. He later remarked: "No little man with a gun was going to turn her away from her friends."[229] The Law Society eventually acted to settle Cliff's complaint, but the remedial road construction did not take place until after the Huxtables left the island.

The Neighbor is Subdued: A Lesson Learned

One night Cliff came home to find barbed wire stretched across his gate. The sight of barbed wire became the proverbial last straw. Cliff's patience and long-suffering came to an abrupt end. During the exchange that followed, Cliff told his neighbor that he did not want to place him in an institution, but that he was going to do so because that's where he belonged. Cliff described the offender's canny response: "He laughed this sort of mad cackle and replied, 'If you could do that you would have done that months ago.' Cliff retorted: "No, I don't want to put you away, but you are forcing me to put you away. If you would behave yourself, I would never make a move to put you away. But one more move and you're in. Don't think I can't."[230] The neighbor removed the barbed wire. No further incidents arose.

Looking back on the experience, Cliff described the life-lesson that he learned from the ongoing dangerous confrontations with his neighbor: "And I learned something important that I needed to know before I went to St. Helena. Just because you're a Bahá'í and you try and love the human race, you are not there to be used as a doormat or anything else. You can love them. You can serve. But you are not there to be abused. You are noble creatures. You are very privileged noble creatures because you have been given this message, and you are not here to be abused."[231]

Advice From Cliff's Physicians: Two Years of Bed Rest (1965)

The accumulated stress from his responsibilities at home and school and with his neighbor brought Cliff's mental and physical health to the breaking point. He consulted physicians. Early in 1965, specialists in Vancouver had recommended that he have Catherine institutionalized, and Gavin placed with relatives, so that Cliff could have a much-needed two-year period of convalescence in order to recover his impaired health. But Cliff could never countenance such a drastic recommendation. By this time, the Huxtables realized that life on Salt Spring had become unbearable. They began seeking a workable solution elsewhere. Another island, St. Helena in the South Atlantic, was beginning to look attractive as a viable solution, but it initially seemed "a bridge too far."

The Turning Point: The Winnipeg National Convention (May 1965)

Catherine had been witnessing Cliff's slow but steady decline. Although she loved her husband deeply, she also depended on him to be functional. When Cliff was at such a low point, Hand of the Cause of God John Robarts provided some much needed love and moral support. Cliff described their meeting:

> Usually I sleep well, but I woke up in the middle of the night feeling absolutely miserable and angry. I sat bolt upright, shook my fist at the heavens, and shouted at God, 'What are You doing to us? We are trying to help You!' Not long after that John Robarts came out—a "one of" visit—and I told him how bad it was. He didn't come out here [Salt Spring Island]. He invited us to the Empress Hotel for tea in Victoria. He hugged us and listened to us. I told him what was going on, and he hugged me again and he said, 'Oh Cliff, God loves you for that.' Cliff remonstrated but Mr. Robarts replied, 'He loves you for that. You know where it's coming from.'[232]

Mr. Robarts' comforting words and moral support helped to momentarily assuage Cliff's grief. By then the Gulf Islands had become administratively part of the Canadian Bahá'í community; they were no longer "virgin territory." At the annual British Columbia Regional Convention, Cliff was elected a delegate to the National Convention in Winnipeg. Although he appreciated receiving the confidence of the friends, Cliff was feeling so demoralized that he did not want to go. Money was again in short supply, but Catherine encouraged him by saying, "Please go. I'm praying for a miracle." Catherine's remark struck to the core. Cliff went.

The National Convention turned out to be his consolation and reward. It brought healing to his broken spirit and showed him that "the way of the righteous is made plain." (Proverbs 15:19). His old friends from Ontario, Douglas Martin, Winnifred Harvey, Doug Wilson, Michael Rochester, Don Dainty, Ron Nablo, Husayn Banani, all listened as he recounted the trials that he and Catherine had been going through at their pioneering post. Although Cliff Huxtable was not normally a man given easily either to complaining or to tears, he wept on his friends' shoulders; and they wept with him. True to the Bahá'í spirit that animated them, Cliff's friends responded by pouring out their loving-kindness and understanding. In 1978, Cliff remembered his friends' kindness with a memorable line of gratitude: "Bahá'í friendships are the most precious thing in this world."[233]

Hand of the Cause of God, Mr. Zikrullah Khádem (1904–1986), was present. To the assembled delegates, he told the inspiring story of the Iraqi general and Knight of Bahá'u'lláh, Munír Vakíl, well-known to Mr. Khádem because of his visits to Iraq on behalf of the Guardian. Mr. Vakíl was a well-to-do, middle-aged man whose heart had responded immediately to the call of Shoghi Effendi to open virgin territories during the Ten Year Plan (1953–1963). Following a consultation with Mr. Khádem, Mr. Vakíl abandoned the material comforts of his home and career after choosing a very challenging goal—Kuria Maria, a remote group of five islands in the Arabian Sea, 25 miles (40 km.) off the south-east coast of the Sultanate of Oman. The island he landed on had a population of about 60 inhabitants. The conditions were so primitive that they barely sustained life. The subsistence diet consisted of fish that were baked on hot rocks in the sun. Because no shelter was to be found anywhere on the island, Mr. Vakíl was obliged to build himself a stone hut.

The presence of this "refined and advanced man" attracted the attention of the island's inhabitants who inquired why he had come. Mr. Vakíl told them in all simplicity that he came because he loved them. (To what extent he was able to teach the Faith openly is not clear at this point.) Under such trying conditions, his health continued to decline; he lost weight. Shoghi Effendi recalled him because he had other duties for him to perform, but Mr. Vakíl begged the Guardian to stay. His greatest desire was to remain at his post, even at the cost of his health. Shoghi Effendi's unerring sense of guidance probably saved the general's life. In the end, he refused Mr. Vakíl's request to stay. Mr. Khádem met the Iraqi pioneer upon his return to Baghdad, "frail, exhausted and very ill." When Mr. Vakíl recounted to the assembled friends his experiences on Kuria Maria, another unidentified believer was so moved that he spontaneously arose: 'I am prepared to replace him. We cannot leave a pioneering post vacant.' At the end of his story, Mr. Khádem's voice broke: "Friends, won't you stand up and serve the Cause?"[234]

St. Helena Island Becomes a Canadian Goal

Before Cliff attended the National Convention, the Huxtables had been consulting for months to find a way out of their dilemma. During their consultations, they kept zeroing in on St. Helena, one of the most isolated islands in the world, 1200 miles (1950 km.) to the west of northern Namibia in southwest Africa. Although St. Helena presented a number of advantages, the Huxtables decided against it, mainly because of its extreme remoteness.

But the possibility of pioneering to St. Helena suddenly resurfaced at the National Convention. During the proceedings, when the overseas goals were announced, St. Helena Island was included among them. Although St. Helena had previously fallen under the jurisdiction of the American National Spiritual Assembly, the Universal House of Justice decided to transfer the goal to Canada. During a conversation with Husayn Banani, who was fully aware of the Huxtables' dire straits, he encouraged Cliff with the simple comment: "You know, it would be wonderful if you and Catherine could go." That night, a few of Cliff's friends offered to hold an all-night prayer vigil to receive the guidance, strength and courage Cliff so urgently needed to make a decision. All through the night, they prayed: "That night I did something that I had never done before or since. I stayed up with a number of the friends and prayed all night. In the morning, I knew that we were going to St. Helena."

-8-
ADIEU SALT SPRING ISLAND:
The Canadian Teaching Trip (1965–1966)

The Sudden Decision to Pioneer to St. Helena Island

Cliff phoned Catherine the same morning from the National Convention. Although Catherine had been praying for a miracle, she was momentarily stunned by Cliff's sudden announcement. A long silence followed. She had mixed feelings about Cliff's proposal, but encouraged by her husband's renewed vitality, clearly reflected in his voice, she agreed: "Well, I prayed for a miracle. Let's go."[235] Some four months after they arrived on St. Helena, Catherine reflected back on that moment in a sixteen-page letter to Rúhíyyih Khánum, written on August 27, 1966, from the Hussey Charity School, named for its former use, an old house owned by Colonel Gilpin on Napoleon Street in the capital, Jamestown. Cliff's decision came as a sudden certainty, but despite her immediate approval, Catherine needed the day to process the change:

> And so there was that memorable convention at which Cliff lost his head and found his heart!! He cried, he sang, he prayed all night, and on the last day phoned me and said he wanted to volunteer for us to fill St. Helena. I just about dropped dead on the spot—this was a real bolt from the blue and I felt far too tired to move <u>anywhere</u>, let alone to a tiny top of a volcano in the middle of an ocean! However, we had been in such despair and Cliff sounded so revitalized, I left it up to him. He was there and I wasn't, and if he felt, in that rarefied atmosphere, that we should go to St. Helena then I'd go along with it, God willing. Through the power in the prayers I actually felt enthusiastic about it by the time Cliff reached home, late that night.[236]

In her letter of May 26, 1965, to Diana Dainty, written in the same

8 ∞ Adieu Salt Spring

month as the National Convention took place, Catherine looked forward to the stimulation of the long trip, despite her fatigue: "I am getting happier and happier about going to St. Helena. It may be hard to find the energy to cope with the trip but new sights and people are so stimulating to me, I usually get an extra burst of energy." Although the decision to leave Salt Spring Island was made in May, the Huxtables were not able to leave until some five months later, on October 13, 1965. Their "dream-house" waterfront property off Beddis Road did not sell easily. Because they had no savings, the Huxtables had to sell all the furnishings they had just acquired the year before to pay for the expense of a 13,000 mile (21,000 km.) land, sea and air voyage.

The Huxtables' departure from Salt Spring Island was a lonely affair, attended by no one. The Bennetts, who would have normally been there, were absent because Fletcher was ill. Cliff could not risk exposing himself to contagion and passing it on to Catherine. By a strange turn-of-events, their antagonistic neighbor was the one who gave them their final send-off. Cliff recalled their last moments on the island:

> It was raining the day that we had to leave, and I couldn't get the trailer up the hill. Mr. ___ came and pulled us up with his tractor and shook hands with me at the top of the road. When it came time to go, Fletcher had the mumps and the last hand I shook was ___'s. We went down to the Fulford dock. It was drizzling. We parked and waited for the ferry. And I can remember getting out of the car, and sitting on the doorstep of the trailer and eating an apple and feeling really sad because I thought I was going to live in this place for the rest of my life. This is a really wonderful island.[237]

Canada Meets the Huxtables: Inspiring Pioneers to Arise

In consultation with the NSA, the Huxtables planned a five-month travel-teaching trip from British Columbia to Montreal. The NSA knew that if anyone could inspire the Canadian community to contribute to filling the goals of the

Nine Year Plan (1964–1973), the Huxtables would certainly qualify as credible pioneers. Catherine and Cliff also looked forward to meeting the friends. Catherine wrote that after spending six years on an island, they "felt the need of seeing a lot of Bahá'ís and getting our batteries recharged before tackling St. Helena."

For the journey east, Cliff had purchased a 1957 DeSoto automobile, powerful enough to pull an eighteen-by-eight-foot, two-ton, house trailer that was spacious enough to allow Catherine to turn around in her wheelchair. A delighted three-year-old Gavin slept on the top bunk. The trailer was heated because they knew that on their trip to Montreal, the departure point for St. Helena, they would have to contend with the inevitable snowstorms and icy roads of the Canadian winter. Occasionally, they had to put up at a motel.

The original travel-teaching itinerary was to have included the prairie provinces of Alberta, Saskatchewan and Manitoba, but in its letter of November 4, 1965, concerned that such a demanding trip would further tire the already exhausted Huxtables, the Canadian NSA revised the schedule: "The Assembly is concerned that, under no circumstances, should you deplete your energies and resources in such a way as to interfere with the primary project of filling the St. Helena goal."[238] It requested, instead, that the Huxtables should go directly to Ontario from British Columbia, without travel-teaching in the prairie provinces, and to detour through the United States to avoid the snow belt. However, some adjustments had to be made because the Huxtables had planned to say farewell to old friends on their way east.

Although it has not been possible to reconstruct precisely their complete itinerary, Cliff Huxtable has indicated that they crossed British Columbia, visited Bahá'í communities in Alberta and Saskatchewan, including Regina to visit Angus and Bobbie Cowan; turned south to Montana; went on to Milwaukee; south to the House of Worship in Wilmette, Illinois; east to Windsor, Ontario; north-east to Toronto, then further east to Montreal, the departure-point for St. Helena.[239] In her letter of August 27, 1966, to Rúhíyyih Khánum, Catherine wrote that they spoke to sixteen different groups.

In Cliff's letter of September 12, 1966, to Gil Humphreys of Salt Spring Island, he mentions, without referring to the Bahá'í Faith, passing through the following cities,: Richmond, Princeton, Penticton, Vernon, Golden (British Co-

8 ∞ Adieu Salt Spring

lumbia), Calgary, Lethbridge (Alberta), Regina (Saskatchewan), Winnipeg (Manitoba), Milwaukee (Wisconsin), Chicago (Illinois), Windsor, and Toronto (Ontario), Montreal (Quebec). We cannot be sure that the Huxtables visited Bahá'ís in all these locations, but we do know that they met their fellow-believers in at least the following cities: Calgary—Catherine mentions the "happy singing of the Calgary Bahá'ís"—Lethbridge where they had a memorable visit with Jack and Enid Wrate and family; Regina, where they visited the Cowans; Milwaukee, where they visited Beth and Dr. Jack McKenty; Windsor, where they met with an enthusiastic group of Bahá'ís; Kitchener, where they visited with Michael and Elizabeth Rochester for a few days; Toronto, where they visited Elizabeth and Douglas Martin and held meetings around the city; and Montreal where they spoke at meetings held at the Maxwell Home, the national Bahá'í shrine. The memorable Lethbridge, Milwaukee, Windsor and Montreal stops are described more fully below.

Vote of Confidence from World War I Flying Ace Don MacLaren and his Wife Verna

The first stop the Huxtables made was in Sidney, British Columbia, where they stayed with Verna and Don MacLaren, the World War I flying ace. Don had been led to the Faith by Verna in 1952. In his later years, Don spoke very reluctantly about his military exploits, but he became an enthusiastic promoter of the Bahá'í teachings. He served on the NSA from 1954 to 1957. Don became a noted figure in Canadian military and aviation history. He was "one of Canada's most decorated World War I pilots, a pioneer in Canada's aviation industry, and the first employee of Trans-Canada Airlines, the predecessor of Air Canada."[240] Following their visit, Don wrote to the Huxtables in care of the NSA on November 29, 1965. He and Verna were supportive of their upcoming pioneering move, despite the misgivings expressed by some of the friends. Don's eloquent, forthright, and perceptive message of Godspeed must have been received as great encouragement:

> You know, of course, there has been much eyebrow lifting and sucking of teeth over your decision to pioneer in the South Atlantic Island. We have done some of that ourselves. This

may be a natural reaction to what most of us in our comfortable, secure cocoons think may be a rash and reckless adventure. . . . The old order is stuffy, arrogant, pompous and jealous; it always has been in colonial possessions. They may think of your message as less than the dust, but there will be a seed sown and a lamp lighted which will never go out, and you know that many thousands of your Bahá'í friends all over the world will know you are there. . . . All pioneering is reckless in its own way, and so was the first aeroplane flight; we can do little to encourage you but pray that you will be sustained and comforted and that somebody down there will be led to listen to you and believe.[241]

Renewing Their Strength: Inspiring the Friends, Inspiring Themselves

As we look back upon the Canadian travel-teaching trip, it becomes clear that the Huxtables captured the hearts and inspired the imagination of those communities who were fortunate enough to have met them on their journey. In light of the service they had performed in Regina and Salt Spring Island, the able-bodied would find it difficult to excuse themselves from pioneering, especially now that the Huxtables were about to settle in one of the remotest islands in the world. Consciences were searched and hearts were inspired as the Canadian community followed the journey eastward of the thirty-three year-old young woman and her supportive husband and young son.

Although the Huxtables were exhausted when they left Salt Spring Island, and remained in a state of exhaustion throughout their Canadian teaching trip, their faith became revitalized. They relied on prayer, and dug deeply each time they met the friends to tap into the divine source, to find just the right words and spirit of encouragement to assist each community to accomplish the goals of the Nine Year Plan. In the process, they became the direct recipients of divine confirmations. Although the well of their spirits often felt as if it had run completely dry, the revitalizing waters of Bahá'u'lláh's inspiration would flow freely at the meetings. Their efforts were amply rewarded. Catherine wrote: "But invariably the talks we gave revived our spirits—our sense of conviction and determination to go on, our faith in unfailing divine assistance."

Catherine and Cliff tried different teaching styles that they had never had the opportunity to use previously. In one town, they assisted "a very sick community for several weeks," as they poured out the love, healing and guidance provided in the Bahá'í teachings. In another place, Catherine taught a children's class. It gave her particular pleasure to be able to speak to so many groups. She reflected on her early years as a Bahá'í, those few years during which she felt she had so little to offer to the community. She confided in Rúhíyyih Khánum:

> Years before I had thought my time for giving talks was over—that I was not well enough to do it any more. But on that exhausting trip Bahá'u'lláh enabled to me to speak to about sixteen groups—usually briefly, preceding a longer talk by Cliff to Bahá'ís only, but occasionally at firesides too. And I know that some of it was the best I'd ever done.

On the long road to Montreal from Salt Spring Island, the Huxtables discovered that it was not their faith alone that was revitalized. Under the stresses and strains of the baptism of fire that they had to endure on the island, their marriage had been severely tested, but as a teaching team, they discovered that their union grew stronger, as it became an instrument that served the needs of the Divine Plan. Catherine wrote to Rúhíyyih Khánum how their marriage was strengthened by their teaming up to teach the Bahá'í Faith: "We discovered that while there are many things our marriage is not, one thing it definitely *is*, is an instrument for teaching. . . . We found that even such feeble instruments could be channels."

Joyous Visits: Lethbridge, Alberta, Milwaukee, Wisconsin, Windsor, Ontario

On their journey east, three visits stand out as being memorable—their visit to Lethbridge, Alberta; their detour to Milwaukee, Wisconsin; and their meeting in Windsor, Ontario, just across the river from Detroit. Cliff responded in an email of June 20, 2014, that the visit with the Wrates was one of the highlights of the Canadian teaching trip. Catherine's letter of January 17, 1966, to Enid Wrate, written from Mrs. Heward's home in Toronto, captures the atmosphere of the visit: "We still cherish the memory of our happy stay with you—your loving hospitality, the wonderful close unity of your family and your exemplary service to the Cause we all cherish. Just heard there are new believers in Lethbridge!! What a miracle! We can hardly wait to hear what their names are, in case they are people we met."

Milwaukee: How Beth McKenty Helped Catherine to Fulfill the Guardian's Counsel

During their Milwaukee visit, the Huxtables called on freelance journalist and Auxiliary Board Member, Beth McKenty, and her husband Dr. Jack McKenty. With the assistance of Jack, Beth was the first Bahá'í teacher of the great jazzman, trumpeter John Birks "Dizzy" Gillespie. On the last day of their visit, Catherine described in her letter to Rúhíyyih Khánum what she referred to as "one of the most moving experiences of my entire life." To understand why Catherine was so moved, we need to understand that Beth McKenty became the unknowing instrument for suddenly fulfilling "an almost forgotten prayer" and some advice that Shoghi Effendi had given to Catherine some thirteen years before.

In the previous chapter, I reported the Guardian's advice to Catherine that she could serve the Faith by transcribing the sacred writings into Braille and by making recordings for the blind. Catherine explained to Rúhíyyih Khánum why she wrote the Guardian:

> You see, when I joined the Faith way back in 1952, when I was 20, I wanted desperately to be of some service but in those early months I could not see how I could be of use with advanced muscular dystrophy. I did not think I could give talks, serve on LSA's or committees, and I <u>obviously</u> couldn't possibly go pioneering, much as I longed to!

Catherine received a reply from the Guardian dated October 5, 1953, signed on his behalf by Rúhíyyih Rabbaní. The answer contained a postscript in the handwriting of Shoghi Effendi: "Assuring you of my loving prayers for your success and spiritual advancement, Your true brother, Shoghi."[242] Catherine summarized his response. "His answer was very wonderful," she wrote. Part of the reply was that in view of her condition, he did not know just what it would be possible for Catherine to do, but he suggested that she transcribe some of the Bahá'í sacred writings into Braille or record some Bahá'í literature for the blind.

Despite this clear guidance, Catherine would meet severe obstacles in her desire to execute the Guardian's advice. She suspected that the man from the Canadian National Institute for the Blind was a "religious bigot." The Braille machine that he brought her was so old and stiff that Catherine's weakened arms and fingers became too sore to use it. He denied Catherine's request to make voice recordings because all the records were made by professional actors in New York. He was not even willing to arrange for her to read aloud in person. By the time he died suddenly a year or two later, Catherine had become involved in other things, but she had not forgotten Shoghi Effendi's advice. On her second attempt, the American Service to the Blind committee had advised her to work through the Bahá'í Audio-Visual Aids committee. Anticipating that she could now be of service, Catherine bought a high quality tape recorder with money she had set aside for her funeral before she married. But the committee returned the tapes with the comment that her voice was too weak. "Well, that seemed like the final blow," she wrote, "first my hands too weak, then even my voice!" Discouraged, she shelved the project for the time being.

When that fated November 4 day in 1957 suddenly struck, Catherine grieved the Guardian's death with tears. Not only had the "Sign of God on earth" suddenly disappeared, but she felt she had disappointed Shoghi Effendi. She had not answered his letter because she was waiting until she had accomplished the task. Catherine knew that the Guardian was not interested in good intentions, but in results. She hoped that their pioneering move to Regina would be "an acceptable substitute" for service to the blind. But "God moves in a mysterious way His wonders to perform."[243] On the last day of their stay in Milwaukee, Beth suddenly turned on the tape recorder and handed Catherine one of the Guardian's messages, "The Summons of the Lord of Hosts," and asked her if she would read it for her blind friend Margaret Jensen. Catherine looked at Beth and broke into a flood of tears. Once she had regained her composure, Catherine explained why she had been so moved. Later that day, they drove to Winnetka and had a lovely visit with Margaret Jensen and her family. Once the Huxtables arrived on St. Helena, Margaret and Catherine exchanged audiotapes.

In the same letter of January 17 to Enid Wrate mentioned above, Catherine expressed her admiration for Beth: "We had a blissful time in the McKenty's home. To see Beth struggling to run a home and cope with the usual difficulties of marriage and child-rearing is a moving sight. There is no rest anywhere for that woman. She showered us with love and opportunities to serve, and we left Milwaukee feeling greatly enriched—and nearly out of Kleenex!"

Windsor, Ontario: A "Historic Meeting"

The stopover in December, 1965, in Windsor, Ontario, was a particularly joyous meeting. It occurred at the home of Gale and Jameson "Jamie" Bond, Knights of Bahá'u'lláh for the District of Franklin (1953–1963). Along with the Huxtables, who had not yet been named Knights of Bahá'u'lláh, one other Knight was present. Bruce Matthew had opened Labrador to the Bahá'í Faith in 1954. Tom Garraway who became the pioneer successor to the Bonds in the District of Franklin was also there. Tom later served as a secondary school teacher at the Maxwell International School at Shawnigan Lake, British Columbia. (The school closed its doors on its twentieth anniversary in 2008, and now operates as one of the global network of Dwight schools that offer an international baccalaureate). Also present were Gerald Robarts, who is, at this writing (2015), still living in Windsor, as well as Jan Jasion, historian and former pioneer to Poland, now living in France, and a number of other local Bahá'ís.

Jamie Bond remarked that the meeting was "historic" because those present had lived in the four corners of Canada. The Bonds had been the most northerly Canadian Bahá'ís, Gerald Robarts was living at the southernmost point of the country in Windsor, the Huxtables had settled in one of the farthest points west, and Bruce Matthew had lived in Goose Bay, Labrador in the east. (Bruce later lived further east in St. John's, Newfoundland.) Although Cliff hardly knew Gerald from their years at Forest Hill Collegiate because he had been a year ahead of Cliff, in his brother Weston's class, they enjoyed getting reacquainted. As it turned out, five Knights of Bahá'u'lláh were present at that happy gathering, all of them feeling closely bonded in the satisfaction that came with knowing that they had been faithful to the call of the Guardian.

Toronto and Montreal: Highs and Lows

The high spirits generated by their teaching-trip were suddenly rudely grounded once they arrived in Toronto on December 16, 1965. They spent a month at Mrs. Heward's, who had by then moved to 1 May Street in fashionable Rosedale, after the Colonel's death in Orillia in 1958. At the same time, they visited Cliff's mother, Dorothy, who had been widowed by the car accident mentioned above in the summer of 1961. Catherine's mother and Dorothy Huxtable were not pleased with the choice of remote locations that their children's Bahá'í service involved. In retrospect, we can understand their concern, especially that of Mrs. Heward. The moves west to Regina and Salt Spring Island, and now the upcoming move to an even remoter island in the middle of the South Atlantic Ocean, would deprive Catherine's mother of the precious little time she had left with her daughter. Mrs. Heward made no attempt to conceal her feelings during their visit. Catherine confided in her letter to Rúhíyyih Khánum: "Cliff was made sick and sleepless by the atmosphere of resentment towards him for taking me so far away." On a more forbearing and conciliatory tone, Cliff referred to the same emotional climate that had stifled cordiality in their mothers' homes. In the letter written to Gil Humphreys, Cliff wrote:

> We spent a month with our parents in Toronto. They were upset about our activities and it was not very pleasant. They had no real idea what our lives had been like in the past two years and how desperate we were to find a situation in which we could survive as functioning humans. They also did not have the faith with which Bahá'u'lláh had inspired us. So it was very hard for them.[244]

Catherine outlined the reaction of her mother to their move to faraway St. Helena in a letter to Diana Dainty: "My mother, in England on a trip, has taken our news very hard. She is hoping God will prevent us from making a terrible mistake." However, the same letter throws a different light on the reaction of Dorothy Huxtable: "Surprisingly, Cliff's mother has taken it quite calmly and is glad we are leaving this place."[245] (This discrepancy in Catherine and Cliff's report of Dorothy Huxtable's reaction is perhaps explained by a certain ambivalence on the part of Cliff's mother.) During the following year when Audrey and John Robarts visited Mrs. Heward at 1 May Street, the Robarts tried to allay any remaining hard feelings by explaining that Catherine and Cliff were not sent by any Bahá'í authorities as "missionaries" to Salt Spring and St. Helena islands. In his letter of June 28, 1967, John Robarts related to the Huxtables that he had explained to Mrs. Heward and Mrs. Huxtable that these relocations were made on a voluntary basis.[246] He remained convinced, as he had explained in an earlier letter written on Valentine's Day, following a pleasant dinner and evening visit with the mothers of our pioneers, that "They understand why you pioneered and are proud of you for having done it."[247] It is possible that Mrs. Heward and Mrs. Huxtable were amenable by this time to the explanation of the Hand of the Cause. However, Cliff's reaction to John Robarts' assessment was that he was likely being "overly optimistic."[248]

From Toronto, the Huxtables flew to Ottawa during the last week of January, 1966, and then on to Montreal where they spent six weeks in the Maxwell Home, the only national Bahá'í shrine located in the western world, so designated by the Guardian in a letter of June 20, 1953, to the NSA of Canada because of its association with the visit of "the beloved Master."[249] In Montreal, the Huxtables both fell ill with the flu, but Catherine described how Cliff "dragged himself out of bed almost nightly" to address groups of friends in Sutherland Maxwell's study, located on the ground floor. Catherine recalled how the presence of little Gavin, who loved to visit 'Abdu'l-Bahá's room, lightened the atmosphere of the sacred home: "Gavin, then 3½, loved to go there for his bedtime prayer. He would always climb up and sit on the window sill for it. You were in my thoughts a great deal there and I tried to picture your childhood in that lovely home . . . I think

8 ∞ Adieu Salt Spring

Gavin's carefree laughter and busy little feet in the background helped to bring a more happy, home-like feeling."

Once they reached Montreal, Cliff had momentarily wanted to suspend their trip to St. Helena on the basis of principle. Because their income had dried up, with his strong spirit of independence, Cliff was dead set against the idea of receiving assistance from the Canadian Bahá'í Fund. The importance of settling pioneers during the Nine Year Plan was, however, imperative. The NSA called on Rowland Estall to visit Cliff in the Maxwell home. His first comment was a kindly, "You do not have to go." Then he added: "It is much easier to find the funds than it is to find those who will go." Following a two-minute titanic inner struggle, Cliff decided to continue their journey. He remarked some fifty-years later: "My daily prayers of appreciation include Rowland Estall to this day."[250] Six months after they reached St. Helena Island, Cliff reflected back on the emotional healing generated by their Canadian teaching-trip: "The healing love they [the Bahá'ís] poured out upon us washed away the bitterness engendered by hostile neighbors and my chronic ill-health which had plagued my last years on Salt Spring. You cannot put a price on that kind of medicine."[251]

∞9∞
ST. HELENA ISLAND (1966–1967)

"The Army of the Supreme Concourse prepared the way and the impossible became possible." Cliff Huxtable

The Appeal of the Island

Although St. Helena was indeed one of the remotest places in the world, the sub-tropical climate of the small volcanic island had the advantage of being cooled by the trade winds. There would be no more frigid Canadian winters to endure, but the summers in the low-lying capital of Jamestown were hot and humid. In 1966 the population of the island consisted of about 5500 inhabitants. In St. Helena the Huxtables would not have to learn a foreign language; culturally, the island was British and Canada belonged to the British Commonwealth of Nations. The cost of living would be affordable; Cliff's teaching experience would possibly qualify him for a position; helpers at a reasonable price would be available for Catherine. Before they arrived on St. Helena, the Huxtables fully expected that the steep terrain would hinder the movement of a person in a wheelchair, but on arrival they found the omnipresence of stairs very challenging. (Cliff had to carry Catherine up and down stairs or pull her up and let her down in the wheelchair.) Since the only access to St. Helena was by ship, the Huxtables could expect to see their Canadian friends and family only occasionally. St. Helena would be a challenging pioneering assignment in a very remote location without benefit of the much needed company of friends and family.

On the Way: Renewed Strength at the Guardian's Resting-Place

The six weeks in Montreal flew by; the time to leave Canada had drawn close. On March 9 the Huxtables flew to Dublin where they spent a week with Cliff's brother Wes, who was working as the Canadian Trade Commissioner to the Republic of Ireland, his wife Mary and young son David. From Dublin, they journeyed on to London where they spent a month visiting with the Bahá'í friends and Catherine's beloved "Stouge," Madeleine Ashlin. In London Gavin appeared to be sickly. A blood test was taken, but they did not receive the results before they left the capital. Cliff spoke to a meeting of two hundred British Bahá'ís at the Naw-Rúz Feast where Catherine and Cliff met Jagdish (Jack) Saminaden, a Bahá'í from the island of Mauritius. The Huxtables were pleased to have met Jagdish, and to learn what they could about St. Helena because he had just completed two-and-a-half difficult but successful years of pioneering on St. Helena.

Any stopover in London could not have been complete without a visit to the Guardian's resting-place in the New Southgate Cemetery, a cemetery that despite the name is located in North London. At Shoghi Effendi's graveside, Cliff felt his sense of determination and strength renewed, a force that sustained him through the last difficult leg of their sea voyage and the early weeks on St. Helena. The Huxtables had two days vacation in the maritime county of Hampshire before boarding the ship at the port of Southampton. Along with Mrs. Heward, who had flown over from Toronto to join them in England, they visited with Mrs. Heward's sisters and brother who also lived in Hampshire. They enjoyed a brief visit with Cliff's friend from their Regina days, Alasdair Morrison and his wife. The afternoon before departure, as they were saying goodbye, Alasdair inadvertently smashed Cliff's right thumb in their car door. The compound fracture was agonizing. With a badly broken thumb, Cliff wondered how he would be able to manage moving Catherine in her wheelchair and attend to the needs of little Gavin on board the ship. Mrs. Heward saw them off at Southampton. Cliff mused in the same letter of September 12, 1966, to Salt Spring islander, Gil Humphreys, written from St. Helena six months later: ("I think she was hoping I would smash the other thumb and call the whole thing off. But she was a brick by this time and gave us a loving farewell.")

They sailed away on the RMMV (Royal Mail Motor Vessel) Capetown Castle after settling into cramped quarters. Two days out to sea, Cliff and Catherine had to contend with more than Cliff's painful thumb injury. Their concern over Gavin's health in London was heightened when he awoke delirious with a raging fever of 105 degrees Fahrenheit (40 degrees Celsius). Frantic with worry, Cliff awakened the ship's doctor in the early hours of the morning. The British medical officer was none too pleased, and stomped down to their cabin. He made no diagnosis, but simply advised the Huxtables to break their thermometer and go to bed. (They found out later that Gavin was suffering from glandular fever, more commonly known today as infectious mononucleosis.) In the morning they awoke to find that a bill for five pounds had been slipped under the door. When Cliff complained to the doctor that the bill was excessively high for the services he offered, he threatened to declare that Gavin had measles. The threat, if carried out, would mean that they would not be allowed to land at St. Helena: the Huxtables kept quiet. They prayed "with a vengeance" during the next day that Gavin's fever would abate so that they would not have to disembark at Portugal's island of Madeira to seek further treatment. Cliff later remembered:

> Do you know Gavin's temperature dropped to normal; we were able to take him ashore where we had a lovely tea in Madeira, and go back to the boat. We sailed out of the harbour, and that evening Gavin's temperature shot up again. Anyway, he gradually improved and though sickly on arrival, we were able to land at St. Helena on the 9th of April 1966.[252]

Government Officers Dissuade the Huxtables from Settling in St. Helena

On May 31, 1965, six months before their departure, the Huxtables had written to the Education Office on St. Helena, inquiring about the possibility of employment and the availability of accommodation for Catherine. On July 10, 1965, Education Officer A. W. Johns wrote back apologizing for the "depressing reply" to their inquiry. Johns informed them that the education department could not offer Cliff any teaching position since there were no vacancies for overseas personnel at the time, and that government policy determined that local posts would be reserved for St. Helenians. Johns further notified the Huxtables that the terrain would be unsuitable for a person in a wheelchair, and that there was no ground-level hotel accommodation available.

He advised them further that there was little chance of home ownership because suitable land for building purposes was in private hands and not easily obtainable. Immigration regulations required proof of an income of at least 800 pounds per annum. Cliff had also received a cable from the new government Secretary saying that St. Helena was completely unsuitable for a person in a wheelchair and that they should not come. In spite of this discouraging news, the Huxtables were not dissuaded. Subsequent events revealed that, however remote the possibility seemed of their finding both suitable accommodation and gainful employment, before the end of September they had been able to secure both. They did so in a manner that clearly defied the odds. William Masehla, the secretary of the NSA of South and West Africa, later enthusiastically qualified this turn-of-events as "truly miraculous."[253]

A Triumphant Disembarkation: How Catherine Reached *Terra Firma*

Despite the mishaps of the journey, the Huxtables felt overjoyed as the Capetown Castle sailed into Jamestown Bay on April 9, 1966. Cliff joyfully observed Catherine's disembarkation, as she made her way to *terra firma*:

> We were worn out, but didn't we feel triumphant! Here we were, St. Helena at last! I think it was a Saturday, if I remember correctly, and of course with the ship in everybody was down on the wharf. We were lowered in a lifeboat to the surface of the bay. Seamen helped me wheel her up planks from the ship's lifeboat onto a small platform of planks lashed across the gunwales of a local 30 foot wooden whaler from the days of 'Moby Dick', with a small British Seagull outboard motor on the stern, and off she went. Catherine was a radiant picture in her red-ribboned Madéira 'boater' hat as the little boat pitched and tossed towards shore. At the landing steps, strong brown hands reached out to lift her off, still fastened into her wheelchair, as the whaler skidded by the landing on the crest of a wave and all was well. We wheeled our way along the wharf and up to the hotel where we had a reservation.[254]

Although Cliff felt triumphant on landing after the six month journey from Salt Spring Island, John Robarts empathized with Catherine who had felt dangerously exposed during her transfer to land: "Cathie, you must have had to call on all your inner reserves of faith to go through with that terrifying disembarkation exercise!"[255]

The Bahá'í Community of St. Helena Island

At the time of the Huxtables' arrival, the Bahá'í history of St. Helena was a mere twelve years old. Only one other believer, St. Helenian Basil George, was living on the island. The other two Bahá'ís had left the island to find work. Mrs. Elizabeth Stamp was the Knight of Bahá'u'lláh for St. Helena. The sixty-seven-year-old Irish widow from Boston, USA, arrived there on May 4, 1954, and between occasional off-island visits, remained for a decade until the end of 1964. In his letter of August 16, 1966, to the Huxtables, John Robarts quoted Shoghi Effendi as saying during the Robarts' pilgrimage in January 1955, that Mrs. Stamp was a "heroine" for having pioneered there alone for so long. She had in fact endured considerable psychological distress throughout the decade of her residence. The Mauritian Jagdish Saminaden arrived in St. Helena from London sometime in January 1960, and stayed for two-and-a-half years—again under challenging circumstances. He was the only Bahá'í on the island when Mrs. Stamp was away.

Jagdish was unemployed for the first six months of his residency, but he found a job later in the Treasury Office. After much perseverance, he led Gay Corker, who sang in the church choir, and Basil George, a policeman, to the Faith in 1960–1961. Basil later married a twenty-three-year-old Scottish woman, Barbara George, who first arrived in 1964 on St. Helena as a young VSO teacher (Voluntary Service Overseas). The first Local Spiritual Assembly was formed on April 15, 1973.[256] The George family became, and remain to this day, along with Cliff and his wife, Delia Huxtable, pillars of St. Helena society. On May 17, 2003, in Plantation House, the country residence of the British Governor, Basil George was awarded the insignia of Officer of the British Empire (OBE) for his contribution to education and the promotion of tourism on St. Helena.[257]

How the Huxtables Met Basil George at the Consulate Hotel

The Consulate Hotel was a small building completely unsuitable for a wheelchair. Cliff and Catherine found that steps had to be climbed even to reach the ground floor. Because no bedrooms were located on the ground floor, they had to struggle up a long, steep staircase to reach their room. They had to descend some "very steep and murderous stairs to get to the toilets and washroom." On the first day of their arrival, they heard some people talking on the front veranda when someone spoke the name "Basil." When it turned out to be Basil George, Cliff quietly informed him that they were Baháʾís and invited him up to their room for a chat. The Huxtables enjoyed fellowship with Basil for scarcely two months because he was slated to leave for the United Kingdom in June, to complete his three-year BA in Education. After Basil's departure, our pioneers would find themselves the only two believers on the island. Basil was the first "Saint"—the familiar name for St. Helenians—to have achieved university entrance. As "Europeans" and newcomers, the Huxtables were facing limited employment opportunities, and poor prospects for housing. The general interest in the Baháʾí Faith was virtually nil on St. Helena. Catherine and Cliff deeply regretted Basil's departure; he was greatly missed.[258] They found themselves alone with their son Gavin.

Settling in: Finding Accommodation and Employment

Besides Colonel Heward, another Colonel was to enter the Huxtables' lives at a critical moment. The Huxtables remained at the Consulate Hotel from their arrival on April 9 until the end of May, 1966. With no prospects for suitable accommodation or employment in sight, Cliff "tramped the streets until there was no more hope."[259] In his growing desperation, he was even contemplating building a house out of flattened oil drums, if they could find a piece of land. Just when Cliff was reaching the last knot at the end of his rope, a perceptive and helpful friend intervened. He introduced the Huxtables to Colonel Gilpin, a World War Two commander of the St.Helena Artillery and sometime Acting Governor, who had a vacant ground floor in an old house in Jamestown in the former Hussey Charity School at the top of Napoleon Street.

Although the Colonel had turned down over thirty previous inquiries, his heart softened to Cliff and Catherine, the daughter of a fellow artillery officer. (Echoes of Gil Humphreys' kindness on Salt Spring Island.) The Colonel would offer them the flat at low rent on condition that Cliff would install a bathtub and toilet in one room as well as a kitchen sink. The Colonel would supply the plumbing and bathroom fixtures. Cliff's friend and the Colonel himself provided help on the job. The Colonel lent them some furniture—a scarce commodity on the island—and even pitched in and sewed some drapes! At the end of May, 1966, the Huxtables moved in. The Colonel agreed to let them stay until October when their visa would expire.

In finding employment and accommodation, the Huxtables faced three adverse circumstances: First, they belonged to a religion that the conventionally-minded British colonial administration and the populace on St. Helena viewed as "peculiar." (Anglicanism was the dominant faith.) It was because of the perceived peculiarity of their Faith that Tommy Heuvel, the then Auxiliary Board Member for South and West Africa, expressed surprise in a letter to Basil George that the Huxtables had been granted permission even to land.[260] Second, the Huxtables discovered that North Americans were not well-liked by the British on St. Helena, although Canadians fared somewhat better than Americans in polite society. Third, Cliff suspected that St. Helenians doubted his mental stability for the fact of bringing his wheelchair-bound wife to a steep volcanic island when he faced very slim possibilities of finding employment. As it turned out, however, their intrepid move, although at first viewed as bizarre and foolhardy by some, nonetheless attracted positive attention. It was soon to gain the admiration of the colonial administration from junior government officers right up to the Governor himself.

Cliff's Forced Recovery From Chronic Illness

During their five-month cross-Canada teaching trip, the Huxtables had no opportunity to build up any vital health reserves. Following Cliff's compound fracture of the thumb in England, and Gavin's infectious mononucleosis during the ocean voyage, the Huxtables both succumbed to a flu epidemic just after their arrival on St. Helena. While recovering from the flu and a broken thumb, Cliff had no choice but to install the plumbing in their new flat, if they were to take advantage of the Colonel's offer of quarters.

Barely two months after they moved into Colonel Gilpin's flat, Cliff's chronically strained health suddenly caught up to him. If complete exhaustion were not enough, Cliff had been suffering variously from intestinal influenza, a chest cold, a skin rash, a suspicion of diabetes, and boils. He collapsed in bed, but not before he was able to hire domestic help which took a great weight off his and Catherine's shoulders. Catherine wrote to poet Roger White: "To have to watch helplessly the gradual, complete breakdown of a young man's health has been one of the most horrifying experiences of my life."[261] Cliff's collapse was, however, another proverbial blessing in disguise. At long last, "after years of ill-health and exhaustion,"[262] he would be forced to take the time he needed to recover completely. It was a luxury he had not been able to afford since their last two difficult years on Salt Spring Island. Convalescence required fully two months of bed rest. At the Consulate Hotel, Catherine had been spending long hours in their room while Cliff installed the bathroom and kitchen plumbing in the accommodation provided by Colonel Gilpin. As Cliff healed, they would be able to enjoy some time together and strengthen their bonds of love and affection, while they parented little Gavin with the assistance of hired domestic help. Helpers for Catherine also provided an important bridge to St. Helenian society; through them the Huxtables could meet the helpers' families and friends.

Against All Odds Cliff Finds Gainful Employment: Settling in at 1 Ladder Hill

Cliff had applied for a teaching position in April soon after their arrival. Their visitor's visa was set to expire on October 9. They were living on hope and a prayer as they weighed their chances of employment. One evening our pioneers consulted with a friend "who was wise in the way of colonial governments." They came to the discouraging conclusion that Cliff's chances for a teaching position were slim. Without gainful employment, the Huxtables would have to abandon their pioneering post and make their way back to Canada. But then, just as they were facing these dismal prospects, the tide of their fortunes began to turn in their favor. Two Anglican clerics, who were also members of the school board, motivated perhaps by curiosity as much as kindness, began to take a friendly and inquisitive interest in the Huxtables. Word spread that Cliff had been a secondary school teacher and vice-principal in Canada. Catherine's radiant wheelchair presence, as always, encouraged strangers to become friends. The Huxtables were invited to tea where officials' wives were present; local school board members would drop in for a casual chat.

On August 18, Cliff's thirty-fourth birthday, the rising tide of their good fortune turned fully: the Governor offered Cliff a teaching position. It was the only job available on the island that would suit his qualifications. Cliff requested and was granted a slight increase in salary in recognition of his teacher training and administrative experience. He was appointed on exactly the same terms as any qualified St. Helenian, i.e. without the gratuities, inducements, and paid-leave that were offered to education officers from the United Kingdom. St. Helenians were impressed that Cliff took the job without the inducements that would have doubled his salary.[263] Although the lack of these additional benefits meant a lower salary, the job came with the offer of medical care, accommodation at reasonable rent, and, from the Treasury, the offer to finance the purchase of a car with left-hand steering to facilitate the lifting of Catherine.

On August 24, Cliff became Assistant Education Officer and Headmaster of the Secondary Selective School. At the end of September, the Huxtables moved into a fine old stone house at the top of 1 Ladder Hill. Catherine described the setting: "We will be about 700 feet up but close to town and in a warm, dry part of the island. Mostly cactus grows in the surrounding land but there is a breathtaking view of sea and sky, looking towards the sunsets too. Just a few yards from the school and plenty of neighbours nearby."[264] Public Works agreed to install ramps and to punch a doorway through the sixteen-inch stone wall for the sake of Catherine's mobility.

Once Cliff received his teaching and administrative appointment, clergy, government officials and islanders alike welcomed the Huxtables to St. Helena. Cliff noted: "Now we seem bathed in the sunshine of goodwill when we go into the streets."[265] Cliff's letters to Gil Humphreys and to Douglas Martin of the Canadian NSA, reflect the happiness that Catherine and Cliff felt following the securing of the "beachhead," the military metaphor Cliff had used to describe their situation.[266] These passages reflect the gratitude that the Huxtables felt as the promised divine confirmations eased their straitened circumstances. In his letters to the Bahá'í community, Shoghi Effendi noted a dynamic pattern of growth that he identified as "crisis and victory." His words describe perfectly the positive reversal of circumstances experienced by our pioneers: "They have, in the past, proved themselves capable, in times of crisis, of overleaping the most formidable barriers, and of wresting victory from the jaws of impending defeat."[267] In his letter to the Canadian NSA Cliff wrote:

> Catherine is happy, Gavin is delighted (he says he will stay here to live when we leave!), And I am at least well with every reasonable prospect of remaining so. With interesting and constructive activities, ample household help, and a big contribution yet to be made through the cause of God, we have everything to be thankful for. The island is open now.

Cliff had not forgotten, of course, the stalking shadow of Catherine's gradually failing health, as this following allusion makes clear, but it affirms a favorable outcome. In the same letter to the NSA he wrote: "Of course other crises are looming on the horizon, but we are now confident that they will be followed by victory." His letter to Gil Humphreys, written on September 12, 1966, eloquently reflects the gratitude that filled Cliff's heart:

> My heart is filled with gratitude when I compare life now and our prospects with those we left behind. There is so much we can achieve here now, and under conditions which should help us to thrive rather than be crushed by our efforts at service in survival. We find ourselves much confirmed in that Faith that inspired us to undertake this hazardous journey.

In the closing salutation of the letter to the Canadian NSA, Cliff concluded with this confident affirmation: "The activities of the Army of the Supreme Concourse are quite apparent at the moment. Love, Cliff."

Six Hours that Transformed Hand of the Cause John Robarts and his Wife Audrey Robarts (December 16, 1966)

Sometime during the fall of 1966, the Universal House of Justice informed Hand of the Cause of God John Robarts that his services and those of his wife Audrey would be required once again in their native land. In October, 1953, following Shoghi Effendi's appeal for pioneers during the Ten Year World Plan (1953–1963), the Robarts left their comfortable home at 4 Millbank Avenue in Forest Hill Village, near Toronto, to open Bechuanaland, later Botswana, to the Bahá'í Faith, earning the Robarts and their youngest son, Patrick, the title of Knights of Bahá'u'lláh. After thirteen years of service on the African continent, the Robarts were being recalled to Canada. Hand of the Cause of God William Sears explained to the Huxtables the reason for the Robarts' recall during the Nine Year Plan. Canada had to raise 154 LSAs by 1973, but they had fallen from sixty-eight to fifty—eighteen LSAs behind the number won during the previous Ten Year Plan. In 1966, Canada was required to achieve 104 LSAs in a little more than six years. Mr. Sears wrote: "No doubt this is one of the main reasons that John was called back to Canada."[269] The Robarts would make a short stop on St. Helena on their way back home.

On Monday, December 12, the Robarts departed the port of Cape Town on the Capetown Castle, the same vessel that had conveyed the Huxtables to St. Helena eight months earlier.[270] They were moved to their spiritual depths during their six-hour visit. One of John's comments was later recorded in an NSA letter of February 13, 1967, that his stay with the Huxtables was "an experience like none other in his entire Bahá'í life."[271] The spiritual dynamic that so deeply touched the heart of the Hand of the Cause and his companion in so brief a timespan was created by the following conditions. The Robarts were witnessing firsthand the spirit of sacrifice the Huxtables were making in a remote location, under difficult conditions. They were witnessing also the clear evidence of the divine confirmations that sustained our pioneers. In a letter to the Huxtables, written by the Hand of the Cause from Toronto on February 14, shortly after their return to Canada, he described the transforming power of that visit:

> Your pioneering has had a very special purpose, unlike any other I have ever known. Audrey and I felt it when we were with you and it has really struck us many times since. Where could we find greater evidences of the proofs of the power, the love, the mercy, of God? The friends in Canada, and elsewhere, upon hearing of your example and experiences might well arise as one man and offer themselves. . . . One thing for absolute sure is that our beloved Shoghi Effendi is very very close to you all the time. I felt his presence when we were with you and I am sure you have rejoiced his heart many many times.[272]

A more sobering reason, I discovered, touched the Robarts during their layover. Cliff explained:

> During that wonderful visit John became very aware that Catherine did not have long to live. He drew me aside onto the verandah of our government quarters and compared life to the brief passage of a bird through one cathedral-like window into a large room, and out the other side through a similar window. I had not been dwelling on the shortness of our time together, nor did I after that.[273]

The Huxtables also were greatly encouraged by the visit of the Robarts. Cliff described it as "What a happy day!" but he expressed this regret: "How sad that no one else on the island was aware of the significance of the event!" Cliff went on to explain the value of those precious hours: "It helped us greatly to refocus our efforts and to accept the sometimes trying circumstances of our lives. John's immediate understanding of both the joys and difficulties of teaching in a community like this, and his wise advice are deeply valued."[27]

4

Teaching the Faith on St. Helena Island: The Power of Example

During the eighteen months before Catherine's death, the Huxtables attracted islanders to the Faith mainly by indirect teaching: by forming friendships, winning trust and having natural conversations on spiritual, moral and social themes. Catherine's radiant personality, Cliff's steadfast service to her, their warm hospitality, their free association with St. Helenians of African and mixed descent, and Cliff's effectiveness and integrity as an education officer, a job that required him to visit Saints who lived in the isolated hinterland of Jamestown, gradually won the admiration and respect of locals and employees in the Department of Education. Nevertheless, the Huxtables had to proceed with caution as far as direct teaching was concerned. As long as Cliff worked in the Anglican dominated Department of Education, their interaction with the government of St. Helena would be a sensitive business, even in those waning days of the British colonial empire. Cliff observed that "The clergy is civil but watches us closely and there is some reason to believe with gnashing teeth."[275]

But the sincerely religious, whatever their rank or denomination, came to realize that the Huxtables were God-fearing people, however strange their religion might have at first appeared. They gradually understood that any seriously ill woman in a wheelchair, who had traveled half-way around the world to settle on a remote, hilly island, must have been entirely committed to her chosen Faith. Catherine's letter to the Bahá'ís of Salt Spring Island detailed how living the Bahá'í life is the most effective way to teach the Faith when direct teaching is not advisable:

> Cliff is making very good headway in gaining the confidence of the local people. In the shops, by insisting on waiting his turn instead of being served ahead of brown people, by stopping to chat when out shopping, picking up people walking on the road, going hunting with some, getting one to show him how to make a kite, helping some prepare a local newspaper, writing

a note when someone became seriously ill, giving an old lady his own sandals because her swollen feet would not fit into women's shoes—and so on. This pioneering stint has changed Cliff's heart. He no longer wants to be a hermit. He is thin and tired. He drives himself relentlessly, but he is getting a heart-warming response from <u>many</u> and some islanders <u>tell</u> him, wonderingly, that he is not like the Europeans here.[276]

After their arrival on April 9, 1966, and during the approximately five months the Huxtables lived in Jamestown, they had frequent visitors—so many that Catherine complained that she and Cliff did not have enough time alone. After Cliff secured the principalship of the secondary school that summer, she was looking forward to moving to the house on 1 Ladder Hill to get some relief.[277] This did not mean that interest in the Bahá'í religion was immediately aroused; it was, in fact, slow and sporadic in coming. But every opportunity to engage in direct teaching was warmly, eagerly, and tactfully welcomed. On the first day of Ayyám-i-Há (Intercalary Days), 1967, some new friends came for tea and asked the Huxtables to tell them about the Faith. Catherine afterward exclaimed that "It was heaven!"[278] Other opportunities for direct teaching arose during the eight months preceding Catherine's death. A few of their contacts, Cliff wrote, became willing to read "the odd Bahá'í book."[279] Cliff was not discouraged, however, by the slow response; things were as they should be. "Indeed I feel the time is not yet," he reflected. "Much time and effort are required to build a solid foundation of trust between "Europeans" (ourselves) and St. Helenians."[280]

Governor Sir John Field and Lady Margaret Field

Two influential contacts within the British civil administration helped to predispose government officials and others to look upon the Huxtables favorably. The Governor and his wife, Sir John Osbaldiston and Lady Margaret Field, often invited the Huxtables to private dinners at the Governor's residence, Plantation House. Cliff wrote that Lady Field "is very attached to Catherine." Lady Field had been "a great help in breaking down artificial barriers at the "top."[281] Although the

Governor had at first been wary, and even nervous about Cliff's intentions and his North American qualifications, through a series of conversations, meetings and visits with the Huxtables, Cliff was able to win the Governor's confidence. With Governor Field's background in chemistry, he had been particularly keen on having Cliff introduce the teaching of science into the St. Helenian curriculum, an objective that Cliff, as a former science student and teacher, also shared.

∞ 10 ∞
DEATH AND RESURRECTION: DANCING WITH AN ANGEL (1967)

"Love is as strong as death, as hard as hell." Meister Eckhart

Catherine's Deteriorating Health: Help Gratefully Received

Within nine months of the Huxtables' arrival, Catherine's health had seriously deteriorated. Cliff wrote on January 10, 1967, that his wife was "really very sick."[282] The decline is clearly visible in her last photo taken during the August, 1967 visit of Ken Tinnion and Nina Robarts Tinnion, when compared to the more vibrant, full-faced photos taken earlier in Regina and Salt Spring Island. Catherine received the best medical services found on the island through the care of Dr. John Noaks, the Senior Medical Officer for St. Helena. Catherine liked Dr. Noaks because he was a compassionate, spiritually-minded physician, who was genuinely fond of St. Helenians.

To facilitate Catherine's ever-increasing difficulties with respiration, Cliff's sister Janet had shipped a breathing apparatus that brought some relief each day after "spells." To facilitate concentration, clearer thinking and a more cheerful outlook, after experimenting with various medications, the doctor prescribed a stimulant that had no negative side effects. Catherine welcomed the relief provided by Dr. Noaks' prescription. She wrote to Diana Dainty on July 2, 1967: "I am profoundly thankful." Catherine's radiant spirit was far from being totally eclipsed by the fast-approaching end of her physical life. Cliff wrote to Mrs. Heward about six weeks before she died: "Catherine has never been in better spirits but MD is taking its toll. With the perky pills and breathing machine she is able to do a lot and we have some very deep, meaningful and happy times together."[283]

Soul to Soul Conversations: A Renewal of Love

For his own mental survival, Cliff had never allowed himself to dwell on the limited number of days that remained of life with Catherine. It was a practice he maintained since the beginning of their marriage. He tried to live one day at a time, even though he knew that with each passing day, Catherine's time with Gavin and him was growing shorter. They would need, of course, to talk about the inevitable, but it had been too painful to broach the subject. When at last they began to talk freely about the end of Catherine's life, their earnest conversations brought liberation to them both; their frank, loving dialogue helped to buttress their hearts during those last difficult but rewarding days. As the Huxtables found the courage to face the inevitable together, and to speak about it openly, their hearts grew closer together. Cliff has affirmed that throughout their marriage, Catherine never criticized him, nor did she express annoyance or create distance between herself and her husband. She welcomed him home lovingly each day. Despite the tests they faced, their marriage was a happy one.[284]

In the same letter to Mrs. Heward quoted above, Cliff wrote: "Thank God the channels of communication are wide open and we are very much in love. It makes it all so much easier." Those days became a time of ingathering—a time to enjoy the satisfaction that comes with knowing that Catherine's life had been well-lived, a time to savor quiet moments, and to find joy in what they had accomplished together, and despite Catherine's growing weakness, to speak of future plans. Open communication also applied to the tone of letters sent either by Cliff or Catherine to their friends. Catherine was able to continue letter writing virtually to the end of her life, although her former pace had slowed considerably from lack of energy. Even as her voice was failing, she kept writing. Cliff kept close friends and relatives informed of Catherine's condition until the moment of her death. A month before Catherine's passing, Cliff remarked in a letter to the Rochesters: "Afraid scores and scores [of letters] still unanswered."[285] The Huxtables' Canadian teaching-trip in 1965–1966 had earned them hundreds of friends and admirers. Cliff's letter of October 14, 1967, to Enid and Jack Wrate in Lethbridge, Alberta, mentions that over a hundred letters were waiting to be answered. The Bahá'ís at home wrote our pioneers a continual stream of supportive letters that greatly buoyed up Catherine and Cliff's spirits until the final moment and, for Cliff, during the time of bereavement following Catherine's death.

10 ∞ Death and Resurrection

One Mind and Heart: Facing Catherine's Last Days Together

The loving bond that had been created between our pioneers in the declining months of Catherine's life came through a hard struggle. Cliff's job as Headmaster of the Secondary Selective School, his work in teacher-training and curriculum development, not only provided the necessary income the Huxtables required for daily living, but also gave Cliff the sense that he was making a worthwhile contribution to improve the quality of education on St. Helena. He seemed to be more resigned to the slow pace of the Bahá'í teaching work than Catherine; he knew that much time and labor would be required to make inroads for the Faith in the face of the strong position enjoyed by the "establishment" on the island. Although St. Helenians had become more friendly after Cliff was hired, little interest was shown in learning about the Bahá'í Faith. Veritable bright spots illumined the Huxtables' day when St. Helenians or the English residents of the island made inquiries about the Faith.

As Catherine's health declined, and although the Huxtables had "very loyal and helpful" housekeepers, Cliff naturally wanted to spend as much time as possible with his wife. He remarked: "Though we often don't feel very useful to the Cause under these conditions, we know that we are in the best possible situation at the moment."[286] For Catherine, who spent long daytime hours resting at home, the situation initially looked very different—at least regarding her perceived inability to serve the Faith. Her usual frankness and honesty came to the fore in a letter written to Diana Dainty on July 2, 1967. As she looked back over the past year, a year that had required her to make "great adjustments" to her invalid condition, she wrote:

> It seemed like I wasn't going to be able to be of any use here at all, and looking after Gavin here was particularly difficult in some ways. I often felt rebellious and miserable about being here. At times I felt that only one pioneer had come here—Cliff, and that I was only a reluctant tagger-alonger. I don't want your pity or to depress you—only want to show that there was another side to the glowing report John Robarts seems to have given in Canada!

Gradually, however, through a series of practical steps, Catherine found that she was able to transform her former negative attitude into one of positive acceptance:

> But little by little certain changes have occurred. One by one the things I feared or worried about have been sorted out, either by talks with my doctor (who automatically visits me weekly without my asking, which means a lot), or with Cliff or through changes in outward circumstances or through reflection (those long hours in bed).

Catherine explained to Diana that she found Roger White's article "Point a Loving Camera" particularly helpful in making the fewer contacts she had with people "more meaningful."[287] Although Pamela Webster and Ann Kerr Linden had long before remarked on Catherine's captivating greeting and magnetic interaction with her friends, she felt that she could still improve on giving her guests her undivided attention: "I became more particular about the way I look at people—especially important in this little place where every detail is noticed. This has brought visible results."

Catherine wrote of direct teaching more often than Cliff; it was naturally on her mind as she inched closer to death's door. She was greatly heartened when these opportunities presented themselves:

> The other thing that is making both Cliff and I [sic] much happier and more relaxed these days is that at last we seem to have found a true seeker, and several doors seem to be opening in rapid succession. We are both able to do direct teaching now, and relations with both St. Helena people and overseas whites are better than ever before.

Finally, Catherine shared her feelings with Diana Dainty about her marriage, family life and approaching death, and the slow transformation that had occurred through more open, loving communication:

> Our marriage has become healed again in the last ten months or so. Talking frankly about my trip to the Abha Kingdom, and its many ramifications for him, Gavin and me has been a very great bounty and brought us so close. Our times together and with Gavin are very happy and we have great discussions about our work here, the people, etc.

Those ongoing therapeutic conversations with Cliff about Catherine's approaching death ultimately brought her great reassurance and peace of mind. Earlier, the young mother had naturally been troubled at the prospect of death at age thirty-five: "Several times I felt that death was just around the corner, and several aspects of this troubled me a lot," she wrote to Diana. Her tried and true method of expressing her deepest feelings, whether through speaking or writing, along with the good counsel of her husband, her doctor's compassionate care, Roger White's insightful article, and any opportunities for direct teaching, all conspired favorably to make Catherine's last year one in which she moved further into that rare but liberating state of contentment that Bahá'ís call "radiant acquiescence."

Her Final Days: Joining the Centenary of the Proclamation of Bahá'u'lláh (October 24, 1967)

Barely two weeks before she died, Cliff wrote in his letter of October 14 to Enid and Jack Wrate, a succinct description of Catherine's physical and mental state, their life at home and the place of contentment and gratitude that they had both reached simultaneously:

> Catherine is in excellent spiritual shape—as good or better than I have ever seen her. Her condition has deteriorated greatly in the past year and she is by and large an invalid now. She does not expect to live long and in view of the daily struggle to eat, rest, breathe, dress etc. we cannot wish it on her. With

the help of some perky pills her mind and spirit are as active as ever, but we have had to cut social activities to the bone—her body just cannot keep up, nor can mine. She is one of the truly great souls. We have household help that really wants to be of service, excellent medical attention, a reasonably comfortable home and a job to be done. We often say this is the best place for us at this stage. When everything is right it is marvellous how everything fits. Climate, pace of life, my job, etc. are all geared to our circumstances, and we do have opportunities to serve the Cause even though it appears that both hands are tied behind our backs. This would not have been possible for us in Canada. Much love to you all, Cliff

In 1967 the Universal House of Justice had called for a centenary celebration to mark Bahá'u'lláh's proclamation to the kings, rulers, religious leaders and peoples of the world. To honor the centenary befittingly, the House of Justice decided to present Bahá'u'lláh's message to world leaders of the day. They chose to publish His announcement in a special edition entitled *The Proclamation of Bahá'u'lláh*, to be presented to Heads of State, and a general edition that would be made available to the Bahá'í community in English, French, German, Italian and Spanish. The Huxtables were able to join in the world-wide proclamation of Bahá'u'lláh's teachings to a "leading clergyman and his wife." Cliff outlined the circumstances in a letter of November 13, 1967 to the Rochesters:

> The evening before Catherine died, we proclaimed the nature of the Faith (couldn't be avoided against our better judgment) to a leading clergyman and his wife. C. wanted to stay up for an hour after they left and we felt the evening was God-designed—and felt we could accept whatever the repercussions. We were happy to take part in the World-wide Proclamation.

10 ∞ Death and Resurrection

Taking Flight: Early Morning (October 25, 1967)

No indication was given in the letter of October 14 from Cliff to Enid and Jack Wrate, eleven days before Catherine's death, that she was about to leave the world. Even when you expect death—and Cliff had seen all the unmistakable approaching signs—its dreadful visitation still comes unexpectedly. Cliff confided in the Rochesters in his letter of November 13 cited above: "But I had no idea her passing was so imminent." In a graphic letter to Mrs. Heward, Cliff described Catherine's final moments. Her son-in-law did not shroud his words in delicacy to protect a mother's feelings. He wanted Helen Heward to know the exact circumstances of her daughter's death, just as she would have known them had she been at Catherine's side. At the time of writing, Catherine's mortal remains still lay in bed where she had breathed her last, only two-and-a-quarter hours before:

> #1 Ladder Hill, St. Helena, Island, South Atlantic
> Wednesday, October 25, 1967
> 4:30 AM
>
> Dear Mrs. Heward,
> Catherine's unconquerable spirit winged its flight to the Abha Kingdom at about 2:15 AM this morning. She was sick all day yesterday (Tuesday) and stayed in bed. She was short of oxygen and the breathing apparatus, though used often, did not bring her full relief. I was called home from school in the morning. There were great pauses and blanks in her conversation. Doctor said nothing to be done. She rallied somewhat in the evening and then slept peacefully from 8:30 to 10:30 PM and again from 11 to 1 AM. It took half an hour to get her comfortably adjusted for the night, and I was just dozing off beside her when she repeated earnestly several times "I want to die." Then she asked if it was so dark because she had gone blind. I turned the light on briefly and she was reassured. After

a few minutes quiet, she started to gurgle. I phoned the doctor, propped her up and held her, tried to give her the breathing apparatus—all to no avail. It was all over in 15 minutes—no struggle on her part.

Cannot but be happy for her release after the past year but unbelievable that our beloved is no longer with us. Gavin was awake a few minutes ago (coughing) and I explained it to him. He took it very well—wanted to and did come to the bedroom to say goodbye to Mummy—Reactions for all of us later. In recent letters, John Robarts, Hand of the Cause of God, has proclaimed Catherine a heroine and saint of the Bahá'í Dispensation and has rightfully declared that the whole Bahá'í world will be grieved at her passing. You and I have the bounty of special association with her. May our lives prove us worthy. Love, Cliff

Even in her last hours, as she rested on the brink of eternity, Catherine's sense of duty remained strong. Earlier on, she reminded Cliff about Gavin's necessities for the coming school day: "Then she tried to say a lot about household details, like putting out Gavin's clothes for the morning." It is so entirely fitting that Catherine died in Cliff's arms. She would have wanted it no other way, as the final moment on their earthly journey together, performed by the noble body and soul of the man who carried her many times during their seventeen years of friendship, love and married life. Sometime before she died, Catherine left a special love letter for Gavin in care of his father to be delivered to their son at an appropriate future time. Among the last words spoken to Cliff were "I love you."[288]

Cliff's Announcement to the Bahá'í International Community: A Funeral Like no Other on St. Helena Island

"Dear Cliff....I was very moved by your account of Catherine's funeral: it is somehow very important to know how people one loves spend their last hours and

10 ∞ Death and Resurrection

how they come to their graves and to have some glimmering of where their bodies lie."
Madeleine Ashlin Davis

Catherine's funeral can be experienced no better than by reading Cliff's eloquent letter describing the event. His letter bears witness to the power of the heroism, love and sacrifice that drew to Catherine's graveside a solemn and supportive crowd of mourners that represented clerics, the business class, civil servants, laborers, and ordinary citizens alike, including complete strangers—and prostitutes. Cliff's letter also testifies to the determinative role played by his wife in his social and spiritual education:

> November 1967
> Dear Friends,
> Catherine's saintly, heroic, and glorious spirit passed away to the next world at 2 A.M. October 25th. The end came suddenly after only one day of total discomfort. She had every useful medical aid. Her last words were an earnest, but not anguished prayer, "I want to die". She lived to nurture a discouraged youth she had met 17 years ago, into a husband and a man, to bear our son Gavin and give him an excellent introduction to life, to see him begin his schooling, to pioneer for the Baháʼí World Faith from Toronto to Regina, then to the Gulf Islands, and finally to St. Helena 13,000 miles away in the South Atlantic—always overcoming incredible tests and difficulties in addition to her crippling disease. She touched the hearts, illumined the spirits, challenged and inspired the courage, of all who were fortunate enough to meet her. She trampled every base desire beneath her feet, and turning to God for sustenance, reached out to suffering humanity with a pure and radiant heart to offer this new message of love and fulfillment. Her life was a triumph over almost every conceivable personal difficulty. The third evening after her passing she came to me in a state of indescribable joy

and we danced together in perfect harmony. I praise God for the bounty of being her partner.

During the past six months our external activities were severely curtailed and we led a quiet and intimate family life such as we had never known. Catherine prepared Gavin well and left him a farewell note which will mean much to him as he matures.

Catherine is buried high in the center of the island overlooking the majestic scenery of St. Helena to the South Atlantic beyond. We spoke often of her death. As a newcomer and outsider to this insular community, I expected her funeral to be the loneliest journey of my life. Over 80 cards and letters of sympathy poured into the house; ranging in sources from the Bishop to an impoverished leper. Although no one was asked to attend, and the burial was during working hours, and I refused to comply with the local custom of hiring buses for the "professional" funeral goers, it was the biggest funeral procession I had seen since our arrival 19 months ago.

The Governor, clergy, labourers, servants, businessmen, housewives, clerks and administrators, shopkeepers, schoolchildren, and streetwalkers—all were there.

The Governor's wife, the Vicar of Jamestown, our servants, education officers, and a police constable (four brown, three white) read the Bahá'í sacred writings at her graveside. All stood deeply moved and silent, through the chill wind and rain, until the earth had been replaced. Then the people came forward and heaped the entire grave with bouquets and wreaths of fresh flowers. Many were astonished that so many could be found at this season. When all had departed, I scattered some earth from the courtyard of Bahá'u'lláh's tomb over Catherine's grave and recited the Tablet of Ahmad.

10 ∞ Death and Resurrection

It was not a lonely journey; and the 27 cables from the Queen Charlotte Islands in the Northwest, to Swaziland in the Southeast, made it less so. I was particularly touched to hear that the Baháʼís were holding a memorial service in Toronto, and that our mothers were attending. Catherine's mother arrives toward the end of this month, the doctor predicts good health for me after a few months rest, and we are surrounded with practical offers of assistance. With love,

Cliff Huxtable.

Catherine's was the only funeral Governor and Lady Field attended during the Governor's six year tenure on the island. At 3:44 p.m., October 25, Douglas Martin sent a telegram to his fellow NSA member, Michael Rochester: "Grieved inform you passing this morning Cathy Huxtable Arranging Toronto Memorial Sunday Stop Can you assist John [Robarts] behalf NSA Doug". Among the hundreds of letters of sympathy and condolence Cliff received was the following message from the National Pioneer Committee of Canada:

January 8, 1968

Dearest Clifford,

Several of the friends in the Ottawa area received your letter describing Catherine's death. It was deeply moving, Cliff, and I'm sure many of us were moved to silent prayer right on the spot. Speaking for Diana and myself, many's the time that we thought of the both of you with a great deal of warmth in our hearts. Your sacrifices are a constant reminder to the two of us to stay on the track, and we are certainly not alone! All others here hope and pray for your continuing victories and particularly that good health will return to you soon.

Deepest love and affection,

Don Dainty for the National Pioneer Committee

Michael Rochester's Vision of Catherine Running Free

Two extraordinary visions of Catherine have been recorded following her death. The waking visions experienced by Michael Rochester and Cliff Huxtable both confirmed her newfound ecstasy, that much longed for freedom and joy that was realized at last. Less intense and personal than Cliff's ecstatic dance with Catherine, but impressively vivid nonetheless, Michael Rochester described to Cliff what he saw in his letter of November 13, 1967, written from St. John's, Newfoundland:

> The morning after the news of her passing came, I was standing before a window in our house looking out on a long hillside of pines and firs which stretches as far as you can see behind the house, and thinking of Catherine. Suddenly and vividly I had a vision of her running down a grassy slope, with her arms spread wide and her hair streaming back in the wind of her running. Her face was radiant with a look of the most inexpressible joy. And into my mind came that verse of the prophet Isaiah, 'They that wait upon the Lord shall renew their strength; they shall mount up with wings as eagles; they shall run and not be weary; they shall walk and not faint.' How intensely happy she must be!

The Rapture: Dancing With an Angel

In recounting the following vision, it would be fitting to change the great Meister Eckhart's saying, cited at the head of this chapter, to the comparative degree: "Love is stronger than death, but harder than hell." The Huxtables' life together fully exemplifies Eckhart's saying. However one understands the word "resurrection," it testifies to the power of the Spirit over the physical fact of death. In His talk on "Visions, and Communication with Spirits," 'Abdu'l-Bahá validates the existence of such a phenomenon when He refers to "the revelations of the Prophets, and the spiritual discoveries of the elect."[289] Cliff's resurrection vision of Catherine, on the third evening after her death, is an undeniable confirmation

10 ∞ Death and Resurrection

for those who believe in the immortality of the soul that death cannot be the final end. Because Catherine's appearance to Cliff occurred when he was fully awake, it qualifies as a true vision, not a dream.

The long history of religion, mysticism, and the Baháʼí Faith itself are replete with visions that qualify as true representations of reality, representations that produce awesome, inspiring and hopeful effects on hearts and minds. Waking visions of the departed also underscore one of religion's foundational teachings: the immortality of the soul that remains faithful to God, and its habitation in paradise. Cliff's general announcement of Catherine's death alluded to the visitation: "The third evening after her passing, she came to me in a state of indescribable joy and we danced together in perfect harmony. I praise God for the bounty of being her partner." However, in his letter of November 13, 1967, to the Rochesters, Cliff gave further details about what transpired on that evening of joyous reunion. He was alone, listening to music, when the vision began in the upper right-hand corner of the room:

> The following Friday evening we danced to Mantovani's Swedish Rhapsody. I have never experienced a human contact so real! She was beautiful in a full, long, white gown gathered at the waist—C's face of her late teens only radiant beyond anything in this world—and how she danced! She is very close, appreciative & understanding—has been praying for us—already beautifully protected from some very dangerous situations—I feel steadied up now & able to cope again. There is no death. Much love, Cliff.

Regarding the execution of the Will of God, let us recall that Catherine's most heartfelt desire was to dance, a longing that was denied to her because of muscular dystrophy. The reader will recall from chapter 3 that, on the night when they met, Cliff had started across the floor of the hall at Victoria College to ask Catherine to dance, but turned back suddenly when he noticed that she was sitting in a wheelchair. But this time, there was no turning back. The dance was fully realized; the embrace was complete, and in a way that neither one could have imagined on that autumn evening in 1950. Cliff's description of Catherine's visitation suggests a few powerful symbols: the white gown is the bridal gown, the symbol of the soul's purity, worn at the wedding feast when the soul is united with its Creator; the dance is the dance of ecstasy, the final state promised by God to the faithful soul; the dance is the rapturous reunion of two souls who were fully restored to complete union and wholeness, a union that they were not able to enjoy fully while Catherine suffered from her illness.

The Memorial Service and Launching the Centenary Proclamation (October 29, 1967)

The Canadian NSA's response to the Universal House of Justice's call to launch a centenary proclamation was to announce a Proclamation Conference that was held in Toronto on Sunday, October 29, 1967. The NSA also decided that a thirty-minute memorial dedicated to the life of Catherine Huxtable should be added to the program. The conference and the memorial were attended by about 400 people. Catherine's mother Helen and Cliff's mother Dorothy, and her husband from her second marriage, Harold Window, sat in the front row. The conference was attended by Hand of the Cause, John Robarts, his wife Audrey, and all members of the Canadian NSA. In a heartfelt letter, John Robarts reported later to Cliff: "I think we all felt an extremely strong flow of the spirit through that room."[290]

The NSA asked Michael Rochester to deliver the eulogy on its behalf. His tribute is eloquent, elegant and succinct—an economy of expression that captures in relatively few words the essence of Catherine's life and service. We should bear in mind that at the time of Catherine's passing, she and Cliff had not yet been named Knights of Bahá'u'lláh by the Universal House of Justice. Michael's comment below that they must occupy a similar station to the Knights of Bahá'u'lláh because they opened a virgin goal during the Ten Year Crusade anticipates that appointment two years later.

I reproduce the eulogy in full here. I have retained the passing reference to his vision of Catherine that is mentioned in the section above:

10 ∞ Death and Resurrection

"Catherine Heward Huxtable— her name recalls so vividly to so many people that gentle beautiful girl with the infectious smile whose quiet friendship has meant so much to those whose hearts were troubled, whose self-effacing courage has been such a shining example.

She was still a young girl when she was found to have muscular dystrophy, and within a few years was unable to walk and had to be in a wheelchair. So often people in Catherine's situation are described as "confined to a wheelchair," but while she was indeed physically confined, the word is completely inappropriate for the freedom of her spirit.

When I first met her some sixteen years ago, she had been given no more than another five years of life. In fact, however, she lived more than ten years beyond that limit, and in that decade wrote her name in imperishable letters in the book of Canadian Bahá'í history and accomplished services which would have been remarkable enough had she been in perfect physical health.

She and Cliff Huxtable made their declaration of faith in Bahá'u'lláh together in 1952, and three years later they were married. They longed to pioneer for the Cause and finally, despite the very real difficulties presented by her physical handicap,[291] they broke the pattern into which her life had seemed to be cast and left Toronto to go as pioneers to Regina. This was in 1957, and in later years Rúhíyyih Khánum told them that their name as pioneers had been on a piece of paper in the Guardian's pocket on the day of his passing.[292]

For two years they helped a strong community to grow in Regina, then in 1959 turned their eyes to the Gulf Islands of British Columbia, which the Guardian had permitted the NSA of Canada to take as an alternative to the extremely difficult goal of Anticosti. Though they were never named by Shoghi Effendi as Knights of Bahá'u'lláh, I think she and Cliff must surely occupy a similar station, as the first pioneers to arrive in a virgin goal of the Ten Year Crusade.

Their years on the Gulf islands, though hard in many ways, bore wonderful fruits—to their great happiness their son Gavin was born in 1962, and new believers came into the Cause in the islands so that by Ridván 1964 a goal of the Nine Year Plan was won by the formation of the first Local Spiritual Assembly there.

Having contributed so much to the accomplishment of the first Canadian goal of the Plan, she and Cliff decided to pioneer to another island goal, St. Helena, set in the vast emptiness of the South Atlantic Ocean. Many of the newer believers, who did not know Catherine and Cliff from their Toronto days, will remember with pleasure their visits to Bahá'í communities as they crossed Canada en route to St. Helena, where they arrived at Ridván 1966. There they have faced and overcome enormous hardships and tests and there, four days ago, Catherine left this world.

For all of us who love her, the sense of loss is full of pain, but this pain is not unmixed because we cannot but be glad, for her sake, that the brilliant soul's long struggle within the cage of the body has ended.

The morning after the cable came from Cliff to tell us of her passing, I was standing before a window looking out on a hillside and thinking of her. Suddenly and vividly I had a vision of Catherine, running down a grassy windswept slope, with her arms outspread—those arms which in this world could hardly lift a teacup—with her hair streaming back in the wind and with a look of inexpressible joy on her face. And I thought of the words of the prophet Isaiah "They that wait upon the Lord shall renew their strength; they shall mount up with wings as eagles;

10 ∞ Death and Resurrection

they shall run and not be weary; they shall walk and not faint."

We—her Bahá'í brothers and sisters—can hardly imagine her tremendous happiness now that she is in the presence of the Holy Ones whom she so deeply loved, and of the Master ['Abdu'l-Bahá] and Shoghi Effendi whose faithful servant she so truly was."[293]

Rúhíyyih Khánum Extols Catherine's Life During her South American Teaching Tour (1967–1968)

As mentioned above, Rúhíyyih Khánum and Catherine continued to exchange occasional friendly letters both before and after the Huxtables met the Guardian's helpmate at the home of Ann and Sven Kerr in West Vancouver in the spring of 1960. In a letter written on February 25, 1955, Rúhíyyih Khánum thanked Catherine for sending her a piece of jewelry:

> Dear Catherine—Thank you so much for the lovely broach [sic] and the thoughts that went with it. We are all—as always—very busy here; work, pilgrims, mail. But it is a thrilling life and a privileged one. The beloved Guardian is well and always eager to hear news of the advance of the 10 Year Plan! Much love, Rúhíyyih[294]

When Catherine died, Hand of the Cause of God John Robarts was advised by wire. Because the NSA did not have Rúhíyyih Khánum's South American address, they requested that Mr. Robarts "advise her directly."[295] Rúhíyyih Khánum wrote to Cliff in care of the NSA, assuring him of "her deep sympathy in the passing of Catherine and of her prayers for the progress of Catherine's spirit."[296] The NSA asked John Robarts and Michael Rochester to assist in planning the memorial service in Toronto.

At the time of Catherine's passing, Rúhíyyih Khánum, accompanied by her cousin Jeanne Bolles, was on a teaching tour of South America. From the Falkland Islands, Margaret Leonard, wife of Knight of Bahá'u'lláh, John Leonard, attended the conferences given by Rúhíyyih Khánum in Buenos Aires and Montevideo. Margaret wrote that on the last night of the meetings in Montevideo, Madame Rabbaní told "the beautiful story of Cathy's life." In a letter of condolence to Cliff, Margaret wrote: "She suggested to the friends present that Cathy's life was an inspiration to us all, that she demonstrated what faith and courage really mean." Jeanne Bolles related to Margaret that "Rúhíyyih Khánum had felt impelled to tell this story wherever she went." Margaret continued: "You can see by this that Cathy's life of suffering is now inspiring not only her particular friends but many unknown to her."[297]

∞11∞
CATHERINE HEWARD HUXTABLE: A LIFE REMEMBERED

A Love That Could Not Wait

The foregoing narrative has depicted the story of two remarkable individuals who contributed to the local, national and international development of the Bahá'í Faith, a couple who made a lasting impression, not only on those who shared their circle of faith, but also on those who stood at its fringes. Catherine's life stands out as living testimony to the power of the Bahá'í Revelation, not merely to provide comfort and meaning to one who was facing an early death, but also to empower and transform her spirit, despite—or because of—the adversities the Huxtables faced together throughout their twelve year marriage.

Bahá'u'lláh has revealed: "And yet, is not the object of every Revelation to effect a transformation in the whole character of mankind, a transformation that shall manifest itself both outwardly and inwardly, that shall affect both its inner life and external conditions?"[298] Shoghi Effendi wrote the ultimate statement on the attainment of individual spiritual transformation: "One thing and only one thing will unfailingly and alone secure the undoubted triumph of this sacred Cause, namely, the extent to which our own inner life and private character mirror forth in their manifold aspects the splendor of those eternal principles proclaimed by Bahá'u'lláh."[299] Catherine's life was a living demonstration of the essential requirements alluded to in these sacred texts. The transformation of her spirit was gained at the cost of great sacrifice, without which high spiritual attainment cannot be gained.

Despite the fact that she lived under the creeping menace of a fatal illness, Catherine arose to serve the Faith she loved so well with a resolute courage that captured the imagination and won the admiration of those who witnessed her consecration. The sweetness of her disposition, and the gentility of her character only augmented the love and affection she radiated. From the moment she became a Bahá'í in 1952, and because she was acutely aware that her life would be cut short, Catherine determined that she would not die without making a significant contribution: "Only by centering myself in the Covenant of God can my life or death have any significance. If I have a private prayer, it's this: Let my life and death count in the Faith!"[300]

Her significant contribution lay, of course, nowhere else but in pioneering for the Faith she had so eagerly embraced in 1952. But beyond that, Catherine's physical move, admirable in its own right, manifested at the same time a spirit of the gracious acceptance of her disability, coupled with a defiance, even a heroism that may well serve as model for what may be achieved by those who must face a life of adversity and affliction. But hers, we have to remember, was not an instant transformation. Catherine struggled to grow into the spirit of service that she ultimately came to choose. Following her enrollment, she thought that muscular dystrophy would prevent her from serving, be it on an LSA, a committee, or as fireside speaker, let alone as pioneer. We are all heartened by the fact that, with the steady support of her helpmate, she grew to overcome her former doubts and misgivings.

Moved by Shoghi Effendi's verbal directive to the Toronto Bahá'ís to disperse, delivered by Winnifred Harvey following her pilgrimage in 1956, and by the Guardian's sudden death in 1957, the actions she took with Cliff were inspired by an urgent resolve to make her significant contribution while there was yet time. Catherine's life provides an outstanding example of one who took seriously the Báb's stirring charge to the Letters of the Living: "Heed not your weaknesses and frailty; fix your gaze upon the invincible power of the Lord, your God, the Almighty."[301]

No Plaster Saint

Catherine was humble enough not to take any personal credit for her spiritual attainments. She attributed the achievement of her full and successful life, not only to Cliff and her mother, Helen Bury Heward, but ultimately to "Bahá'u'lláh, whose teachings will give anyone courage and power to fulfill their dreams."[302] *In Life and Holiness* (1964), the prolific Trappist monk, Thomas Merton (1915–1968), critiqued the negative stereotype of "the plaster saint." Merton

11 ∞ A Life Remembered

deplored the stereotype as projecting an image of holiness that was unattractive and unrealistic, as doing religion a disservice by depriving saints of their humanity and vitality. Catherine Huxtable was no plaster saint. Her life manifested a healthy balance of warm humanity, spiritual sensitivity, and the dedication of a true believer. The spiritual virtues that she possessed, which have been explored in the pages above, were harmoniously blended with a radiance, comeliness, good humor, an innocent sense of mischief and playfulness, loving-kindness, determination and frankness. Most importantly, Catherine's spirituality was greatly enhanced by that mode of service that was sure to win the admiration of Shoghi Effendi—action! When all but a few of her fellow Torontonians responded to the Guardian's call, the Huxtables determined that muscular dystrophy could not be an excuse for not arising to pioneer.

The spirit in which this Knight of Bahá'u'lláh patiently faced her daily trials did not prevent her from fully experiencing life's joys and satisfactions, even during the final days of her life. She excelled in the art of making delicate, intricate petit point pictures and jewelry. She enjoyed reading, although she admitted to wrestling with the abstractions of modern poetry. Despite being bright and perceptive, she was not naturally drawn to the niceties of intellectual analysis and those distinctions that could too easily lead to the spirit of contention which greatly upset her. She enjoyed jazz, classical music, cinema, theatre and especially dance. Catherine loved people and cultivated social relationships. Wherever she lived, she became a good neighbor. As long as her health permitted, she opened her home to friend and stranger alike. When she became a mother, with the welcome acceptance of domestic help, she threw herself into the challenging new role that had unexpectedly come upon her.

But her first, last and greatest love was the Faith of Bahá'u'lláh. It gave her life meaning, purpose and direction. She understood that its teachings were indispensable to the salvation of humanity and to the steady development of her own soul and the souls of others. For the fifteen years that she lived consciously as a Bahá'í, Catherine Huxtable determined that she would give her all for the promotion of the Faith's life-giving teachings. Her life demonstrates that attaining well-being and happiness is indeed possible for anyone who has to face adverse conditions, be they emotional, mental or physical—and she experienced all three. Although outwardly she was confined to a wheelchair, her spirit could not be imprisoned. It soared at times to heights that few able-bodied persons have known.

In his 1974 biographical tribute, Weston Huxtable drew attention mainly to his sister-in-law's admirable humanity, although a few have not hesitated in proclaiming Catherine one of the saints and heroines of the Bahá'í dispensation. According to Cliff Huxtable and to Eileen White Collins, this last judgment belonged to Hand of the Cause of God, John Robarts. In Cliff's letter to Mrs. Heward, quoted in the preceding chapter, written only two-and-a-quarter-hours after her passing, he wrote: "In recent letters John Robarts, Hand of the Cause of God, has proclaimed Catherine a heroine and saint of the Bahá'í Dispensation and has rightfully declared that the whole Bahá'í world will be grieved at her passing." Gale Burland's letter of January 28, 1967, written from Oakville, Ontario, to the Huxtables quotes John Robarts as follows from a gathering of the friends: "John's words went deep, please God—and among them as he looked at us, and he was very moved, and so were we—were these: 'You know, friends, on St. Helena I'm convinced that we have not just two heroes or two saints—but two saints and two heroes.'" When Catherine died, in his letter to Cliff, John Robarts wrote a simple but telling phrase: "She has died a martyr's death."[303]

Another Hand of the Cause, Zikrullah Khádem, also had high regard for Catherine's spiritual station. While Mr. Khádem was speaking during the 1970 Canadian National Convention, Michael Rochester noted a comment that Mr. Khádem made about Catherine. He repeated a statement of Shoghi Effendi that the courageous Canadian pioneer to Bulgaria, Marion Jack (1866–1954), was "distinguished not by her ability but by her spirit of detachment . . . " Mr. Khádem then went on to say: "Catherine Huxtable is next to Marion Jack." It is not exactly clear, as Michael Rochester has indicated, what exactly he meant: did she stand next to "General Jack"[304] in detachment?; next to her in spiritual stature?; next to her in courage?[305]

It is not too far-fetched to conclude, considering that he was speaking of Canadian pioneers, that Mr. Khádem meant next in rank. And, after reviewing carefully the circumstances of her life, and in view of the considered opinions others have made, it is not a gratuitous interpretation of Mr. Khádem's words to conclude that this was his meaning. It is not speculation to say that both Canadian pioneers showed extraordinary and exemplary courage and detachment in the face of adversity: In Marion Jack's case, in the face of poverty, want, old age, poor health, and the dangers of war; and for Catherine Huxtable, the courage and detachment she manifested in acquiescing to a life-shortening illness, in becoming a wheelchair pioneer, as she faced the challenges of moving long distances, finding helpers, morally supporting her husband while he looked for work, taking on motherhood, raising her son for the five years of life that yet remained to her, making friends and teaching the Faith in virgin territories—all this as she gradually succumbed to being an invalid who had to face death at the age of 35.

It is also clear from poet Roger White's deft and psychologically sensitive pen-portrait of Catherine, that he shared the same opinion as John Robarts, no less than the man who was closest to her. Roger wrote: "Wherever she went she was described as a saint, a heroine and a true Bahá'í."[306] Cliff Huxtable also expressed this view in the first line of the inspiring letter he wrote announcing Catherine's death, a line that I repeat here: "Dear Friends, Catherine's saintly, heroic, and glorious spirit passed to the next world at 2 A.M. October 25th." He was categorical in this email of November 6, 2013, to me: "Beyond doubt, Catherine is a heroine, an angel and a saint." These words were not used carelessly; they were based on years of the closest association.

In our Spiritual Struggles we are as Salmon Spawning

In chapter 7, I quoted Bernice Boulding Crooks that she marveled at the courage Catherine showed in battling her condition. Eileen Collins made the same observation. The heroism of Catherine's spirit was beautifully expressed in some of the most memorable lines that she wrote in her letter to the Bahá'ís of Salt Spring Island, on March 6, 1967, seven months before her death. In that letter, she used the analogy of the spawning salmon as a simple, but original and effective metaphor for spiritual struggle, not only for the individual, but for all humanity. We know now that Catherine's words were fully demonstrated by her deeds:

> Dear friends: the obstacles are many here. The obstacles are many where you are. We are all fighting upstream. I like to think of the salmon. He has plenty of problems to overcome and has to fight upstream too. Everything is pulling him back to the ocean to join the other kinds of fishes, but if he does, his kind will not survive. There is a power in him to struggle on, attain the goal and win the victory. That power in him is beyond all reasonable expectation. It is God-given. We too can win our victory and overcome terrible tests because we too have a God-given power within us. Our power is our knowledge of Bahá'u'lláh, our love for Him and our faith in Him. It can conquer the rocks of opposition, the downward pull of materialism, comforts, illness . . . if we allow ourselves to be pulled back, our kind—the human kind, will not survive.

The Huxtables consciously chose to place themselves in challenging pioneering situations, knowing full well that in so doing they would be tested. Bahá'u'lláh's Hidden Word comes to mind: "O SON OF MAN! The true lover yearneth for tribulation even as doth the rebel for forgiveness and the sinful for mercy."[307] But rare are those who dare. The situations of adversity they would face would require them to sink or swim. Indeed, they felt at times that they had failed in their mission, but they never gave up. In referring to their choice of St. Helena Island, Paisley Glen in her "In Memoriam" tribute "Catherine Heward Huxtable" (1967), wrote that the Huxtables chose "to tread a path which it seemed even angels feared."[308] We should not form any misconceived notions from Paisley Glen's words that the Huxtables were somehow pathologically fond of suffering. Their choices were dictated by the limited number of years that yet remained to Catherine and their mutual desire to contribute significantly to the implantation of the Bahá'í Faith in remote areas.

Although the Huxtables could not have foreseen the extent to which they would be tested when they arrived on Salt Spring Island and later on St. Helena, and although the situations in which they found themselves temporarily broke them, still they found the strength, through prayer, perseverance, and divine assistance, to endure and not give up. And, despite the many challenges they faced, the promised divine assistance always reached them. The pattern of their life, as Paisley Glen perceptively noted, was "trials and confirmations."[309]

At the end of her life, Catherine was filled with contentment and gratitude; she looked forward to her release after years of long-suffering. During her dying days, she knew the peace and serenity that come with the knowledge that she used up every last ounce of strength in the service of the Cause she loved so much. The last battle she fought, as she lay convulsed by the throes of death, was mercifully short. For Catherine, death was no shrouded "grim reaper," but the merciful angel of deliverance who bore her up on wings of joy.

St. Helena Island Contains a Hidden Treasure

The title of Wes Huxtable's biographical outline of Catherine's life, "A Conqueror for St. Helena," reflects the military metaphor that is used frequently in the Bahá'í sacred writings and the epistolary of Shoghi Effendi. But as I have explained in chapter 1, the title should not give offense as being overly triumphant, simply because it refers to the conquering of self—the only victory, 'Abdu'l-Bahá tell us, that is worth the fight. Although her name will undoubtedly be revered in the annals of the global Ten Year Plan, it is a fact—unlike her experiences in Toronto, Regina and Salt Spring Island—that no one became a Bahá'í through Catherine's direct teaching during the eighteen months that she lived on St. Helena. The reader should not misconstrue this observation as any minimization of her accomplishment. A far more subtle and mysterious spiritual dynamic was at work. The spirit that motivates any sincere act should not be measured by the sole criterion of *immediate* results. The fact that Catherine laid down her life on St. Helena will be a source of blessing for all St. Helenians for centuries to come, once they will have recognized the hidden treasure that once lived among them. The sacrifice that the wheelchair pioneer shares with her husband will undoubtedly inspire generations as yet unborn, both on St. Helena and around the world. In another sense, her legacy belongs to the greatness that 'Abdu'l-Bahá predicted for Canada in one of the two tablets written to that nation in the *Tablets of the Divine Plan* (1916–1917).

Dealing with Depression

We have seen in chapter 10 that during the last year of her life, Dr. John Noaks prescribed a stimulant to relieve Catherine's depression. In a letter written to Diana Dainty from the Kerrs' in West Vancouver, just weeks before the Huxtables arrived on Salt Spring Island in 1959, Catherine referred to lapsing into periodic "terrific depressions."[310] I should say here that one or more biochemical factors were no doubt involved in Catherine's bouts with this debilitating mood disorder. As was indicated in chapter 7, Cliff had been diagnosed by Dr. Bourdillon with an underactive thyroid while they were living on Salt Spring Island. Depression can be one of its side effects. In fact, Catherine wrote in her annual letter that both she and Cliff had been prescribed medication for an underactive thyroid.[311] The condition was remedied for Cliff through medication, but while the thyroxin pills brought her temporary relief, Catherine continued to battle with depression. (The central nervous system and the endocrine glands are more directly affected by certain types of muscular dystrophy). She endured and fought periodic depression until Dr. Noaks prescribed a stimulant. She wrote to Diana Dainty that she was grateful for the remedy.

True to her frankness, Catherine did not hesitate to disabuse others of their false impression if they praised her glowingly when she was in a "spiritual slump." She came to understand, however, that her depressions had nothing to do with the well-being of her soul. She concluded that she would not be held responsible for "all the nasty things one is inclined to do, think or say under such conditions."[312] In the same letter to Diana Dainty, she wrote that she suffered from guilt and despair at those times when she felt she was being less than cordial. But then, Catherine Huxtable, like so many other conscientious spiritual strivers, was simply being too hard on herself.

However, she gained "new insights," and with them some relief from the burdens of conscience, by reading chapter 9, "The Dark Night of the Soul," in Evelyn Underhill's classic work *Mysticism* (1911), and Abbé de Tourville's little booklet, *Letters of Direction* (trans. 1939). She wrote to Diana that what she judged to be lapses of conduct when she was suffering from depression would not be held against her by a loving and merciful God. She wrote that her understanding "may be implied in Bahá'u'lláh's teaching about the soul being unaffected by illness—just veiled, or cut off from experiencing its qualities." The words of Ann Kerr Linden bear repeating here: "You could feel that she was a person who had suffered intensely. She was at times in despair about what she was facing, and she experienced fear, frustration and worry, but she was not sunk by it. She was connected to God."[313]

The Testimony of Dr. Albin T. Jousse

Before closing this tribute, one more testimony throws light on the example of Catherine's life. Although the self is difficult to conquer in an absolute sense, I think it is true to say that the spirit of Catherine Huxtable's magnanimity conquered the weakness of her body. It is a fact that she outlived the medical prognosis of her projected life-span by fifteen years. Catherine's Toronto specialist, Dr. Albin T. Jousse, the director of the Lyndhurst Spinal Cord Center, a facility founded in 1945 that treated injured Canadian veterans returning from World War II, a man who had himself succeeded in the face of physical disability, wrote to Catherine shortly before her death. In response to her farewell letter, he expressed the conviction that the example of Catherine's life and influence was beyond any certain evaluation: "I have no doubt, however, that your life has been greatly prolonged by your high motivation, and I quite agree with you that it has been very full. I think your influence has undoubtedly been much greater than that of most humans and much greater than anyone could evaluate . . ."[314] Did Dr. Jousse intuit with these prescient words the spiritual legacy that Catherine would ultimately bequeath?

With Cliff's help, the upper class Torontonian overcame the challenges of her condition and her surroundings because she knew she was a pioneer, a realization that gave her deep joy, motivation, and satisfaction. Although the approach of death at thirty-five years of age once filled her with the anxious and conflicted emotions of a young mother who must abandon a much loved, thriving, sunny little boy, Catherine fully accepted that inevitable, God-ordained phenomenon that all must face. The last words she spoke to Cliff in the early hours of October 25, 1967, the determined but not anxious, simple utterance,

"I want to die", indicate not only that Catherine Huxtable had grown flesh-and-bone weary of her long years of suffering, but also that she had fully acquiesced to the will of God.

Her Rejection of the Stereotype of the Suffering Saint

Catherine Huxtable would probably smile at the attributions of saintliness and heroism, perhaps even remonstrate with anyone who would apply these descriptors to her. For great souls are not trapped by the image that others might make of them. She had already rejected the label that others would attribute to her when she said to one of her unnamed friends on the eve of their departure for St. Helena: "I don't aspire to be a saint; I would rather be one of God's teddy bears. I am really no different from anyone else. It is just that I know that I shall have less time than others."[315]

It was, of course, precisely the precious commodity of scarce time that galvanized her, and in the end made her life significantly different from that of her able-bodied friends, despite her heartfelt desire to be perceived and treated just like everyone else. Although Catherine acted naturally, and rejected any stereotype of the suffering saint, her special destiny, nonetheless, was to show all who were graced by her presence, that a life of adversity can produce the finest spirit of humanity. The lives of Catherine and Clifford Huxtable validate the old truth that noble souls will still lay down their lives for a cause—"one universal Cause, one common Faith," proclaimed by the Unifier of humanity as "the sovereign remedy and mightiest instrument for the healing of the world."[316]

∞12∞
AFTERWORD

- At this writing (2016), Knight of Bahá'u'lláh Cliff Huxtable, is still living on St. Helena Island, where he serves as a member of the Local Spiritual Assembly and sometime delegate to the Annual Convention of the Bahá'ís of South Africa. On August 13, 1969, Cliff married Delia Duncan, a St. Helenian who later became a Bahá'í. Their two children, Jane and Robert, are now living and working in Canada. Cliff and Delia travel to Canada from time to time to see old friends, but mostly to visit their children and grandchildren.
- Cliff and Catherine's son, Gavin Clifford Huxtable, who was born in 1962 when the Huxtables were living on Salt Spring Island, lived on St. Helena until he was fifteen years old. He completed his high school classes in Toronto, while he lived with his grandmother Heward. Studies at the University of British Columbia followed. Gavin is currently living in Ontario.
- Bernice Boulding Crooks, Catherine's companion-helper during the Huxtables' stay in Regina and Salt Spring Island, passed away while this book was being written. She died on June 16, 2014, on Saturna, one of the southern Gulf Islands of British Columbia. She was in her seventy-fifth year. Bernice was the first Bahá'í to have enrolled in the Gulf Islands, although she lived the greater part of her Bahá'í life as an isolated believer. She testified to Catherine's indomitable courage and that the Huxtables were agents of transformation in her own life. She is survived by her four children, Sam, Sandra, Shelly, Clifford, and her former husband Barry Crooks.
- Catherine's mother, Helen Bury Heward, outlived Colonel Heward by some forty-four years. She died in 2002 at the advanced age of ninety-eight years. Colonel Heward passed away in 1958, at the age of ninety.

- Catherine's sister Julia Wynne Harvie passed away in 1992, at the age of sixty-four.
- Madeleine Ashlin Davis, the other "Stouge," Catherine's much loved childhood friend from Toronto, moved to England and married a pediatrician, Dr. John Davis. Faithful to their friendship, Madeleine and Catherine exchanged letters until the end of Catherine's life. Madeleine passed away from cancer in 1993.
- The Reverend Pamela Webster, Catherine's longtime, devoted correspondent, introduced Catherine to the Unitarian church in Toronto where their spiritual search began. Pamela testified to the unforgettable quality of Catherine's faith and capacity to love. She is currently serving as an Episcopal priest in Ely, Minnesota, after having had a positive Bahá'í experience for some eight years.
- Ann Kerr Linden, a friend and contemporary of Reverend Pamela Webster, is still practicing as a psychiatric social worker in Toronto, following the death of her husband Sven Kerr in 2014. She testified to the palpable faith radiated by Catherine Huxtable.
- Fletcher Bennett died on July 31, 2013, and at his request is buried in Central Cemetery on Salt Spring Island in the same section as my parents Joyce Mary Halsted McLean and Allan James McLean, and other Salt Spring Bahá'ís, including the Danish-Canadian Tom Volquardsen, one of the pioneers who replaced the Huxtables when they left for St. Helena.
- Cliff Huxtable attended Fletcher Bennett's funeral and marveled at the positive effect of the Bahá'í Faith on the Bennetts' children and grand-children. Cliff was happy that he lived to see the flowering of the seeds that Catherine and he had planted on Salt Spring Island a half-century before.
- Fletcher's widow, Elinor Bennett, died peacefully on May 29, 2014, just two weeks after our last telephone interview about the early days of the Bahá'í community on Salt Spring Island. She is buried alongside her husband Fletcher in Central Cemetery on Salt Spring Island.

∞13∞
TRIBUTES TO CATHERINE AND CLIFF HUXTABLE

"She has died a martyr's death.... I am sure the day will come when people will travel to St. Helena from all over the world just to say a prayer at the grave of Catherine Huxtable." Hand of the Cause of God John Robarts in a letter to Cliff Huxtable, December 7, 1967.

"She was at times so radiant you could hardly bear to look at her." Beth McKenty speaking of Catherine to author.

"Cliff, I can never thank you enough for telling me of the Cause." Michael Rochester to the Huxtables, handwritten on the back of a letter from the National Teaching Committee.

"She had come to our home near Toronto to speak to some interested young people about the Bahá'í Faith and as they listened intently, their eyes never leaving her beautiful face, I wondered at the power in the soft-spoken words that held them spellbound." Joyce Mary Halsted McLean, mother of author, during the 1989 announcement of the Catherine Huxtable scholarship, celebrating twenty-five years of the Bahá'í Community on Salt Spring Island.

"She is in my very bones and my soul." Catherine's childhood friend, Madeleine Ashlin Davis, writing to Cliff after hearing of Catherine's death.

"Dear Cliff, what can I say? I feel I must tell you how I saw long ago when Stouge fell in love with you how you transformed her life, and how you made her happy, and how you gave peace to her. And your devotion to her, and your sheer physical effort on her behalf I count as one of the most remarkable human endeavours I have ever been privileged to see." Madeleine Ashlin Davis

"Her life on earth was such a heavenly miracle; her eternal life in that Exalted Realm will certainly be no less." Enid Wrate to Cliff Huxtable

"What a priceless gift you gave me—no wonder I can't thank you [enough] for it. From the time of those days when I was privileged to see how you served your family, I have never for a moment been discontented or unhappy with my own role of servitude, and I have understood the nobility of man." Enid Wrate to Cliff Huxtable on hearing of Catherine's death

"We know of course that all those who were privileged to come into contact with her in person or by her wonderful letters, can never be quite the same again and so much of what I am striving to be is largely because of the privileged position I had long years ago and being in daily contact with my little sister." Julia Heward Harvie to Cliff Huxtable

"I have always been so completely happy in having you as my brother-in-law, Cliff and I thank you with all my heart for giving Catherine the richest years of her life and I believe I know how very much you have meant to her." Julia Heward Harvie to Cliff Huxtable

"I wouldn't be a Bahá'í today if it hadn't been for her." Cliff Huxtable

∞14∞
MEMORABLE QUOTATIONS

"I came to St. Helena without illusions. I expected to find it very hard and I do. But I am glad I came for I am on my chosen highway, the path of service in the Cause of God, and I know my destination—nearness to God." Catherine Huxtable

"In our early days, when she was alone being driven in her car, she would on occasion suddenly and without warning break into a loud and perfect rendition of a Nelly Lutcher song. So delightfully out of character!" Cliff Huxtable

"They may think of your message as less than the dust, but there will be a seed sown and a lamp lighted which will never go out, and you know that many thousands of your Bahá'í friends all over the world will know you are there." Don MacLaren, World War I Flying Ace and early founder of Canada's aviation industry, letter of November 29, 1965, as the Huxtables made their way to St. Helena Island.

"I have never forgotten that night, in 1954, in Toronto, when the pair of you came down the aisle of that auditorium to greet me. I watched you come, all the way even though there was a fair sized group around me. There was such a sweetness on both your faces. A beauty." Florence Mayberry, on learning of Catherine's death.[317]

REPORTED SAYINGS OF FRANCIS ST. GEORGE SPENDLOVE

The following quotations of George Spendlove were reported by Cliff Huxtable in a letter of January 7, 1966, to the Canadian NSA. Parenthetical remarks by Cliff.

"If you don't know your heroes, they don't belong to you."

"Every door is open until it is slammed shut in your face." (On deciding what to do and on overcoming obstacles.)

"Nothing is as it seems." (To the overenthusiastic concerning an "easy" possibility.)

"Be careful! The Bahá'ís are very precious people." (On crossing the street in heavy traffic.)

"Always call to be sure it is convenient before dropping in on a friend." (But his door was always open.)

"I never stay at a home unless invited by the husband." (Either the non-Bahá'í or the Bahá'ís.)

"And did you do it?" (On being informed by someone of the "old guard" that 'Abdu'l-Bahá told him/her to do such and such. That made them quiet every time.)

"Have you prayed about it? I don't know any better than you. Ask God then act." (To one seeking his advice)

"God loves you very much. You will scarcely believe what is happening when you begin to realize how much God loves you." (To the woebegone Bahá'í)

OTHER REPORTED SAYINGS OF GEORGE SPENDLOVE

"Be very careful what you pray for; you may get it." (Quoted in *The Canadian Báhá'í News*, September, 1967, p. 4.)

14 ∞ Memorable Quotations

"God can change everything, even your past." (from my aunt Hope Halsted Hubbert to author) [My aunt explained that he meant that God can change the way we look at our past.]

"There is no such thing as a coincidence in life."[318]

∞Appendix I∞
A CHILD MEETS CATHERINE HEWARD HUXTABLE

A few vague memories of Catherine Huxtable linger from my childhood. One of them has been prompted by the following lines written in 1989 by my mother, Joyce McLean, quoted above, on the occasion of the 25 anniversary celebration of the establishment of the Local Spiritual Assembly of Salt Spring Island, British Columbia in 1964. On December 2, in a public address in Central Hall, where the first public talk had been given by Mrs. Helen Wilks on May 18, 1963, the LSA announced the establishment of the Catherine Huxtable Scholarship, which was offered to all students of the Gulf Islands. On that occasion my mother said:

> Our family first met Cathy Heward in the fall of 1952 when she was twenty-years-old, and she immediately captured our hearts. She had come to our home near Toronto to speak to some interested young people about the Baháʼí Faith and as they listened intently, their eyes never leaving her beautiful face, I wondered at the power in the soft-spoken words that held them spellbound . . ." (From the archives of the Salt Spring Island LSA)

I would have been seven years old at that time of Catherine's visit to our home. If I did in fact witness that gathering, I cannot clearly distinguish now what is true memory from imagination. But it was a family wedding on May 1, 1955, that created the first and only vivid memory of Catherine. As often happens in one's senior years, this memory remains as clear now in my seventy-first year as the day it occurred. My mother's youngest sister, Edna Halsted, was being married to Ronald Nablo. That joyful occasion afforded the opportunity of a brief, passing meeting between a twenty-three-year-old woman in a wheelchair and a ten-year-old child, nephew of the bride.

My mother and Michael Rochester had been put in charge of arranging the wedding; they chose a rental hall in West Toronto. As young as I was, it was still clear to me that this occasion would be special. At home, a flurry of anticipation and excitement preceded the wedding. Mother dressed my younger brother Steve and me in blue blazers, white shirts and grey flannel trousers, and fitted us with neckties—an accessory that we had seen being worn only by men. It made us feel officially more grown up. I had never seen our older sister Mary Lou looking so sophisticated: she wore a bright party dress. Dad wore a suit, not his usual casual attire. Although I no longer remember what mother wore, a few black and white snapshots of the McLean children taken at the wedding survive. Although children are sometimes reluctant and shy before a camera, we were all smiling freely at the happy event.

I suddenly came face to face with Catherine who was sitting just in front of a doorway. I stood still and gazed at her, wondering, I suppose, at the sight of a woman in a wheelchair. But Catherine, sensing my dilemma, lost no time and took the initiative. With her playful sense of humor, she smiled and winked at me. Raising her right hand, she fired off a bullet in my direction, accompanied by the sound of a mock pistol shot. In that brief moment, Catherine Huxtable entered the world of my consciousness. For six more decades, her memory was revived in passing conversations with Joyce McLean, Don and Diana Dainty, Ronald and Edna Nablo, Elizabeth and Michael Rochester and others, until she came to life again in the pages of this book.

∞Appendix 2∞
HOW THE HUXTABLES WERE NAMED KNIGHTS OF BAHÁ'U'LLÁH

*The following material is based on the information supplied by Michael Rochester in emails of April 22 and July 20, 2014, to author.

- On January 1, 1968, Michael wrote to the Hand of the Cause of God John Robarts, following a conversation they had had about who were the Knights of Bahá'u'lláh to Canadian goals. An extract from that letter reads: "I have often wondered whether Cliff and Catherine Huxtable could be regarded as Knights of Bahá'u'lláh since they opened the Gulf Islands, which the Guardian had, before his passing, approved as an alternative to Anticosti [Island]."

- In light of this letter, on January 3, 1968, Mr. Robarts wrote to the Hands of the Cause residing in the Holy Land regarding the status of Patrick Robarts, Mr. Robarts' son, as a Knight of Bahá'u'lláh. The Guardian had written "and son" on his World Crusade map, beside the names of John and Audrey Robarts for Bechuanaland (now Botswana). Patrick's name did not subsequently appear on the Roll of Honor after Shoghi Effendi's passing, despite the fact that Shoghi Effendi had declared Patrick to be a Knight during the Robarts' pilgrimage in January 1955. In that same letter, Mr. Robarts wrote: "Also it is my opinion that the names of Clifford and Catherine Huxtable should be included. They opened the Gulf Islands which the Guardian had approved as an alternate goal to Anticosti."

- On September 14, 1969, the Hands of the Cause in the Holy Land, wrote to Mr. Robarts confirming that the Universal House of Justice had decided to add Patrick's name to the illuminated Roll of Honor.

- The letter continued: "You will also be happy to know that after receiving your recommendation, and after review of all the facts bearing on the question, the

House of Justice has also decided that both Clifford and Catherine Huxtable should be listed as Knights of Bahá'u'lláh for the Gulf Islands, which the Guardian approved as an alternate to Anticosti, as a virgin goal of the Ten Year Crusade…"

- On December 1, 1969, Mr. Robarts wrote to the Canadian NSA informing them of the decision of the Universal House of Justice.

- Thus, ten years after the Huxtables arrived in the Gulf Islands, and twelve years after Shoghi Effendi's death, Catherine and Clifford Huxtable were named Knights of Bahá'u'lláh for the Gulf Islands.

- Catherine died two years before she was named a Knight of Bahá'u'lláh.

∞Appendix 3∞
TIMELINE OF THE LIVES OF CATHERINE AND CLIFFORD HUXTABLE

1932. Catherine Rudyerd Heward is born on January 6 in the village of Charlwood, Surrey, England.

1939. Colonel Stephen A. Heward and Helen Heward move Catherine and her sister Julia Wynne to Toronto; they settle at 7 Clarendon Crescent a few blocks south of the boundary of Forest Hill Village; Catherine begins her elementary education at Havergal College (Anglican), a private school for girls.

1940. Catherine first meets her childhood friend, Madeleine Ashlin, later Davis, at Havergal College; they nickname one another "Stouge;" they remain bosom friends for life.

1942. Catherine is diagnosed with muscular dystrophy.

1945. Catherine graduates to secondary school at Bishop Strachan School (Anglican), a private school for girls.

1947. Catherine is forced to begin to use the wheelchair, but she resists it for the next two years.

1948/49. Cliff learns about the Bahá'í Faith from his brother Weston who becomes a Bahá'í through Gerald Robarts, one of the three sons of the future Hand of the Cause, John Robarts and Audrey Robarts, while Wes and Gerald are attending Forest Hill Collegiate.

1949. Cliff's life suddenly changes when he accidentally injures a young boy in the head after he throws a rock over a bridge in east Toronto; his spiritually aware science teacher Hiles Carter gives him wise, loving counsel to help him deal with the accident; it is a calamity that eventually becomes a providence.

1949. Catherine withdraws from Bishop Strachan School because of her weakened condition; she meets Ann Cartwright (later Kerr Linden) and Pamela Ball (later Webster); Catherine takes a sea-journey to England with her mother and sister Julia; she begins to live again after she experiences an epiphany; she overcomes her sadness and awakens to the beauty of trees, the arts and music; her self-confidence increases.

1950. Madeleine Ashlin moves to Brazil from Havergal College to join her father; Cliff and Catherine meet at the Fall Freshman Dance at Victoria College, the University of Toronto; Cliff crosses the floor to ask Catherine to dance, then realizes that she is in a wheelchair; Joyce Sachs (later Asquith) introduces them; a group of friends visits the Hewards' following the dance; Cliff has the strong intuition that he is going to marry Catherine.

1950. Through Pamela Ball Webster, Catherine investigates the Unitarian church; Catherine becomes a Unitarian at First Unitarian Toronto where the Reverend William Phillip Jenkins is minister; Cliff tells Catherine about the Bahá'í Faith.

1950–1952. Cliff and Catherine discuss Unitarianism and attend Bahá'í firesides together; their courtship begins; within two years they decide to marry.

1952. Catherine and Cliff attend Elizabeth Manser (later Rochester's) fireside where they meet their spiritual mentor, George Spendlove; it is a life-changing moment for them both.

1952. During the month of April, Catherine and Cliff become Bahá'ís at the home of John and Audrey Robarts at 4 Millbank Avenue in Forest Hill Village; because of muscular dystrophy, Catherine decides to break off the relationship with Cliff, but she has a change of heart with Cliff's reassurance; marriage has to wait until Cliff graduates from university.

1954. Cliff graduates from the University of Toronto.

1955. Cliff and Catherine marry at 7 Clarendon Crescent; the Unitarian Reverend Jenkins officiates because the Bahá'í marriage ceremony does not yet have legal status in Ontario; Don Dainty performs the Bahá'í ceremony on behalf of the LSA of Toronto; George Spendlove attends, "toasts" the bride and groom and amuses the guests during his speech; the Huxtables honeymoon in the vicinity of the Bahá'í House of Worship in Wilmette, Illinois.

1955–1957. The Huxtables begin married life in their bed-sitting apartment at 7 Clarendon Crescent; they both serve on the Toronto LSA; they begin firesides at home; Cliff finds a job in sales for Canadian Laboratory Supplies and then in teaching at Western Technical and Commercial High School; Catherine is employed with petit point work for Marina Creations; Winnifred Harvey returns from pilgrimage (1956) and meets with the Toronto Bahá'ís to deliver the Guardian's emphatic message that they should disperse from the city.

1957–1959. Following Shoghi Effendi's sudden death, and despite Catherine's disability, the Huxtables decide to pioneer to Regina to strengthen the fallen LSA; they are accompanied by Eileen White (later Collins) who assists Catherine as companion-helper; Cliff finds a job as a representative in adult education; seventeen-year-old Bernice Boulding (later Crooks) becomes Catherine's companion-helper after Eileen's marriage to Albert Vail; during their summer vacation (1958) to West Vancouver, the Huxtables become intrigued by the view of the Gulf islands; after a successful period of Bahá'í teaching, the Regina LSA is reformed.

1959–1961. The Huxtables pioneer to the Gulf Islands, settling on Salt Spring Island; Cliff works for local "baron" Gavin Mouat as a self-employed laborer and deckhand on the ferries; Gavin convinces Cliff to apply for the short-term position of principal of the Saturna Island Elementary School; the application is successful.

1962–1964. Gavin Clifford Huxtable is born on Salt Spring Island; Cliff becomes a teacher and joint vice-principal at the Salt Spring Island High School; the first LSA of the Gulf Islands is formed on Salt Spring Island (1964).

1964–1965. Cliff's health deteriorates because of the serious stresses of professional and domestic responsibilities; the Huxtables endure mischief and threats of violence from an emotionally disturbed neighbor; medical specialists in Vancouver recommend that Cliff take two years of bed rest; Cliff attends the Bahá'í National Convention in Winnipeg; the Huxtables decide to pioneer to St. Helena Island in the South Atlantic.

1965–1966. After leaving Salt Spring Island, the Huxtables begin a five-month travel-teaching trip across Canada as far as Montreal to inspire the Bahá'ís to win the goals of the Nine Year Plan.

1966. After visiting Dublin, London and Hampshire, U.K., the Huxtables sail from Southampton on the Capetown Castle; they arrive on St. Helena on April 9, 1966; St. Helenian Bahá'í, Basil George, leaves for university in the UK in June, 1966; the Huxtables remain as the only Bahá'ís on the island; temporary accommodation is found at the Consulate Hotel and later at Colonel Gilpin's flat on Napoleon Street; exhausted and sick, Cliff collapses in bed for two months; on his thirty-fourth birthday (August 18) the Governor offers Cliff a job as teacher and principal of the Secondary Selective School; they move to their first home at the top of 1 Ladder Hill; Hand of the Cause John Robarts and his wife Audrey Robarts spent six remarkable hours visiting with Huxtables on their way back to Canada from Africa.

1967. Catherine's health deteriorates rapidly; their love is renewed and their marriage healed as they find the way to talk openly about Catherine's passing; the night before Catherine dies, they proclaim the Faith to a leading clergyman and his wife; Catherine dies in the early hours of October 25, 1967; her funeral is attended by the Governor and his wife and mixed representatives of St. Helenian society; on the third evening after her death, an ecstatic, youthful Catherine, dressed in a bridal gown, appears to Cliff in a radiant vision; the dance that was always denied to them because of Catherine's muscular dystrophy finally takes place; Cliff afterward writes: "There is no death."

∞ Appendix 4 ∞
WRITTEN ON HER GRAVESTONE

"They that have forsaken their country for the purpose of teaching Our Cause—these shall the Faithful Spirit strengthen through its power. . . . Whoso hath attained their presence will glory in their meeting, and all that dwell in every land will be illumined by their memory." — Bahá'u'lláh

"Deeply grieved passing Catherine Huxtable. Assure Cliff and her family fervent prayers Shrines progress her soul. Her devoted heroic services unforgettable."

Cable from the Universal House of Justice to the NSA of South and West Africa, October 30, 1967

Notes

Chapter 1: The Scope of this Book

1. http://en.wikipedia.org/wiki/Knights_of_Bah%C3%A1'u'll%C3%A1h. This webpage mistakenly lists Catherine Huxtable as the only Knight of Bahá'u'lláh for the Gulf Islands, British Columbia. Cliff Huxtable is the other Knight. The date of arrival was October 13, 1959, not September 1959.
2. 2. W. G. Huxtable, "A Conqueror for St. Helena". http://bahai-library.com/huxtable_conqueror_st_helena. The author, Weston "Wes" Huxtable, was Catherine's brother-in-law.
3. For biographical sketches of the lives of all the Hands of the Cause known to date see Barron Harper's *Lights of Fortitude: Glimpses into the Lives of the Hands of the Cause of God* (Oxford: George Ronald Publisher, 1997).

Chapter 2: Catherine's Early Life and Formative Years: England and Toronto (1932–1950)

4. Information on the Heward family has been provided by Cliff Huxtable in detailed emails to author dated November 20, 22, 26, 28, December 3, 2013, February 12, 2014, and an email from Michael Rochester, dated December 9, 2013. This information has been supplemented by my own research.
5. Biographical Dictionary of Architects in Canada (1800–1950) http://dictionaryofarchitectsincanada.org/architects/view/246.
6. Except where otherwise indicated, this section relies on the articles by Wes Huxtable and Roger White mentioned in the Acknowledgements, and on emails dated November 20, 26, 28, 2013, from Cliff Huxtable to author. I have also provided some contextual description supplied by information gleaned from emails from Michael Rochester and

interviews with Pamela Webster and from my own research.
7. Email dated July 25, 2014, from Cliff Huxtable to author.
8. So named because the patient developed a vivid, strawberry colored tongue and rosy rash. In 1941, antibiotics were not yet fully developed or widely prescribed. They effectively cured the disease.
9. For further information on Chief Justice Anglin, see http://www.scc-csc.gc.ca/court-cour/judges-juges/bio-eng.aspx?id=francis-alexander-anglin.
10. Email dated November 20, 2013, from Cliff Huxtable to author.
11. "I die a little more each day," Catherine Heward as told to Ron Kenyon, in *Liberty* magazine, 24. No date.
12. Email dated May 14, 2014, from Cliff Huxtable to author.
13. Telephone interview with Pamela Webster by author, January 28, 2014, and email dated July 8, 2014, from Pamela Webster to author.
14. Telephone interview with Pamela Webster by author, December 10, 2013.
15. Paraphrase of Catherine's comments in a letter to Diana Dainty, March 7, 1960.
16. Except where otherwise indicated, the material in the following three sections has been reproduced from notes taken during a telephone conversation between Ann Kerr Linden and author, December 1, 2013.
17. Email dated November 28, 2013, from Cliff Huxtable to author.
18. Weston G. Huxtable, A Conqueror for St. Helena: A Tribute to Catherine Huxtable, http://bahai-library.com/huxtable_conqueror_st_helena.
19. "She Makes Gay Coasters for Marina Creations," *The Toronto Telegram*, 1956. The date was obliterated on the original article found in the Huxtable papers. Further Internet research was inconclusive.
20. Telephone interview with Pamela Webster by author, December 10, 2013.
21. Email dated December 4, 2013, from Cliff Huxtable to author.
22. Email dated November 10, 2013, from Cliff Huxtable to author.
23. Weston G. Huxtable, *A Conqueror for St. Helena: A Tribute to Catherine Huxtable.* http://bahai-library.com/huxtable_conqueror_st_helena.

24. Email dated December 11, 2013, from Cliff Huxtable to author.
25. Interview with Pamela Webster by author, December 10, 2013.
26. Email dated December 27, 2013, from Cliff Huxtable to author.
27. "Recollections," transcript of a tape-recorded talk made by Cliff Huxtable at the request of the Universal House Justice, St. Helena Island, March (no day), 1978. Copy courtesy of Cliff Huxtable to author.
28. Telephone interview of October 31, 2013, with Ronald Nablo by author.
29. Gerald had two brothers, Aldham (Aldie) and Patrick, and a younger sister Nina, now Nina Tinnion.

Chapter 3: The Freshman Dance, Unitarianism, the Bahá'í Faith (1950–1952)

30. Email dated December 5, 2013, from Cliff Huxtable to author.
31. Telephone interview of December 10, 2013, with Pamela Webster by author.
32. Email dated July 8, 2014, from Pamela Webster to author.
33. Telephone interview of December 10, 2013, with Pamela Webster by author.
34. My thanks to the archivist of First Unitarian in Toronto, Sara Griffiths, for providing me with this information in an email of January 21, 2014.
35. A phrase that originated in the good works performed for the disadvantaged by Toronto's born-again, crusading mayor, William Howland, who was first elected in 1885. See http://www3.bc.sympatico.ca/st_simons/cr9606.htm.
36. Telephone interview of December 10, 2013, with Pamela Webster by author.
37. Letter dated June 22, 1952, from Catherine Heward to Michael Rochester. Michael became a Bahá'í in August of the same year.
38. Telephone interview of December 11, 2013, with Pamela Webster by author.
39. Ibid.
40. Email dated December 11, 2013, from Cliff Huxtable to author.

41. Telephone interview of December 11, 2013, with Pamela Webster by author.
42. A "humanist" here means that Jenkins believed in bettering the condition of humanity, and helping people to help themselves.
43. "William Phillip Jenkins," http://uudb.org/articles/williamphillipjenkins.html.
44. Information provided by Douglas Martin who was serving at the time on the Toronto LSA. Email of December 20, 2013, to author. The date of the legalization of the Bahá'í marriage ceremony in Ontario and British Columbia is given in Shoghi Effendi, *Messages to Canada* (Thornhill: Bahá'í Canada Publications, 1999), p. 281, n. 54.
45. Telephone interview of December 10, 2013, with Pamela Webster by author.
46. Telephone interview of December 11, 2013, with Pamela Webster by author.
47. Telephone interview of December 10, 2013, with Pamela Webster by author.
48. Ibid.
49. Email dated December 17, 2013, from Cliff Huxtable to author.
50. Ibid.
51. This is my formulation of the Bahá'í view of the afterlife, not the statement of anyone attending the firesides.
52. Telephone interview of December 10, 2013, with Pamela Webster by author.
53. Email dated December 17, 2013, from Cliff Huxtable to author.
54. The contents of the following section have been paraphrased from Catherine's letter of August 1, 1952, to Michael Rochester and from an email dated December 11, 2013, from Cliff Huxtable to author.
55. The core activities consist of children's classes, youth empowerment activities, devotionals and study circles.
56. "I would like to comment that it has been found over the entire world that the most effective method of teaching the Faith is the fireside meeting in the home. Every Bahá'í as a part of his spiritual birthright, must teach, and the one avenue where he can do this most effectively is by inviting friends into his home once in 19 days, and gradually

attracting them to the Cause. After the individuals have confidence in the pioneer, and the pioneer in the individuals, then they can be taught and confirmed in the Faith. This method is far more effective than advertising in newspapers, public lectures etc. The Guardian is encouraging the believers over the world, including those on the home fronts, to engage in this method of teaching." From a letter written on behalf of the Guardian to the Bahá'í Group of Key West, Florida, March 31, 1955, in *Bahá'í News*, no. 292, pp. 9–10, quoted in no. 828 of *Lights of Guidance: A Bahá'í Reference File*, Comp. Helen Bassett Hornby, 4th ed. (New Delhi: Bahá'í Publishing Trust, 1996), p. 246.

57. "Headed Exhibit of Canadiana at Museum," Obituary in *The Globe and Mail*, May 11, 1962.
58. Comment from Douglas Martin to author during the annual conference of the Association for Bahá'í Studies in Montreal, Quebec, 2012, celebrating the centenary of 'Abdu'l-Bahá's visit to North America.
59. Email dated January 9, 2014, to author from David Spendlove, son of George and Dorothy Spurr Spendlove.
60. Letter of Shoghi Effendi addressed to George Spendlove, Toronto, Ontario, 11 December 1936, Special Collections, GL1/093/02, Canadian Bahá'í Archives.
61. "In Memoriam," *The Bahá'í World: An International Record*, vol. XIII, 1954–1963 (Haifa: The Universal House of Justice, 1970), pp. 895–899. Although the article was unsigned, Douglas Martin informed me that while he was serving on the Universal House of Justice, it was understood by his colleagues that the author of the article was Rúhíyyih Khánum. Email of December 24, 2013, from Douglas Martin to author. The Guardian's widow knew George Spendlove well from the time of her childhood when he attended Bahá'í meetings in the Maxwell Home in Montreal.
62. Ibid. Although Madame Rabbaní does not mention drooping eyelids, it has been mentioned by several Bahá'ís who knew George Spendlove. I first heard the remark from Husayn Banani at my parents' home in Toronto; it is also apparent in his photographs.
63. Both quotations cited by Rúhíyyih Khánum for George Spendlove's "In Memoriam," *The Bahá'í World*, vol. XIII, 1954–1963, p. 898.

64. Email dated December 11, 2013, from Cliff Huxtable to author.
65. Letter of Shoghi Effendi addressed to George Spendlove, Washington, D.C., U.S.A., July 26,1936, Special Collections, GL1/093/01, Canadian Bahá'í Archives.
66. For the definitive history of this historic Bahá'í family, read Violette Nakhjavani's two volume study, *The Maxwells of Montreal* (Oxford: George Ronald Publisher, 2011 and 2012).
67. The above information is from the transcript of author Marlene Macke's notes of her interview with Cliff Huxtable on August 7, 2000, in Oshawa, Ontario. The interview contains recollections of George Spendlove's life as told by George Spendlove to Cliff Huxtable. The interview features mainly memories of George Spendlove, but it also contains Cliff's brief personal impressions of other Bahá'ís of that time, such as Laura Davis, Douglas Martin, Vera Raginsky, and Winnifred Harvey.
68. "May Ellis Maxwell," compiled by the Universal House of Justice, published in *The Bahá'í World*, vols. I–XII, 1925–1954, pp. 516–28, http://bahai-library.com/may_ellis_maxwell_bw.
69. Rúhíyyih Khánum, "In Memoriam," for George Spendlove, *The Bahá'í World*, vol. XIII, 1954–1963, p. 896.
70. Will C. van den Hoonaard, *The Origins of the Bahá'í Community of Canada, 1898–1948*. (Waterloo: Wilfred Laurier Press, 1998), p. 105.
71. From Marlene Macke's transcript of her interview with Cliff Huxtable on August 7, 2000, in Oshawa, Ontario. During my few visits in 2014 to the home of George's son, David Spendlove, and his wife Rosemary in Ottawa, he showed me an impressive collection of his father's academic articles in archaeology.
72. Ibid.
73. Emails dated January 7, 2014, from Elizabeth Rochester, and email dated December 10, 2013, from Michael Rochester to author.
74. Email dated January 7, 2014, from Elizabeth Rochester to author.
75. The artist Joyce Frances Devlin told me during a personal interview held in her home in Burritts Rapids, Ontario, on December 7, 2013, that when she first encountered the Bahá'í Faith as a young art student in Vancouver, the meetings seemed to be filled with old ladies with white hair.

76. Email dated November 22, 2013, from Cliff Huxtable to author. The source of the phrase "sweet Bahá'í and Bahá'í" is found in the third stanza of the poem "The Seven Spiritual Stages of Mrs. Marmaduke Moore" by the master of light verse Ogden Nash. Thanks to Michael Rochester for the reference.
77. Marlene Macke, *Take My Love to the Friends: The Story of Laura R. Davis*. (St. Marys: Chestnut Park Press, 2009). The account of Laura's pilgrimage is found on pp. 203–213.
78. Email dated December 19, 2013, from Elizabeth Rochester to author.
79. Email dated November 22, 2013, from Cliff Huxtable to author.
80. Email dated December 11, 2013, from Cliff Huxtable to author.
81. Email dated December 19, 2013, from Cliff Huxtable to author.
82. "Recollections," transcript of a talk given by Cliff Huxtable, St. Helena Island, March, 1978. (no day).
83. The reference to the radio talk is found in Madeleine Ashlin's letters to Catherine dated December 6, 1952, and February 6, 1953. (Canadian Bahá'í Archives). Catherine's fireside talk at my parents' home was mentioned in my mother's announcement of the Catherine Huxtable Scholarship on the occasion of the twenty-fifth anniversary of the establishment of the Local Spiritual Assembly of the Bahá'ís of the Gulf Islands, December 2, 1989, at Mahon Hall in Ganges, Salt Spring Island. Thanks to the LSA of Salt Spring Island for providing an archival copy of my mother's remarks.
84. Douglas Martin, email dated December 10, 2013, to author.
85. Email dated December 19, 2013, from Elizabeth Rochester to author.
86. Catherine's approximate height was provided by Cliff Huxtable in an email of August 22, 2014, to author.
87. Telephone interview of December 10, 2013, with Pamela Webster by author.
88. Ibid.
89. Email dated July 10, 2014, from Pamela Webster to author. Additional information was found at the website http://exlibris.pbworks.com/w/page/30050262/Katharine%20Lucy%20Ball.
90. Telephone interview of December 10, 2013, with Pamela Webster by author.

91. Ibid.
92. This judgment is based on numerous examples of Catherine's descriptions of the individuals that came into the Huxtables' lives, that were found in various letters in the Huxtable papers.
93. Telephone interview of December 11, 2013, with Pamela Webster by author.
94. Telephone interview of December 13, 2013, with Pamela Webster by author.
95. Telephone interview of December 11, 2013, with Pamela Webster by author.
96. Ibid.

Chapter 4: The Summer Letters to Michael Rochester: Catherine's Life and Faith (1952)

97. Email dated April 16, 2014, from Cliff Huxtable to author.
98. Mike prefers to be called "Michael" the name by which he has been known.
99. The details in the next three sentences, including the name of the author, were found at http://leavesandpages.com/2013/02/26/review-a-lamp-is-heavy-by-sheila-mackay-russell/.
100. Email dated March 6, 2014, to author. Harlan Ober was an early American Bahá'í (1881–1962) who married Grace Robarts, the aunt of Hand of the Cause John Robarts. They married at the suggestion of 'Abdu'l-Bahá, who presided at their wedding in 1912. Harlan was an active travel-teacher and public speaker who also served on the Executive Board of the Bahá'í Temple Unity and the NSA of the United States and Canada. After the passing of Grace Robarts, he remarried and in 1956, pioneered to Pretoria, South Africa where he became a member of the Auxiliary Board. Husband and wife, Gladys and Ben Weeden served Shoghi Effendi in various capacities at the Bahá'í World Centre from 1947–1952. Their duties included contacting government officials on behalf of the Guardian. Both were appointed members to the first International Bahá'í Council (1951–1952), the precursor of the Universal House of Justice, first elected in 1963.

101. Mike Rochester to Catherine Huxtable, "Saturday evening" [postmark unclear Jul 18 '52], Cliff Huxtable Papers, 1063-1-1-1, Canadian Bahá'í Archives.
102. Audrey FitzGerald Robarts (1905–2000) was the wife of the Hand of the Cause John Aldham Robarts (1901–1991). He was appointed by Shoghi Effendi among the third contingent of Hands of the Cause in 1957 while he and Audrey were pioneering in Southern Rhodesia, now Zimbabwe.
103. "John Leonard was steadfast in Falklands," *The American Bahá'í*, July 13, 2006. My thanks to archivist Roger Dahl for providing photocopies of the material on John Leonard's life.
104. A short concise article written for a dictionary or encyclopedia
105. Many thanks to Pauline Igao for her informative emails dated March 7 and 9, 2014.
106. Except where otherwise indicated, the following information was provided to author in an email of July 10, 2014, and in a telephone interview with Pamela Webster by author, December 11, 2013.
107. Pam [Webster] to Cathy Huxtable, Sunday, May [15], 1960, Catherine Huxtable Papers, 1016-4-4-230, Canadian Bahá'í Archives. Pamela wrote "Cambridge, Maine," but Michael Rochester who knew the McClellans well informed me the location was Massachusetts.
108. Especially in her letter dated May 28, 1960, in which Pamela enumerated her teacher's qualities. They included the use of primary Bahá'í scriptural sources, patience, consistence, and love. Pamela wrote that she was fortunate because she and Catherine were "first real friends." Pam [Webster] to Catherine Huxtable, 2-4 March 1962, Catherine Huxtable Papers, 1016-4-3-212, Canadian Bahá'í Archives.
109. Pam [Webster] to Catherine Huxtable, March 2-4, 1962, Catherine Huxtable Papers, 1016-4-3-212, Canadian Bahá'í Archives.
110. Nora Nablo Moore is the sister of my uncle-by-marriage Ronald Nablo.
111. Ross Woodman died peacefully at home in London, Ontario, on March 20, 2014. He was the last surviving member of the original Canadian NSA elected in 1948 at the Maxwell Home in Montreal. In 1993, he received the Distinguished Scholar Award from the Keats–

Shelley Association of America.
112. Jamie Bond was probably returning to Coral Harbour on Southampton Island, District of Keewatin, at the northern end of Hudson Bay, where he served as the first pioneer to the Canadian Arctic (1950–1953). In the spring of 1953, he and his wife Gale Bond pioneered to the District of Franklin (1953–1963), in the Northwest Territories, today Nunavut, a service for which they were named Knights of Bahá'u'lláh by Shoghi Effendi. Jamie had pioneered previously to Northern Ontario, then to Charlottetown, Prince Edward Island. Mr. Bond had been greatly inspired by 'Abdu'l-Bahá's two tablets to Canada in the Tablets of the Divine Plan. He also served later on the National Spiritual Assembly of New Zealand. Thanks to Michael Rochester for the information contained in this endnote and the circumstances surrounding his meeting with Jamie Bond. Emails dated February 24 and 27, 2014 to author. Other details from Shoghi Effendi, *Messages to Canada*, p. 280, n. 39.
113. Catherine was not aware at the time of writing that Michael Rochester had already met Jamie Bond at supper in Hart House at the University of Toronto sometime between September 1950 and May 1951. As it turned out, the two men served together on the National Spiritual Assembly of the Bahá'ís of Canada for the fifteen years during which Jameson Bond served on that institution (1967–1982). Michael Rochester's years of service on that same body totalled twenty-nine years (1963–1992).
114. The deep river is in fact the Ottawa River that reaches its greatest depth of 402 feet (122 meters) at the town of Deep River that housed employees for nearby Chalk River. Both towns had their own nuclear laboratories. Deep River and Chalk River are 6 miles (11 km.) distant from one another.
115. Michael's response is quoted by Catherine in her letter dated August 12, 1952.
116. "Dr. Koch and Glyoxylyide/Malonide," http://www.cancerinform.org/kocha.html.
117. Letter to Don and Diana Dainty dated March 7, 1960.
118. Email dated August 27, 2014, from Cliff Huxtable to author.

Chapter 5: Courtship and Marriage: Life in Toronto (1950–1957)

119. Email dated December 10, 2013, from Cliff Huxtable to author.
120. Ibid.
121. Bahá'u'lláh, "Questions and Answers," *The Kitáb-i-Aqdas*, no. 13, pp. 110–111.
122. Email dated December 18, 2013, from Cliff Huxtable to author.
123. Ibid.
124. Ibid.
125. Ibid.
126. D. Window to Cliff Huxtable, 24 February 1968, Cliff Huxtable Papers, 1063-1-1-11, Canadian Bahá'í Archives.
127. Email dated November 19, 2013, from Cliff Huxtable to author.
128. Julia [Harvie] to Mr. and Mrs. C.S. Huxtable, 9 May 1955, Catherine Huxtable Papers, 1016-2-4-99, Canadian Bahá'í Archives.
129. Email dated December 17, 2013, from Cliff Huxtable to author.
130. Email dated December 4, 2013, from Cliff Huxtable to author.
131. Mimeographed letter from the Huxtable papers, December 1959.
132. Janet Huxtable was Cliff's sister. She was engaged to be married to John Hus, a man who was raised in the Dutch East Indies. About the time of her marriage, Janet withdrew from Bahá'í activities. Her marriage to John Hus failed, and she later married their doctor Herman Austrian. Email dated November 23, 2013, from Cliff Huxtable to author.
133. For the fuller explanation of this project with the blind, see the details of the Huxtables' Canadian teaching-trip in chapter 8, and the visit with Beth and Jack McKenty in Milwaukee, Wisconsin.
134. Email dated December 3, 2014, from Cliff Huxtable to author.
135. Will C. van den Hoonaard, *The Origins of the Bahá'í Community in Canada, 1898–1948*, p. 185.
136. See Will C. van den Hoonaard's "Shopflocher, Siegfried (1877–1953)". http://www.bahai-encyclopedia-project.org/index.php?view=article&catid=56%3Aa-selection-of-articles&id=

69%3Aschopflocher-siegfried&option=com_content&Itemid=74. The article also contains passing references to Lorol.
137. Letter dated October 1, 1982, written by Winnifred Harvey to her niece Heather Harvey. Many thanks to Heather Harvey for providing me with a copy of Winnifred's letter. Winnifred wrote that the first Bahá'í talk she heard in Winnipeg was given by Sylvia King, who emphasized too much that the Guardian was not a pope. She was more impressed by Rowland Estall's persistence, his pointed questions and the discussions they had together.
138. Emails dated January 3, 2014, and October 2, 2014, from Heather Harvey to author.
139. The first western pilgrim house was located at 4 Haparsim Street but was replaced at the request of 'Abdu'l-Bahá and funded by the generosity of William Harry Randall. The building was completed during the ministry of Shoghi Effendi. Currently it is occupied by the department of the Secretariat and other offices.
140. "Recollections," from a transcript of a tape-recorded talk by Cliff Huxtable, St. Helena Island, March, 1978.
141. "Recollections," pp. 3–4.

Chapter 6: Regina, Saskatchewan: Pioneers Building Community (1957–1959)

142. "It is not sufficient to pray diligently for guidance, but this prayer must be followed by meditation as to the best methods of action and then action itself. Even if the action should not immediately produce results, or perhaps not be entirely correct, that does not make so much difference, because prayers can only be answered through action and if someone's action is wrong, God can use that method of showing the pathway which is right." "Prayers Answered Through Action," from a letter written on behalf of Shoghi Effendi to an individual believer, August 22, 1957, in *Lights of Guidance*, p. 461, no. 1508.
143. Shoghi Effendi, *Messages to Canada*, letter dated 13 January, 1956, written on behalf of the Guardian, p. 232.
144. Email from Will van den Hoonaard dated March 25, 2014 to author. Dr. van den Hoonaard remembers that the information on the

duration of Mary Zabolotny McCulloch's stay came from Knights of Bahá'u'lláh, Jameson and Gale Bond. See also Shoghi Effendi, *Messages to Canada*, letter dated 18 July, 1957, written on behalf of the Guardian, p. 264.

145. "Recollections," from a transcript of a tape-recorded talk by Cliff Huxtable, St. Helena Island, March, 1978.

146. Cliff Huxtable, "The Opening of the Gulf Islands to the Bahá'í Faith by Knights of Bahá'u'lláh, Catherine Heward Huxtable and Cliff Huxtable," transcript of a tape-recorded talk, July 31, 1998, Salt Spring Island. Personal copy of author.

147. The account in the next two sections is based on a telephone interview with Eileen Collins by author on November 30, 2013, and an email to author dated July 19, 2014.

148. Roger White's first collection of poems, *Another Song Another Season: Poems and Portrayals* (George Ronald Publisher, 1979) was a great success with the Bahá'í community and made his reputation as a poet among his fellow Bahá'ís. Among his other poetic works that followed were *The Witness of Pebbles* (1981), *Occasions of Grace* (1992), and a novella, *A Sudden Music* (1983). Facing death by terminal cancer, Roger wrote some of his simplest but profoundest verse in his last slim volume entitled *The Language of There* (New Leaf, 1992).

149. "Recollections," transcript of a tape-recorded talk by Cliff Huxtable, March 1978, St. Helena Island.

150. Letter dated January 25, 1958, from Catherine Huxtable to Don and Diana Dainty.

151. Before he left for Regina, Cliff Huxtable described his job in a mimeographed letter to friends, December 14, 1957.

152. Information about Catherine's personal teaching activities was provided by Eileen Collins in a telephone interview of November 30, 2013, by author.

153. Email dated June 26, 2014, from Eileen Collins to author.

154. Will C. van den Hoonaard, *The Origins of the Bahá'í Community of Canada, 1898–1948* (Waterloo: Wilfred Laurier Press, 1998), pp. 220–221.

155. "Let us also bear in mind that the keynote of the Cause of God is not dictatorial authority but humble fellowship, not arbitrary power, but

the spirit of frank and loving consultation." Shoghi Effendi, *Bahá'í Administration: Selected Messages, 1922–1932* (Wilmette, IL: Bahá'í Publishing Trust, 1974), p. 63.
156. Will C. van den Hoonaard in *The Origins of the Bahá'í Community of Canada, 1898–1948*, p. 221.
157. Rúhíyyih Khánum to Catherine Huxtable, April 13, 1958, Catherine Huxtable Papers, 1016-2-1-81, Canadian Bahá'í Archives.
158. The Huxtables' annual letter, December, 1958.
159. Cliff Huxtable, "Recollections," transcript of tape-recorded talk, St. Helena Island, March, 1978.
160. Catherine Huxtable's letter to the Daintys, dated March 26, 1959.
161. These family names are taken from Shoghi Effendi, *Bahá'í Administration: Selected Messages, 1922–1932* (Wilmette, IL: Bahá'í Publishing Trust, 1974) pp. 44–51.
162. Letter dated March 26, 1959, from Catherine Huxtable to Don and Diana Dainty and email dated June 26, 2014, from Eileen Collins to author.
163. See Patricia Verge, *Angus: From the Heart* (Cochrane, Alberta: Springtime Publishing, 1999), pp. 43-51.
164. Angus Cowan served on the NSA from 1953–1957 and 1961–1970. "Angus Cowan (1914–1986)," http://bahainews.ca/en/node/954.
165. Patricia Verge, *Angus: From the Heart*, p. 49.
166. Email dated October 22, 2014 from Cliff Huxtable to author.
167. Patricia Verge, *Angus: From the Heart*, p. 49.
168. Ibid., p. 46.
169. The above anecdote was sent by Cliff Huxtable in an email dated September 12, 2014, to author.
170. Email dated September 12, 2014, from Cliff Huxtable to author.
171. The District of Keewatin was a large territory fanning out from the northwest shore of Hudson Bay. Dick Stanton settled in Baker Lake, a hamlet that is located near to Canada's central-point.
172. Annual letter from Catherine Huxtable, December, 1959.
173. Roger White, "Catherine Heward Huxtable, Knight of Bahá'u'lláh, 1932–1967," *The Bahá'í World (1963–1968)*, vol. XIV, pp. 313–315.
174. 'Abdu'l-Bahá, "The Two Natures in Man", *Paris Talks* (London: Bahá'í

Publishing Trust, 1969), pp. 60–62.
175. Shoghi Effendi, *Citadel of Faith: Messages to America, 1947–1957.* (Wilmette, IL: Bahá'í Publishing Trust, 1965), p. 13.
176. Shoghi Effendi, *Messages to Canada.* (Thornhill: Bahá'í Canada Publications, 2nd ed., 1999), p. 160.

Chapter 7: West to the Gulf Islands: The Joy and Trials of Knighthood (1959–1965)

177. The above clarification was supplied by Cliff Huxtable in an email dated September 30, 2014, to author.
178. Email from Will van den Hoonaard dated March 25, 2014, to author.
179. The island is now owned and managed by the government of the province of Quebec as a game reserve and park that attracts between 3000–4000 hunters annually.
180. Mimeographed annual letter dated December, 1959, written by the Huxtables from Salt Spring Island.
181. "Recollections," transcript of a talk given by Cliff Huxtable, St. Helena, Island, March, 1978. (no day).
182. A former resident told me that in 1968, the population was generally acknowledged to be 1500 throughout the year, but swelled to 2500 during the summer.
183. Cliff Huxtable, "The Opening of the Gulf Islands to the Bahá'í Faith by Knights of Bahá'u'lláh, Catherine Heward Huxtable and Cliff Huxtable," transcript, personal copy of author.
184. Annual mimeographed letter of the Huxtables dated December, 1959.
185. "Company History," http://www.mouatstrading.com/history.html. The Mouats' descendants, with their in-laws, the Toynbees, purchased the company's assets in 1969. In the year 2000, the Toynbees and Mouats expanded ownership to include the Almond and Bell families who now manage the family enterprise.
186. For further details on the Mouats' business enterprises on Salt Spring Island, see "A Hundred Years in the Heart of Salt Spring," *Times Colonist* (Victoria), November 18, 2007.
187. Cliff Huxtable, "The Opening of the Gulf Islands to the Bahá'í Faith

by Knights of Bahá'u'lláh, Catherine Heward Huxtable and Cliff Huxtable," transcript.
188. Letter of Shoghi Effendi addressed to Miss Catherine Heward, Toronto, Ontario, Canada, October 5, 1953, Catherine Huxtable Papers, 1016-2-1-77, Canadian Bahá'í Archives .
189. This endnote covers four different items from the Catherine Huxtable Papers in the Canadian Bahá'í Archives: Rúhíyyih to Catherine Heward, February 25,1955, 1016-2-1-78; Rúhíyyih to Catherine Huxtable, April 13,1958, 1016-2-1-81; Rúhíyyih to Catherine Huxtable, February 9, 1963, 1016-2-1-79; Rúhíyyih Rabbaní to Catherine Huxtable, July1, 1963, 1016-2-1-80. The 1966 letter was provided by Cliff Huxtable.
190. Regrettably, this portrait along with two cases of Joyce Devlin's paintings and sketches were destroyed by an emotionally disturbed woman who bought her house while the art work was being stored there. From a personal interview with Joyce Devlin, December 7, 2013.
191. From notes taken during a personal interview with Joyce Frances Devlin by author at her home in Buritts Rapids, Ontario, December 7, 2013.
192. Thanks to Norma E. Hoyle for bringing Steve Fletcher's anecdote to my attention. Quoted with his permission from personal copy of Steve Fletcher.
193. From a mimeographed annual letter of the Huxtables, November, 1960.
194. Telephone interview of May 12, 2014, with Elinor Bennett by author.
195. The following information is based on a telephone interview with Bernice Boulding Crooks on April 25, 2014, and her death-notice on Saturna Island written by Priscilla Ewbank in Island Tides, July 24, 2014.
196. The Chinook word "Skookum" has been explained in the section above. "Bluff" means blunt, frank or hearty.
197. Email dated July 29, 2014, from Cliff Huxtable to author.
198. From the Huxtables' annual letter from Regina, December, 1958.
199. On the back of a small black-and-white photograph, stamp-dated October 1959, Catherine wrote in green ink: "This pic is of me and our

"daughter" Birdie, taken in September, in West Vancouver. Birdie has declared her wish to become a Bahá'í!"
200. "Japanese Canadians," http://www.thecanadianencyclopedia.ca/en/article/japanese-canadians/.
201. Telephone interview with Bernice Crooks by author, April 25, 2014.
202. Email dated March 26, 2014, from Cliff Huxtable to author.
203. Cliff Huxtable, "The Opening of the Gulf Islands to the Bahá'í Faith by Knights of Bahá'u'lláh, Catherine Heward Huxtable and Cliff Huxtable," transcript of a tape-recorded talk made by author, July 31, 1998, Salt Spring Island.
204. Telephone interview with Elinor Bennett by author, May 14, 2014.
205. Ibid.
206. Ibid.
207. The names of the then serving, former or future NSA members were: Angus Cowan, Peggy Ross, Husayn Banani, Tom Anaquod, Michael Rochester, Douglas Martin, Rowland Estall, Elizabeth Rochester, Glen Eyford.
208. Marjorie Merrick was the mother of Diana Merrick Dainty mentioned above.
209. Quotations from Elinor Bennett in this section are taken from a telephone interview by author, May 14, 2014.
210. Email dated March 14, 2014, from Cliff Huxtable to author.
211. The Huxtables' annual letter, December, 1963.
212. The information contained in this section is taken from telephone interviews with Elinor Bennett by author on April 29 and May 14, 2014.
213. "Garden of Ridvan, Baghdad," http://en.wikipedia.org/wiki/Garden_of_Ridv%C3%A1n,_Baghdad.
214. My thanks to Professor Necati Alkan for clarifying the role of the respective Ottoman governors of Baghdad. Email dated May 29, 2015, to author.
215. These individuals were identified from a black-and-white photograph supplied by Cliff Huxtable.
216. The information provided in this section is contained in various annual letters from the Huxtables to their friends and in "Recollections," a

transcript of a talk given by Cliff Huxtable, St. Helena, Island, March, 1978.
217. Cliff Huxtable, "The Opening of the Gulf Islands to the Bahá'í Faith by Knights of Bahá'u'lláh, Catherine Heward Huxtable and Cliff Huxtable," transcript of a tape-recorded talk, July 31, 1998, Salt Spring Island.
218. Ibid.
219. Ibid.
220. Cliff Huxtable, "Recollections," transcript of a talk given by Cliff Huxtable, St. Helena, Island, March, 1978.
221. Cliff Huxtable, "The Opening of the Gulf Islands to the Bahá'í Faith by Knights of Bahá'u'lláh, Catherine Huxtable and Cliff Huxtable," transcript of a tape-recorded talk, July 31, 1998, Salt Spring Island. Emphasis added by author.
222. Telephone interview of December 11, 2013, with Pamela Webster by author.
223. Email dated July 2, 2014, from Pamela Webster to author.
224. Pam Webster to Catherine Huxtable, May 18, 1960, Catherine Huxtable Papers, 1016-4-4-231, Canadian Bahá'í Archives. Pamela wrote that she "simply wallowed in a 30 page masterpiece."
225. Email dated July 2, 2014, from Pamela Webster to author.
226. Cliff Huxtable, "The Opening of the Gulf Islands to the Bahá'í Faith by Knights of Bahá'u'lláh, Catherine Huxtable and Cliff Huxtable," from transcript of a tape-recorded talk, July 31, 1998, Salt Spring Island.
227. Ibid.
228. Ibid.
229. Ibid.
230. Ibid.
231. Ibid.
232. Ibid.
233. Cliff Huxtable, "Recollections," transcript of a talk given by Cliff Huxtable, St. Helena, Island, March, 1978.
234. The last quoted appeal of Mr. Khádem to the National Convention in the above passage is based on Cliff Huxtable's recollections. The story

of Munír Vakíl is taken from Javidukht Khádem, *Zikrullah Khádem: The Itinerant Hand of the Cause of God* (Wilmette, IL: Bahá'í Publishing Trust, 1990), pp. 99–101. A photo of Mr. Vakíl in front of the hut he built himself is found on p. 100. The Guardian's refusal to allow Mr. Vakíl to stay on Kuria Maria is not based on the written recollections of Mr. Khádem in his wife's book, but it was related to the author from Cliff Huxtable's recollections of the address of the Hand of the Cause of God to the Winnipeg National Convention.

Chapter 8: Adieu Salt Spring Island: The Canadian Teaching Trip (1965–1966)

235. Cliff Huxtable, "The Opening of the Gulf Islands to the Bahá'í Faith by Knights of Bahá'u'lláh, Catherine Huxtable and Cliff Huxtable," from the transcript of a tape-recorded talk, July 31, 1998, Salt Spring Island.
236. All quotations from Catherine Huxtable, unless otherwise specified, are taken from her letter of August 27, 1966, to Rúhíyyih Khánum.
237. Cliff Huxtable, "The Opening of the Gulf Islands to the Bahá'í Faith by Knights of Bahá'u'lláh, Catherine Huxtable and Cliff Huxtable," from the transcript of a tape-recorded talk, July 31, 1998, Salt Spring Island.
238. Letter of November 4, 1965 signed by Douglas Martin, Secretary. The Canadian National Office was at that time located at 15 Lola Road, Toronto, Ontario. From the Huxtable papers.
239. Email dated June 27, 2014, from Cliff Huxtable to author.
240. Information on Don MacLaren taken from the Bahá'í Community of Canada website, http://ca.bahai.org/canadian-bah%C3%A1%C3%AD-history/historical-figures/donald-maclaren-1893-%E2%80%93-1988.
241. Letter from Don MacLaren to the Huxtables, November 29, 1965, in the Huxtable papers.
242. Letter of Shoghi Effendi addressed to Miss Catherine Heward, Toronto, Ontario, Canada, October 5, 1953, Catherine Huxtable Papers, 1016-2-1-77, Canadian Bahá'í Archives.

243. From a hymn by William Cowper (1731–1800). The first stanza reads, "God moves in a mysterious way / His wonders to perform; / He plants His footsteps in the sea / And rides upon the storm." The saying has morphed into the abbreviated sentence "God works in mysterious ways." It is sometimes erroneously attributed to the Bible.
244. Letter dated September 12, 1966, from Cliff Huxtable to Gil Humphreys, in the Huxtable papers.
245. Letter dated May 26, 1965, from Catherine Huxtable to Diana Dainty.
246. John A. Robarts to Catherine Huxtable, June 28,1967, Cliff Huxtable Papers, 1063-1-2-37, Canadian Bahá'í Archives.
247. Letter dated February 14, 1967, written by John Robarts to the Huxtables from the Bahá'í National Office, 15 Lola Road, Toronto, Ontario, in the Huxtable papers.
248. Email dated March 21, 2014, from Cliff Huxtable to author.
249. "To this institution [national headquarters] you will soon be adding the Maxwell Home in Montreal, which should be viewed in the nature of a national Shrine, because of its association with the beloved Master, during His visit to Montreal." Shoghi Effendi, *Messages to Canada* (Thornhill: Ontario, Bahá'í Canada Publications, 1999), p. 179.
250. Email dated August 7, 2014, from Cliff Huxtable to author.
251. Letter dated September 12, 1966, from Cliff Huxtable to Gil Humphreys, in the Huxtable papers.

Chapter 9: St. Helena Island (1966–1967)

252. "Recollections," transcript of a tape-recorded talk made by Cliff Huxtable at the request of the Universal House Justice, St. Helena Island, March (no day), 1978. Copy courtesy of Cliff Huxtable to author.
253. Letter dated November 2, 1966, from Mr. William Masehla, secretary of the NSA of South and West Africa, in Huxtable papers.
254. The above account has been conflated from Cliff's verbal and written memories of their arrival contained in the transcript of "Recollections," (1978) and his letter dated December 12, 1966, to Gil Humphreys.

255. Letter dated August 16, 1966, from John Robarts to the Huxtables, in the Huxtable papers.
256. Information on Jagdish Saminaden and Barbara George was found at the website devoted to British Bahá'í history. See https://bahaihistoryuk.wordpress.com/.
257. From "St. Helena: Basil George receives OBE," Juanita Brock, the Saint Helena Herald, May 23, 2003. Accessed at http://sartma.com/art_207_7_46_1.html.
258. The information in the above section was taken from the transcript of Cliff Huxtable's "Recollections." (1978)
259. Letter dated September 12, 1966, from Cliff Huxtable to Gil Humphreys, in the Huxtable papers.
260. From the transcript of Cliff Huxtable's tape-recorded "Recollections," St. Helena Island, March, 1978. Tommy Heuvel's comment is not found in the Huxtable papers; it is repeated by Cliff in a letter dated September 11, 1966, to the Canadian NSA.
261. Catherine Huxtable in a letter to Roger White dated August 10, 1966, in the papers of Michael Rochester.
262. Cliff Huxtable in a letter to the Canadian NSA dated September 11, 1966, in the Huxtable papers.
263. Ibid.
264. Catherine Huxtable in a letter to the Canadian NSA, dated August 24, 1966, in the papers of Michael Rochester.
265. In Cliff Huxtable's letter dated September 11, 1966, to the Canadian NSA.
266. Ibid.
267. Shoghi Effendi, *Dawn of a New Day: Messages to India 1923–1957* (New Delhi: Bahá'í Publishing Trust, n.d.), p. 136.
268. In Cliff Huxtable's letter to the Canadian NSA, dated September 11, 1966.
269. Letter from William Sears dated January 25, 1967, written from Nairobi, Kenya, in the Huxtable papers.
270. Information contained in an undated letter of Auxiliary Board Member Tommy Heuvel, written to the Huxtables, in the Huxtable papers.

271. Douglas Martin, Secretary, National Spiritual Assembly of the Bahá'ís of Canada to Mr. and Mrs. C. Huxtable, February 13,1967, Cliff Huxtable Papers, 1063-1-3-42-2, Canadian Bahá'í Archives.
272. Letter from John Robarts to the Huxtables, dated February 14, 1967, in the Huxtable papers.
273. Email dated September 12, 2014, from Cliff Huxtable to author. John Robarts' image of the bird is drawn from the Venerable Bede's eighth-century *Ecclesiastical History of England.* Bede's text reads: "The present life of man upon earth, O king, seems to me, in comparison with that time which is unknown to us, like to the swift flight of a sparrow through the house wherein you sit at supper in winter, with your ealdormen and thegns, while the fire blazes in the midst, and the hall is warmed, but the wintry storms of rain or snow are raging abroad. The sparrow, flying in at one door and immediately out at another, whilst he is within, is safe from the wintry tempest; but after a short space of fair weather, he immediately vanishes out of your sight, passing from winter into winter again. So this life of man appears for a little while, but of what is to follow or what went before we know nothing at all. If, therefore, this new doctrine [Christianity] tells us something more certain, it seems justly to deserve to be followed." (Chapter XIII) Available online at Project Gutenberg. http://www.gutenberg.org/files/38326/38326-h/38326-h.html
274. Letter dated January 10, 1967, from Cliff Huxtable to the NSA of South and West Africa, in the papers of Michael Rochester.
275. Ibid.
276. Letter dated March 6, 1967, from Catherine Huxtable to the Bahá'ís of the Gulf Islands (Salt Spring and Saturna Islands).
277. Letter dated August 24, 1966, from Catherine Huxtable to the Canadian NSA, in the papers of Michael Rochester.
278. Letter dated March 6, 1967, from Catherine Huxtable to the Bahá'ís of the Gulf Islands. From the archives of the Salt Spring Island LSA.
279. Letter dated January 10, 1967, from Cliff Huxtable to the NSA of South and West Africa, in the papers of Michael Rochester.
280. Ibid.
281. Letter dated January 10, 1967, from Cliff Huxtable to the NSA of

South and West Africa, in the papers of Michael Rochester.

Chapter 10: Death and Resurrection: Dancing with an Angel (1967)

282. Letter dated January 10, 1967, from Cliff Huxtable to the NSA of South and West Africa, in the papers of Michael Rochester.
283. Letter dated September 11, 1967, from Cliff Huxtable to Helen Heward, in the Huxtable papers.
284. Email dated October 22, 2014, from Cliff Huxtable to author.
285. Letter dated September 26, 1967, from Cliff Huxtable to Elizabeth and Michael Rochester, in the Huxtable papers.
286. Ibid.
287. See *The Canadian Bahá'í News*, nos. 198-200, July-September, 1966. This reference reached me courtesy of Michael Rochester.
288. Letter dated November 13, 1967, to Elizabeth and Michael Rochester, in the Huxtable papers.
289. 'Abdu'l-Bahá, *Some Answered Questions*, comp. and trans. by Laura Clifford Barney, 4th ed. (Wilmette, IL: Bahá'í Publishing Trust, 1981), pp. 251–253.
290. Hand of the Cause John A. Robarts to Cliff Huxtable, 7 December 1967, Cliff Huxtable Papers, 1063-1-5-81, Canadian Bahá'í Archives.
291. The word "handicap" used by Michael Rochester was usual parlance at this time.
292. To be accurate, this comment must mean that Shoghi Effendi was aware that the Huxtables intended to pioneer from Toronto to Regina, Saskatchewan, to assist with the reestablishment of the fallen Regina LSA. Shoghi Effendi died on November 4, 1957; the Huxtables did not leave Toronto until December 26, 1957.
293. Handwritten eulogy in the papers of Michael Rochester.
294. Rúhíyyih to Catherine Heward, 25 February 1955, Catherine Huxtable Papers, 1016-2-1-78, Canadian Bahá'í Archives.
295. Letter dated October 25, 1967, to NSA members from Douglas Martin, secretary, in the Huxtable papers.
296. Douglas Martin, Secretary, National Spiritual Assembly of the Bahá'ís of Canada to Cliff Huxtable, February 29,1968, Cliff Huxtable Papers,

1063-1-5-84, Canadian Bahá'í Archives.
297. Margaret Leonard to Cliff Huxtable, March 11,1968, Cliff Huxtable Papers, 1063-1-5-93, Canadian Bahá'í Archives.

Chapter 11: Catherine Heward Huxtable: A Life Remembered (1932–1967)

298. Bahá'u'lláh, *The Kitáb-i-Íqán, The Book of Certitude*. Trans. Shoghi Effendi (Wilmette, IL: Bahá'í Publishing Trust, 2003), p. 240.
299. Shoghi Effendi, *Bahá'í Administration: Selected Messages, 1922–1932* (Wilmette, IL: Bahá'í Publishing Trust, 1974), p. 66.
300. Roger White, quoted in "Catherine Heward Huxtable, Knight of Bahá'u'lláh, 1932–1967," *The Bahá'í World (1963–1968)*, vol. XIV, pp. 313–315.
301. Nabíl-i-A'zam, *The Dawn-Breakers; Nabíl's Narrative of the Early Days of the Bahá'í Revelation*, Trans. Shoghi Effendi (Wilmette, IL: Bahá'í Publishing Trust, 1962), p. 93.
302. Catherine's brother-in-law, Weston Huxtable, quoting Catherine. See W. G. Huxtable, *A Conqueror for St. Helena: A Tribute to Catherine Huxtable*, http://bahai-library.com/huxtable_conqueror_st_helena.
303. Hand of the Cause John A. Robarts to Cliff Huxtable, December 7, 1967, Cliff Huxtable Papers, 1063-1-5-81, Canadian Bahá'í Archives.
304. An appellation given to the outstanding Canadian pioneer Marion Jack by 'Abdu'l-Bahá who was also called an "immortal heroine" by Shoghi Effendi. Rúhíyyih Rabbaní, *The Priceless Pearl* (London: Bahá'í Publishing Trust, 1969), p. 126.
305. Email dated November 5, 2014, from Michael Rochester to author.
306. Roger White, "Catherine Heward Huxtable, Knight of Bahá'u'lláh, 1932–1967," *The Bahá'í World (1963–1968)*, vol. XIV, pp. 313–315.
307. Bahá'u'lláh, *The Hidden Words of Bahá'u'lláh*, Trans. Shoghi Effendi (Wilmette, IL: Bahá'í Publishing Trust, 1989), no. 49, from the Arabic.
308. Although the article was unsigned, Michael Rochester, who was serving on the NSA at that time, informed me that the author was Paisley Glen. "Catherine Heward Huxtable, 1932–1967," *The*

Canadian Bahá'í News, November, 1967, p. 4.
309. Ibid.
310. Letter dated October 7, 1959, from Catherine Huxtable to Diana Dainty.
311. Annual letter from the Huxtables dated November, 1960.
312. Letter dated October 7, 1959, from Catherine Huxtable to Diana Dainty.
313. Telephone interview with Ann Kerr Linden by author, April 8, 2014.
314. W.G. Huxtable quoting from a letter written by Dr. A. T. Jousse to Catherine Huxtable, in *A Conqueror for St. Helena: A Tribute to Catherine Huxtable*, http://bahai-library.com/huxtable_conqueror_st_helena.
315. Roger White, "Catherine Heward Huxtable, Knight of Bahá'u'lláh, 1932–1967," *The Bahá'í World (1963–1968)*, vol. XIV, pp. 313–315.
316. Bahá'u'lláh, *Epistle to the Son of the Wolf*, Trans. Shoghi Effendi (Wilmette, IL: Bahá'í Publishing Trust, 1988), p. 62.

Chapter 14: Memorable Quotations

317. Florence Mayberry to Cliff Huxtable, January 14, 1968, Cliff Huxtable Papers, 1063-1-5-83, Canadian Bahá'í Archives.
318. Hand of the Cause John A. Robarts to Cliff Huxtable, December 7, 1967, Cliff Huxtable Papers, 1063-1-5-81, Canadian Bahá'í Archives.

Bibliography

'Abdu'l-Bahá. *Some Answered Questions*. Compiled and translated by Laura Clifford Barney, 4th ed. Wilmette, IL: Bahá'í Publishing Trust, 1981.

———. *Paris Talks: Addresses Given by 'Abdu'l-Bahá in Paris in 1911–1912*. 11th ed. London: Bahá'í Publishing Trust, 1969.

"A Hundred Years in the Heart of Salt Spring." *Times Colonist* (Victoria). November 18, 2007.

"Angus Cowan (1914–1986)." Canadian Bahá'í News Service. At http://bahainews.ca/en/node/954

Bahá'u'lláh. *Epistle to the Son of the Wolf*. Translated by Shoghi Effendi. Wilmette, IL: Bahá'í Publishing Trust, 1988.

———. *The Hidden Words of Bahá'u'lláh*. Translated by Shoghi Effendi. Wilmette, IL: Bahá'í Publishing Trust, 1989.

———. *The Kitáb-i-Íqán: The Book of Certitude*. Translated by Shoghi Effendi. Wilmette, IL: Bahá'í Publishing Trust, 2003.

———. "Questions and Answers." *The Kitáb-i-Aqdas: The Most Holy Book*. Wilmette, IL: Bahá'í Publishing Trust, 1993.

"Barbara George." U.K. Bahá'í History Project, August 7, 2012. At https://bahaihistoryuk.wordpress.com/

Biographical Dictionary of Architects in Canada (1800-1950). At http://dictionaryofarchitectsincanada.org/architects/view/246

Brock, Juanita. "St. Helena: Basil George receives OBE." *Saint Helena Herald*, May 23, 2003. At http://sartma.com/art_207_7_46_1.html.

"Can anything good come out of Toronto?" *Deep Dove Crier*, June 1996. At http://www3.bc.sympatico.ca/st_simons/cr9606.htm.

"Company History." At the website of Mouat's Trading Co. Ltd. http://www.mouatstrading.com/history.html

"Don MacLaren (1893–1988)." Bahá'í Community of Canada. http://ca.bahai.org/canadian-bah%C3%A1%C3%AD-history/historical-figures/donald-maclaren-1893-%E2%80%93-1988.

"Dr. Koch and Glyoxylyide/Malonide." at the website cancerinform.org. This information was derived from Daniel Haley's book *Politics In Healing*. At http://www.cancerinform.org/kocha.html.

Eddis, Charles. "William Phillip Jenkins." *Dictionary of Unitarian and Universalist Biography*, posted February 15, 2012. At http://uudb.org/articles/williamphillipjenkins.html.

Ewbank, Priscilla. "Bernice [Boulding] Crooks, 1940–2014." *Island Tides*. July 24, 2014.

"F. St. George Spendlove 1897–1962." *Bahá'í World: An International Record*, vol. XIII, 1954–1963. Compiled on behalf of the Universal House of Justice. Haifa: Bahá'í World Center, 1970.

"Firesides More Effective than Publicity." *Bahá'í News*, 292. March 31, 1955.

"Garden of Ridván, Baghdad." Wikipedia. http://en.wikipedia.org/wiki/Garden_of_Ridv%C3%A1n,_Baghdad.

Glen, Paisley. "Catherine Heward Huxtable, 1932–1967." *The Canadian Bahá'í News*, November, 1967.

Harper, Barron. *Lights of Fortitude: Glimpses into the Lives of the Hands of the Cause of God*. Oxford: George Ronald Publisher, 1997.

Huxtable, Cliff. "Recollections." Transcript of a tape-recorded talk. March, 1978 (no day). St. Helena Island.

———. "The Opening of the Gulf Islands to the Bahá'í Faith by Knights of Bahá'u'lláh, Catherine Heward Huxtable and Cliff Huxtable." Transcript of a tape-recorded talk. July 31, 1998, Salt Spring Island.

Huxtable, W. G. "A Conqueror for St. Helena." *Bahá'í News*, 1974–09. http://bahai-library.com/huxtable_conqueror_st_helena.

"Headed Exhibit of Canadiana at Museum" [Obituary of Francis St. George Spendlove]. *The Globe and Mail*. May 11, 1962.

Heward, Catherine and Ron Kenyon. "I die a little more each day." *Liberty*, p. 24, no date.

"Jagdish Saminaden." at the website U.K. Bahá'í Histories, December 9, 2011. https://bahaihistoryuk.wordpress.com/

"Japanese Canadians." http://www.thecanadianencyclopedia.ca/en/article/japanese-canadians/.

"John Leonard was Steadfast in Falklands." *The American Bahá'í*. July 13, 2006.

"Katherine Lucy Ball." At http://exlibris.pbworks.com/w/page/30050262/Katharine%20Lucy%20Ball

Khadem, Javidukht. *Zikrullah Khadem: The Itinerant Hand of the Cause of God.* Wilmette, IL: Bahá'í Publishing Trust, 1990.

"Knights of Bahá'u'lláh." At http://en.wikipedia.org/wiki/Knights_of_Bah%C3%A1'u'll%C3%A1h

Lights of Guidance: A Bahá'í Reference File. Compiled by Helen Bassett Hornby, 4th rev. ed. New Delhi: Bahá'í Publishing Trust, 1996.

Macke, Marlene. *Take My Love to the Friends: The Story of Laura R. Davis.* St. Marys, Canada: Chestnut Park Press, 2009.

———. Transcript of interview with Cliff Huxtable, August 7, 2000. Oshawa, Ontario.

"May Ellis Maxwell." Compiled on behalf of the Universal House of Justice. *The Bahá'í World*, vols. I–XII, 1925–1954. At http://bahai-library.com/may_ellis_maxwell_bw

Nabíl-i-A'zam. *The Dawn-Breakers: Nabíl's Narrative of the Early Days of the Bahá'í Revelation.* Translated by Shoghi Effendi. Wilmette, IL: Bahá'í Publishing Trust, 1962.

Rabbaní, Rúhíyyih *The Priceless Pearl*. London: Bahá'í Publishing Trust, 1969.

Russell, Sheila MacKay. "A Lamp is Heavy." *Leaves and Pages* (blog), February 26, 2013. At http://leavesandpages.com/2013/02/26/review-a-lamp-is-heavy-by-sheila-mackay-russell/.

"She Makes Gay Coasters for Marina Creations," *The Toronto Telegram*, 1956. No date.

"Supreme Court Justice, the Right Honourable Francis Alexander Anglin, P.C." At http://www.scc-csc.gc.ca/court-cour/judges-juges/bio-eng.aspx?id=francis-alexander-anglin.

Shoghi Effendi. *Bahá'í Administration: Selected Messages, 1922–1932.* Wilmette, IL: Bahá'í Publishing Trust, 1974.

———. *Citadel of Faith: Messages to America, 1947–1957.* Wilmette, IL: Bahá'í Publishing Trust, 1965.

———. *Dawn of a New Day: Messages to India, 1923–1957.* New Delhi: Bahá'í Publishing Trust, 1970.

———. *Messages to Canada*. Thornhill: Bahá'í Canada Publications, 2nd ed., 1999.

"The Bahá'í Community of Salt Spring Island, 25 Years (1989)." Archives of the Local Spiritual Assembly of the Bahá'ís of Salt Spring Island, British Columbia, Canada.

Van den Hoonaard, Will C. *The Origins of the Bahá'í Community of Canada, 1898–1948*. Waterloo: Wilfred Laurier Press, 1998.

Verge, Patricia. *Angus: From the Heart*. Cochrane, Alberta: Springtime Publishing, 1999.

White, Roger. "Catherine Heward Huxtable, Knight of Bahá'u'lláh, 1932–1967." *Bahá'í World: An International Record*, vol. XIV, 1963–1968. Compiled on behalf of the Universal House of Justice. Haifa: Bahá'í World Center, 1974.

———. "Point a Loving Camera." *The Canadian Bahá'í News*, nos. 198–200. July–September, 1966.

"William Phillip Jenkins." At http://uudb.org/articles/williamphillipjenkins.html.

INDEX

1953 British Mt. Everest Expedition, 114

'Abdu'l-Bahá: 88, 98, 110, 127, 144, 194; on sainthood, 98; writings, talks, and exhortations, 63, 172, 185
Aboriginal. *See* First Nations
Acco (Israel). *See* Akká
Air Canada, 137
Akká (Israel)
American Service to the Blind, 141
Anaquod, Sophie, 92–93
Anaquod, Tom, 92–93; aids in Huxtables' home purchase, 95; family of, 92
Anderson, Joan, 110
Anderson, Ted, 110
Anglin, Ch. Justice Francis Alexander, 24
anti-fluoridation controversy. *See* Regina, Saskatchewan
Anticosti Island, 99–100, 175, 198–99; initial attempts at pioneering, 81–82
Appleton, Doug, 91
Ashlin Davis, Madeleine, "Stouge", 47 146–47; early friendship, 24–25; introduces Catherine to Pamela Webster, 36; later life, 190; origin of nickname, 24; reaction to Catherine's death, 168–69, 191
Asquith, Joyce (*née* Sachs), 60; introduces Cliff to Catherine, 35–36
Atomic Energy of Canada, 67
Austrian, Dr. Herman, 220 n.132

Báb, quoted, 180
Bach, Marcus, 119
"Back Achers" (Huxtable family farm), 83
Bahá'í Audio–Visual Aids Committee, 141
Bahá'í Faith. *See also* individual Bahá'ís
—and secular education, 114–115;
—legal recognition of marriage: in Saskatchewan, 94; in British Columbia, 113; lack of clergy, as impediment, 94
—meaning of name, 117;
—pioneering, 12, 99–100, 109, 144
—teaching (propagation of the Faith), 41, 52–53, 76, 99, 166
—tenets of the, 23, 30, 71, 83, 98–99; on death, 40; on visions, 173
—Ten Year Crusade, 12, 80
—terminology, 18, 41
—World Congress, 120
Bahá'í House of Worship, Wilmette (Illinois), 75, 136, 201
Bahá'í World Centre, Haifa, Israel, 79
Bahá'u'lláh, 62, 117, 120, 143; centenary of birth, 166; quoted, 29–30, 115, 121, 179, 184
Bahá'u'lláh and the New Era, 53
Ball, Pamela *see* Webster, Rev. Pamela
Banani, Dr. Amin, 116
Banani, Husayn, 116–117, 132, 133
Banani, Musa, 116
Banff, Alberta, 117, 119
Bates, Susan (fictional character), 54
Bechuanaland, 156, 198
Bennett, Elinor, 111, 125; and Bahá'í Faith, 116-121; and "Nought to Six", 114–115; death, 190
Bennett, Fletcher, 125, 135; and Bahá'í Faith, 117, 119–121; death, 117, 190; spiritual search, 115–116
Bennett, Pat, 83
Bolles, Jeanne, 177, 178
Bond, Gale, 47, 88, 91, 142
Bond, Jameson "Jamie", 47, 65–66, 88, 91, 142
Botswana. *See* Bechuanaland

Boulding, Bernice "Birdie", 91, 94, 129
—and Baháʼí Faith, 112–114; enrolls, 113; on Local Spiritual Assembly, 121
—and Huxtables, 91, 100; employment, 111–112; relationship with, 91, 112, 114; impressions of Catherine, 114
—background, 111–114
—death, 114
—friends of, 110
—later life, 189
—marriage and divorce, 113–114; children, 189
Bourdillon, Dr. Robert Benedict, 114–115, 117, 122, 186
Bourdillon, Thomas "Tom", 114
Burland, Gale, 182

Calgary, 126, 137
Campbell, Nancy, 91
Canadian Laboratory Supplies, 76, 202
Canadian National Convention, 1965, 131–133, 202
Canadian National Institute for the Blind, 141
Carter, Hiles, 32, 33, 34, 39, 200
Catherine Huxtable Scholarship, 191, 196
Centenary of the Proclamation of Baháʼu'lláh (1967), 166
Chicago, Illinois, 75, 137
Chosen Highway, The (Blomfield), 61
Church of Christ, Scientist (Christian Science), 42
Cleather, Carol, 91
Cleather, Charles, 91
Collins, Eileen White Vail. *See* White, Eileen
Collins, George, 83
Corker, Gay, 150
Cowan, Angus, 91, 94, 112, 136
—and Baháʼí Faith: in Regina, 84, 93–94; recognition of Baháʼí marriage, 94; member of National Spiritual Assembly, 93; teaching (propagation), 91, 93–94
Cowan, Roberta "Bobbie", 84, 112, 136
—and difficulties in Regina community, 87–89
—restoration of Regina Assembly, 93-94
—teaching (propagation), 91, 94
Crofford, Doug, 92
Crofford, Marian, 92
Cronan, Kay, 113
Crooks, Barry, 113–14, 125, 189

Dainty, Diana (Merrick): correspondence with Catherine, 85–87, 89, 114, 135, 144, 163–65; marriage, 74, 76
Dainty, (Ernest) Don, 83, 132; correspondence
with Huxtables, 85–87, 89, 171; marriage, 74, 76
The Dawnbreakers (Nabíl-i-Zarandí), 56–57
Devlin, Joyce Frances, 108
Dictionary of Falklands Biography, The, 59
District of Franklin, 142
District of Keewatin, 95
Dwight schools, 142
Edinswold, 12, 48, 50, 60, 62, 64
Effendi, Shoghi. *See* Shoghi Effendi
Éire, 146
Ennis, Mabel, 92
Ennis, Verne, 92
Estall, Rowland, 43, 79, 110, 145
Evans, Jack, 123

Field, Sir John Osbaldiston, 159–60,171
Field, Lady Margaret, 159, 171
First Nations: and Baháʼí Faith, 93, 95; and National Spiritual Assembly, 95; pioneering to, 89, 93, 125; teaching, 86. *See also* Anaquod, Tom; Anaquod, Sophie; specific places
Fletcher, Steve, 109
Ford (Winckler), Bahíyyih Randall, 45

Garraway, Tom, 142
George, Barbara, 150
George, Basil, 150–51, 152, 203
Gillespie, John Birks "Dizzy", 140
Gilpin, Colonel, 134, 151–52, 203
Glen, Paisley, 184–85
God Passes By (Shoghi Effendi), 56–57

Index

"Great African Safari", 109
Guardian, The. *See* Shoghi Effendi
Guillet, Bob, 35, 36
Gulf Islands, 12, 131, 196; as goal in Ten Year World Crusade,109; First Local Spiritual Assembly, 120–21; recommended as substitute for Anticosti Island, 81–82; description, 81, 91–100
Gulf Islands Ferry Company, 104
Gwen (maternal aunt of CHH), 53–54

Haifa (Israel), 78–79
Harkness, Jessie, 44
Harvey, Winnifred, 78–79, 82, 132,180, 202
Harvie, Dr. James Norman (brother-in-law of CHH), 20
Hastings, Barbara, 130–131
Havergal College (Toronto), 22, 24, 36
Hepburn, Florence, 123
Heuvel, Tommy, 152
Heward family: attitudes, 36, 64, 71; social standing, 25, 38, 74
—religion in, acceptance of Catherine's beliefs, 40–41; and Anglican Church, 38; and Bahá'í Faith, 40–41
See also individual names
Heward, Catherine Rudyerd. *See* Huxtable, Catherine Rudyerd (*née* Heward)
Heward, Helen Bury (mother of CHH), ancestry, 21, 189; and Catherine's diagnosis, 12, 23; care for Catherine, 20, 122; and Catherine's friends, 27, 36, 48; Catherine's tribute to, 180; and Cliff, 71–72, 143-44; correspondence with Cliff, 161–62, 167, 182; later life, 189; visits Catherine and Cliff in England, 147
Heward (Harvie), Julia Wynne (sister of CHH), 64, 75; care for Catherine, 12, 20, 25; death, 190; marriage, 20; physical appearance, 48; relationship with Catherine, 40, 70, 192; relationship with Cliff, 192; religious convictions, 38, 41
Heward, Lt.-Col. Stephen Augustus (father of CHH), 20-22, 48, 50, 72, 101; career, 20,

21–22, 129; death, 87, 143, 189; health, 64; monetary gift to Catherine and Cliff, 87
Horel, Charles, 103, 104, 114
Hull (Quebec), 79
Humphreys, Gil, 101–102, 114, 136, 147, 155
Humphreys, Nonie, 102
Hussey Charity School, 134, 151–52
Huxtable, Catherine Rudyerd (*née* Heward): appearance, 26; birth and infancy, 21-22; education, 22, 25; employed as needleworker, 28–29, 76; trip to Europe, 25–26. *See also* individual names; muscular dystrophy; specific places
— and Bahá'í Faith, 51; and recording for the blind, 140–142; enrolls, 47; desire to serve, 47; introduced to, 39–40, 43, 45, 47; named Knight of Bahá'u'lláh, 99; teaching (propagation), 47, 53–54, 60–63, 87, 136–139, 158–59, 164
—death, 167–68: decline, 155, 157, 161–66; funeral, 169–71; memorial service, 174–77; readiness for, 161–165, 168, 185 visions of her, 172–74
—health, 77; care for, 20, 23, 84, 96,101, 123, 124, 135; contracts measles, 107–108; contracts scarlet fever, 23; mobility, 24, 28, 75–76, 154; undergoes sterilization operation, 122
—marriage: courtship, 35–36, 67–73; difficulties, 92, 121–122, 125, 139, 159, 161–62; wedding, 73–75; residence at Hewards home, 75–76
—personality, 47–49, 96–98, 118; communicator, 51; egalitarianism, 22–23; friendliness, 28, 109; independence, 96, 109; love of the arts, 25, 26–28, 71; spirituality, 27–29, 97–99, 114; sweetness, 48
—and religion generally: spiritual practice, 96; spiritual search, 30–31, 40; Unitarianism, 36–39
Huxtable, Clifford Stanley "Cliff": ancestry, 71–72; education, 35, 69, 71, 122–23; marriage, 35, 71-73; threatened by neighbor, 127–130. *See also* Bahá'í Faith; individual

names; specific places
—and Bahá'í Faith, 93, 94; attends 1965 National Convention, 131–34; decision to pioneer, 80–84, 99, 134; enrolls, 47; first impressions of, 45; introduction to, 34; role of George Spendlove, 41–47; spiritual growth, 57, 65, 78; teaching (propagation), 136–39, 158–59
—and Catherine's death, 155, 157, 161–63, 165–68; vision of dancing with, 172–174
—health problems: car accident, 121–22; collapse, 153; fractured thumb, 147,152–53; stress, 122, 130–31
—occupation: Atomic Energy of Canada, 67 Canadian Laboratory Supplies, 76; car dealership, 87; ferry, 106–07; manual labor, 103–05; Ontario Hydro, 31
—schoolteaching: in Toronto, 76; in Regina, 82–83, 85, 92; on Gulf Islands, 107–08, 115, 123–24, 125, 130–31; on St. Helena, 148, 150–51, 153–54
—spiritual search, 39; accidentally injures a boy, 31–33; role of Hiles Carter, 32; role of Wes Huxtable, 33–34; Unitarianism, 39–40, 71
Huxtable, David (nephew of CSH), 91
Huxtable, Delia (née Duncan, wife of CSH), 150, 189
Huxtable, Dorothy (mother of CSH), 72–73, 143–44, 174
Huxtable, Gavin Clifford (son of CSH and CHH): 122, 136, 155, 163, 165, 189; and 'Abdu'l-Bahá's room, 144–45; and Catherine's death, 168; birth, 118–119; ill with mononucleosis, 147–148
Huxtable, Rev. George Gellard (great-grandfather of CSH), 72
Huxtable, Jane (daughter of CSH and DDH), 189
Huxtable, Janet (sister of CSH), 83, 161
Huxtable, Mary (sister-in-law of CSH), 91
Huxtable, (George) Reuben (father of CSH), 72–73, 121
Huxtable, Robert (son of CSH and DDH), 189

Huxtable, Weston "Wes" (brother of CSH), 143; and Bahá'í Faith, 33–34; best man at wedding, 74; visits Huxtables, 91; in Dublin, 146; writes short biography of Catherine, 182, 185

Ireland. See Éire

Jack, Marion, 98, 182, 183
Jansch, Dr., 108, 129
Jasion, Jan, 142
Jenkins, Rev. William Phillip, 38, 39, 74, 201
Jensen, Margaret, 142
Johnny, Geraldine, 125
Johns, A.W., 148
Jones, Art, 107, 123
Jousse, Dr. Albin T., 187

Kerr Linden, Ann (née Cartwright): friendship with Catherine, 27–29, 49; hosts Rúhíyyih Khánum, 108, 187
Kerr, Sven, 29, 91, 100, 108
Khánum, Rúhíyyih. See Rúhíyyih Khánum
Khádem, Zikhrullah, 98, 132–133, 182–183
Kivalliq region, 95
Knight of Bahá'u'lláh: meaning, 12; how the Huxtables received the title, 99, 198–99
—others appearing in text: John Leonard, 57–60; Zabolotny, Mary (McCulloch), 81, 100; Richard Stanton, 95–96; Joan and Ted Anderson, 110; Munir Vakil, 132–133; Gale and Jameson Bond, 142; Bruce Matthew, 142; Elizabeth Stamp, 150; John, Audrey, and Patrick Robarts, 156
Konrad, Zygmunt, 56

Labrador, 142
Leacock, Stephen, 21
Leonard, John, 57–60, 177–178
Leonard, Margaret, 60, 177–178
Lethbridge (Alberta), 119, 137, 139,140, 162
Letters of Direction (de Tourville), 186
Levy, John Alfred. See John Leonard
Life and Holiness (Merton), 180
Linden, Ann Kerr (née Cartwright): 91, 100,

Index

108, 190; impressions of Catherine, 27–29, 49, 164, 187
Luth, Lisa, 120–121
Luth, Walter, 120–121

Macke, Marlene, 46
MacLaren, Don, 93, 137–138, 193
MacLaren, Verna, 137
MacLeod, Kay, 119
Magdalen Islands, 81
Manser (Rochester), Elizabeth "Liz": 65, 71, 83, 137, 201; impressions of Catherine, 48; role in Huxtables' conversion, 40, 44–46
Manser, Jessie Harkness, 44
Marina Creations, 29
Marriage, Bahá'í, legal recognition of: in Saskatchewan, 94; in British Columbia, 113
Martin, J. Douglas: 1965 National Convention, 132; attends George Spendlove's firesides, 42; at Catherine's death, 171; at Huxtables' wedding, 74; Huxtables visit in Toronto, 37; impressions of Catherine, 47
Martin, Elizabeth, 47
Masehla, William, 149
Matthew, Bruce, 142–143
Maxwell, Mary. *See* Rúhíyyih Khánum
Maxwell, William Sutherland, 85, 86, 98, 144
Maxwell International School, 142
Mayberry, Florence, 193
McCulloch, Mary (Zabolotny). *See* Zabolotny, Mary
McKenty, Beth, 119, 137, 140, 142, 191
McKenty, Dr. Jack, 137
McLean, Allan James, 190
McLean, Joyce Mary Halsted, 190, 191, 196–197
Merrick, Marjorie, 117
Merton, Thomas, 180–81
Milwaukee (Wisconsin), 136, 137, 139–142
Mills, Margaret, 59
Moen, Edna, 119, 120, 121, 122
Moen, Patty, 119
Montréal (Québec), 79, 82, 135–137, 144–146; and Catherine's family, 21; and Cliff's family, 72; and George Spendlove, 42–44,
Moore, Nora Nablo. *See* Nablo, Nora (Moore)
Morrison, Alasdair, 147
Mouat, Gavin Colvin, 114, 118, 202; assists Huxtables, 104–106; background, 104–105; death, 104–105
Muscular dystrophy: Catherine's diagnosis, 20, 23, 30, 69, 200
—Catherine's attitude toward: and Bahá'í Faith, 86–87, 108, 140–142, 180, 181; and marriage, 68–70, 152; physical limitations, 28–29, 97–98, 173; spiritual search, 30–31
—medical aspects: 108, 161,186; care for, 20, 23–24, 84; treatment of, 69–70, 186; physical effects of, 23–25, 48, 96, 97; and childbirth, 118–119; depression, 161, 166, 186–187
Mysticism (Shook), 186

Nablo, Edna (Halsted), 33, 196, 197
Nablo (Moore), Nora, 64
Nablo, Ronald, 132, 196
Nakhjavani, Violette, 109
National Spiritual Assembly of the United States of America, 133
National Spiritual Assembly of Canada advises Huxtables, 82, 135–136, 145. *See also* individual names
—administrative actions of, 133, 174; pertaining to Gulf Islands, 81, 83, 99, 121; teaching and consolidation, 54, 116, 119
—correspondence: with Shoghi Effendi, 144 with Cliff Huxtable, 155–56; on Catherine's death, 171, 174, 177, 193–194.

Native Americans. See First Nations
Nine Year Plan (1964–1973), 121, 135–136, 138, 145, 156, 176
Noaks, Dr. John, 161, 186
"Nought to Six", 114–115
Nunavut, 95

Ontario Hydro, 31
Orillia (Ontario), 20, 23, 50, 143
Ottawa, 67, 72, 78–79, 82, 144, 171
Owen, Don, 28
Oxford University Mountaineering Club, 114

Paice, Patricia, 91

Rabbani, Shoghi. *See* Shoghi Effendi
Rabbani, Madame. *See* Rúhíyyih Khánum
Raginsky, Harry, 82
Raginsky, Vera, 82
Regina, Saskatchewan, 29, 39, 47, 76, 81–99
—Aboriginal community, 90, 92–94;
—Huxtables' homes, description of, 85–86, 95
—Baháʼí community: children and youth, 92; loss of Local Spiritual Assembly, 82–83; re–establishment of LSA, 90; teaching initiatives in, 90, 93–95; tests and difficulties, 87–89
Renewal of Civilization, The (Hofman), 61
Robarts, Aldham "Aldie", 212 n. 29
Robarts, Audrey (FitzGerald), 33, 174; firesides, 40, 45–47, 71; role in Huxtables' conversion, 57; visits Catherine's mother, 144; visits Huxtables on St. Helena's, 156-58
Robarts, Gerald, 33, 142, 200
Robarts, John, 33, 70, 91, 150, 163; awareness of Catherine's impending death, 157; encourages Cliff in pioneering, 131; firesides, 40, 45–47; following Catherine's death, 171, 174, 177; reflections on Catherine, 97–98, 182, 191; role in Huxtables' naming as Knight, 198–99; role in Huxtables' conversion, 57; as traveling teacher, 116; visits Catherine's mother, 144; visits Huxtables on St. Helena's, 156–58; visits Regina, 90
Robarts, Patrick, 156, 198
Robarts family: pioneer to Bechuanaland (Botswana), 156; visit Huxtables on St. Helena, 156–158
Robinson, Wey, 28
Rochester, Elizabeth Manser, 83; firesides, 40; reflections on post-World War II generation, 45; becomes Baháʼí, 45; reflections on Catherine, 47–48; Huxtables visit en route to St. Helena,137; correspondence with Cliff, 162, 166–167
Rochester, Michael, 37, 83,182, 191, 197; becomes Baháʼí, 55; career, 50; as caregiver to Catherine, 96; and Catherine's death, 171–72, 174–77; correspondence with Catherine, 26, 36, 49–70, 76–77; correspondence with Cliff, 162, 166–167; delivers Catherine's eulogy, 174–77; encourages Catherine in her relationship with Cliff, 68–69; encourages Cliff in pioneering, 132; friendship with Cliff, 50; Huxtables visit en route to St. Helena, 137; receives news of Catherine's death, 171; role in Huxtables' naming as Knights, 198; vision of Catherine running, 172
Ross, Peggy, 91, 119–120
Royal Ontario Museum, 25, 41, 44
Rúhíyyih Khánum, corresponds with Catherine, 90, 108, 175, 177; and George Spendlove, 42, 44; and pioneers, 109, 175; meets Huxtables, 108–109; sits for portrait, 108
Russ (Cliff's co-worker), 31

Sachs, Joyce *see* Asquith, Joyce (Sachs)
Salt Spring Island, generally, 76, 87, 99–133; Baháʼí travel teachers to, 116–17; Catherine's fascination with, 91, 95; description, 100–101; first Local Spiritual Assembly, 120–21; internment of Japanese community, 113
Saminaden, Jagdish "Jack", 147, 150
Saskatchewan, Canada, generally, 81–99; and recognition of Baháʼí marriage, 94; Huxtables move to, 84–86
Saturna Island, 106–108
Saulteaux Nation, 93
Saunders, Kate, 120–21
Schmalenberg, Nona, 92
Schmalenberg, Phil, 92
Schmitt, Gunter "Gordon", 92
Schmitt, Margaret, 92
Schopflocher, Lorol, 79

Index

Schopflocher, Siegfried "Freddie", 79
Sears, William, 116, 156
Shirley (Cliff's cousin), 91
Shoghi Effendi, call for pioneers, 78–80; death, 44; and goals of Ten Year Plan, 81–82, 132–33; and naming of Knights, 198; on propagation of Faith, 155; praise of eminent Bahá'ís, 98, 116, 150, 179, 182; quoted, 89,179; and teaching, 41–42; "The Summons of the Lord of Hosts", 142
—and Huxtables: 99; advises Catherine, 108, 140–41; Catherine dreams of, 78; Huxtables visit grave, 147
See also Spendlove, Francis St. George; Ten Year Crusade
Silversides, Leslie, 89
Silversides, Mabel, 89
Smallwood, Margo, 59
Some Answered Questions, 63
Spendlove, Dorothy G. Spurr, 42
Spendlove, Francis St. George: 41–44, 80; influence on Huxtables, 45–47, 57; at Huxtables' wedding, 74–75; sayings of, 193–95
St. Helena Island, 12–14, 16, 28, 146–160; challenges for the handicapped, 146, 148–150; description, 146, 149–151; housing, 151–152, 154; Huxtables befriended by Governor and Lady Field, 159–160; parents' reactions to move, 144; in Roger White's writing, 97; visit from Robarts family, 156–158
—religions represented on
  Anglican Church, 152, 154, 158
  Bahá'í Faith, pioneering, 131, 133; Bahá'í community, 150–151; Local Spiritual Assembly of, 150; teaching efforts, 158–159
Stamp, Elizabeth, 150
Stanton, Richard "Dick", 98
Stee, Marjorie, 76
Stevens, Georgina, 91
Stewart (Atwater), Marcia, 59
Swaziland, 109, 171

Tablets of the Divine Plan ('Abdu'l-Bahá), 185
Take My Love to the Friends (Macke), 46
Ten Year Crusade (1953–1963), 12, 99–100, 109, 156
Tinnion, Ken, 161
Tinnion, Nina (Robarts), 161
Toronto Local Spiritual Assembly, 76, 79, 80
Toronto Bahá'í community, 41–47, 76, 78–80
Tourville, Abbé Henri de, 186
Trans–Canada Airlines, 137

Underhill, Evelyn, 186
Universal House of Justice, 59, 80, 166; and Centenary Proclamation, 174; names Huxtables Knights of Bahá'u'lláh, 99; and pioneering goals, 133, 156
University of Toronto, 37, 48; and Clifford Huxtable, 35, 50, 70–71, 201; and George Spendlove, 25, 44; and Michael Rochester, 50, 56; and Weston Huxtable, 33
University of Victoria, 76, 123
Uxbridge, Ontario, 83

Vail, Albert, 91–92, 111; as caregiver to Catherine, 96
Vakíl, Munír, 132–33
van den Hoonard, Dr. Will C., 89
Vancouver, 81, 108–109
Vancouver Island, 81
Volquardsen, Tom, 190

Waddell, Stuart, 76
Webster, Arthur "Pat", 126
Webster, Rev. Pamela (*née* Ball), 27–29; education, 39; explores Bahá'í Faith, 60–63; family of, 48; on her friendship with Catherine, 126–27; ordained in Episcopal Church, 63; personality, 37; reflections on Catherine, 40, 48–49, 60, 164; spiritual nature, 37, 39; and Unitarianism, 36–38; visits Catherine on Salt Spring Island, 126
Weeden, Ben, 56
White, Eileen Vail (Mrs. George Collins), 82–84, accompanies Huxtables to Regina, 84, 87–90; and Bahá'í Faith, 83, 91; friendship

with Catherine, 96–98; marries Albert Vail,
    91
White, Roger, 82–83, 91, 153, 164–65;
    reflections on Catherine, 97, 183
Wilks, Helen, 120, 196
Winckler, Bahíyyih Randall *See* Ford, (*née*
    Ford), 45
Windsor, Ontario, 84, 136–37, 139, 142–43
Window, Harold (Cliff's stepfather), 73, 174
Winnipeg, 79, 137; 1965 National
    Convention, 131–33
Woodman, Ross, 64–65
World War II, 22, 74, 187; effect on Huxtables'
    generation, 45; Japanese internment, 113
Wrate, Enid, 137, 162, 165, 167, 192;
Catherine's correspondence with, 139–40, 142
Wrate, Jack, 137, 162. 165

Your Experience as a Bahá'í (booklet for new
    believers), 54

Zabolotny (McCulloch), Mary, 81, 100

About the Author

Jack McLean (b. 1945 Toronto) is a Bahá'í scholar, writer and poet. After pursuing studies in French history and literature at the University of Paris (Sorbonne), he graduated with distinction with an M.A. in the History of Religions from the University of Ottawa. He has won two awards from the Association for Bahá'í Studies North America: one in creative writing for poetry (1994) and a distinguished scholarship award (2013) in the book category for his in-depth study of the writings of Shoghi Effendi, *A Celestial Burning: A Selective Study of the Writings of Shoghi Effendi*.

Along with numerous articles in Bahá'í theology, spirituality and essays on topical subjects, available at his website, Jack has published the following books: *Dimensions in Spirituality* (George Ronald 1994); *Revisioning the Sacred: New Perspectives on a Bahá'í Theology* (editor-contributor Kalimat Press 1997); *Under the Divine Lote Tree: Essays and Reflections* (George Ronald 1999); *A Celestial Burning: A Selective Study of the Writings of Shoghi Effendi* (Bahá'í Publishing Trust of India 2012).

From 2001-2013 Jack wrote the Bahá'í responses to a weekly question on the Ottawa Citizen's "Ask the Religion Experts" page.

Visit him at www.jack-mclean.com